Funny Dostoevsky

Funny Dostoevsky

New Perspectives on the Dostoevskian
Light Side

Edited by Lynn Ellen Patyk and Irina Erman

BLOOMSBURY ACADEMIC
NEW YORK • LONDON • OXFORD • NEW DELHI • SYDNEY

BLOOMSBURY ACADEMIC
Bloomsbury Publishing Inc, 1359 Broadway, New York, NY 10018, USA
Bloomsbury Publishing Plc, 50 Bedford Square, London, WC1B 3DP, UK
Bloomsbury Publishing Ireland, 29 Earlsfort Terrace, Dublin 2, D02 AY28, Ireland

BLOOMSBURY, BLOOMSBURY ACADEMIC and the Diana logo
are trademarks of Bloomsbury Publishing Plc

First published in the United States of America 2024
Paperback edition published 2026

Copyright © 2024 Lynn Ellen Patyk and Irina Erman

Each chapter © Contributors

For legal purposes the Acknowledgments on p. ix constitute an
extension of this copyright page.

Cover design: Eleanor Rose
Cover images: Portrait of Fyodor Dostoyevsky by Vasily Perov, 1872, oil on canvas.
Tretyakov Gallery, Moscow, Russia. Photo © VCG Wilson / Corbis / Getty Image;

Additional Image © Andy Ryan / Getty Images

All rights reserved. No part of this publication may be: i) reproduced or transmitted in any form, electronic or mechanical, including photocopying, recording or by means of any information storage or retrieval system without prior permission in writing from the publishers; or ii) used or reproduced in any way for the training, development or operation of artificial intelligence (AI) technologies, including generative AI technologies. The rights holders expressly reserve this publication from the text and data mining exception as per Article 4(3) of the Digital Single Market Directive (EU) 2019/790.

Bloomsbury Publishing Inc does not have any control over, or responsibility for, any third-party websites referred to or in this book. All internet addresses given in this book were correct at the time of going to press. The author and publisher regret any inconvenience caused if addresses have changed or sites have ceased to exist, but can accept no responsibility for any such changes.

Library of Congress Cataloging-in-Publication Data
Names: Patyk, Lynn Ellen, editor. | Erman, Irina, editor.
Title: Funny Dostoevsky : new perspectives on the Dostoevskian
light side / edited by Lynn Ellen Patyk and Irina Erman.
Description: New York : Bloomsbury Academic, 2024. |
Includes bibliographical references and index.
Identifiers: LCCN 2023046627 (print) | LCCN 2023046628 (ebook) |
ISBN 9798765109786 (hardback) | ISBN 9798765109793 (paperback) |
ISBN 9798765109809 (ebook) | ISBN 9798765109816 (pdf)
Subjects: LCSH: Dostoyevsky, Fyodor, 1821–1881–Humor. | Dostoyevsky,
Fyodor, 1821–1881–Criticism and interpretation. | Russian wit and
humor. | Russian literature–19th century–History and criticism
Classification: LCC PG3328.Z7 H8527 2024 (print) | LCC PG3328.Z7
(ebook) | DDC 891.73/3–dc23/eng/20240205
LC record available at https://lccn.loc.gov/2023046627
LC ebook record available at https://lccn.loc.gov/2023046628

ISBN: HB: 979-8-7651-0978-6
PB: 979-8-7651-0979-3
ePDF: 979-8-7651-0981-6
eBook: 979-8-7651-0980-9

Typeset by Integra Software Services Pvt. Ltd.

For product safety related questions contact productsafety@bloomsbury.com.

To find out more about our authors and books visit www.bloomsbury.com and
sign up for our newsletters.

This book is dedicated to the brilliant, talented, and funny women who have shaped our academic trajectories and our lives.

Contents

List of Figures	viii
Acknowledgments	ix
A Note from the Editors	x
Introduction: The De-seriousification of Dostoevsky *Lynn Ellen Patyk*	1
1 Bakhtin and the Laughing Genres on the Brink of Total War *Caryl Emerson*	25
2 Funny Dostoevsky in Translation: How Funny Is He? *Tatyana Kovalevskaya*	51
3 Raskolnikov's Red Nose: The Slapstick Comedy of Dostoevsky's Serious Protagonists *Fiona Bell*	71
4 Sensations of Laughter: Mind and Matter in *The Brothers Karamazov* *Melissa Frazier*	99
5 Having the Last Laugh: Ontological Jokes and Dostoevsky's Comedic Genius *Alina Wyman*	121
6 "Too Dragged Out, Can't Understand a Thing": The Impatience of Youth in *Demons* *Chloe Papadopoulos*	149
7 Restorative Parody from *Devils* to *Hamilton* *Susanne Fusso*	171
8 The Funny and the Furious: Laughter and Gender in Dostoevsky *Irina Erman*	191
Notes on Contributors	221
Index	223

Figures

3.1 Groucho Marx sees his double in the "mirror" in the 1933 film *Duck Soup* (45:00) — 79
3.2 Tramp gets stuck in the factory gears in *Modern Times* (15:07) — 81
3.3 Tramp's cellmate, the hardened criminal, doing embroidery in *Modern Times* (23:56) — 89
3.4 Ellen and Tramp walking toward the horizon at the end of *Modern Times* (1:26:24) — 94

Acknowledgments

If *Funny Dostoevsky* has a birthplace, it may be a very generic sports bar near Fenway Park in Boston where we (the co-editors, not the royal we) laughed our heads off over drinks after a full day conferencing at the 2019 International Dostoevsky Society's triennial Symposium. We don't remember what we were laughing about—probably not Dostoevsky—but it was also a reunion of sorts. Both of us had done our doctoral work in the Slavic Department at Stanford University, and although we didn't belong to the same cohort, we were both Monika Greenleaf's and Gabriella Safran's students. Monika "brought us together" in an intellectual sense, was a mentor to us both, shaped our sensibilities, and nurtured original, unconventional approaches to just about everything. Gabriella Safran also stimulated and supported adventurous thinking with infallible good humor and a completely infectious laugh.

So perhaps *Funny Dostoevsky* was born at Stanford before it emerged during the Covid Summer doldrums of 2020, when we hatched the idea for the conference "Beyond Carnival: Funny Dostoevsky." We are grateful to all the remote conference's genial participants, and especially to our terrific discussants, including Monika Greenleaf, Yuri Corrigan, Caryl Emerson, Elizabeth Geballe, and Kate Holland. And finally, without each other as co-editors on the same zany wavelength, funny Dostoevsky would have been, well, a lot less fun.

A Note from the Editors

For transliteration that occurs throughout the text, we have used a modified Library of Congress system of transliteration. Well-known Russian names appear in forms most familiar to Anglophone readers (Dostoev*sky* instead of Dostoev*skii*), and we have used -y instead of -ii and -ya instead of -ia (Golyadkin instead of Goliadkin, Nastasya instead of Nastas'ia) in these cases. In regard to contentious translation choices, we have retained author preferences for translating Dostoevsky's *Besy* as either *The Devils* or *Demons*. Where we cite Dostoevsky's works in the original Russian, our volume refers to the Academy edition of *The Complete Works of Fyodor M. Dostoevsky* (*Polnoe sobranie sochinenii F. M. Dostoevskogo v tridsati tomakh* = *PSS*) by volume and page number.

Introduction: The De-seriousification of Dostoevsky

Lynn Ellen Patyk

You can deny seriousness, but not play.

—Johan Huizinga, *Homo Ludens*[1]

In late middle age, when health issues forced him to spend summers in Germany upon doctor's orders, Dostoevsky wrote his beloved wife Anna almost every day and filled his letters with melancholy and tender longing for her and their children in Russia, as well as with the most bitter and slashing complaints about almost everything else. Yet in a July 9 (21), 1876 letter from Bad Ems, an anecdote from his train journey takes center stage. As far as we can tell, the anecdote has not made it into any of Dostoevsky's biographies, but because Dostoevsky took such obvious care and relish in the retelling, we quote it in full:

> We stopped ten minutes, before that it had been a long time since we stopped, and everyone, naturally, ran to the place pour Hommes [for men], and suddenly, at the very height of activity, into the place pour Hommes, full of about two dozen visitors, *there came running* a well-dressed lady, by all indications an Englishwoman. She probably was in *great need*, because she had run almost to the middle of the room before noticing her mistake, that is, that she had come into Männer [men] instead of going in next door to the section für die Frauen [for women]. She stopped suddenly, as though thunderstruck, with a look of profound and frightened amazement that lasted no longer than a second, and then suddenly shrieked extremely loudly, or rather, squealed, exactly the way you sometimes do when you get suddenly frightened, and then threw her hands up in front of her, with a sweeping motion, and lifting them a little over her head, in such a way that the swishing made a sound. I should note that she saw everything,

---

[1] J. Huizinga, *Homo Ludens: A Study of the Play Element in Culture*. (London: Routledge, 2002), 3.

that is, literally *everything* and in all frankness, because no one had the time to conceal anything, and, on the contrary, everyone was looking at her in the same sort of stupefaction. Then after throwing up her hands she suddenly covered her face with both palms and, after turning around rather slowly (everything was lost, it was all over, there was no reason to rush!), her entire figure inclined forward, she left the *facility*, deliberately and not without grandness. I don't know whether she went to für die Frauen; if she was an Englishwoman, I think she died right there and then from shame. But it's noteworthy that there was no laughter. The Germans were all gloomily silent, while in Russia people would surely have laughed and guffawed with delight.[2]

Dostoevsky leaves no doubt as to what his reaction was, and his exacting recreation of the scene invites his young wife to share the guffaws of delight with him. We use this anecdote to launch our study of funny Dostoevsky. It is Exhibit A in our Hall of Evidence, unjustly neglected, that Dostoevsky cherished humor and comedy and had refined his techniques of comedic narration so that the humorous aspects are drawn out and get full play. The foreign language euphemisms, the minutely described gender-stereotyped gestures, the repetitions to make sure the audience gets the point, the big and unavoidable reveal ("no one had time to conceal anything"), and finally, the Englishwoman's savaged/salvaged dignity. This is a story of crushing humiliation for all and (possible) resurrection told in an entirely comic key that Dostoevsky revisits or perhaps in part creates, for no other purpose than his own and his wife's amusement.

As Dostoevsky notes, it was—is—fully possible to take the scandalous situation, which featured the violation of still extant social taboos, seriously. But even though he was clearly among the exposed parties he chose *not to*. He attributes his choice to his Russianness, and the anecdote affords him opportunities to indulge in national stereotypes: gloomy Germans, proper Englishwomen, and unbuttoned (in this case literally) Russians. The fact that it's also a humorous anecdote about a situation taken all too seriously (except by Dostoevsky) also suits our main purposes: to question what is funny and what is not, who considers what funny (and who considers it not) along with all the other issues that bedevil laughter and comedy not only in Dostoevsky but in the study of humor through the millennia.

---

[2] Fyodor Dostoevsky, *Polnoe sobranie sochinenii i pisem v tridtsati tomakh*. Edited by V. G. Bazanov, et al. (Leningrad: Nauka, 1986) 29(2): 92–3. Hereafter cited as *PSS*. Fyodor Dostoevsky, *Complete Letters*, vol 4 1872–7. Edited and Translated by David A. Lowe (Ann Arbor, MI: Ardis, 1991), 294–5.

In this millennia-long study, there is a paradox that Dostoevsky would relish as he relished all paradoxes, especially humorous ones. Perhaps his most beloved paradox and the one that crowns our volume he attributes to Ivan Karamazov's devil regarding life itself: "People take this whole comedy for something serious, despite all their undeniable intelligence. That is their tragedy."³ The double tragedy, in other words, is that people take comedy for tragedy and that life's comedy is therefore lost on them. Comedy and humor have had a strange tendency to get lost—lost in the more literal sense, as was the lost second book of Aristotle's *Poetics* (reputedly on comedy)—and lost in a more figurative sense, as in "lost in translation" or lost on audiences who simply miss the tonal and cognitive shift effected by comedy. The literary theorist Mikhail Bakhtin went so far as to posit that laughter had been historically lost, as irreverent ribaldry, the healthy two-way laughter of carnival, has been suppressed through the progressive "seriousification" of the novel and of Western culture more generally.⁴

Arguably, Dostoevsky has been subject to this same seriousification, and the literary-critical project has been complicit in it. While his contemporaries clearly perceived his comic genius as closely akin to Nikolai Gogol's,⁵ the bitterly partisan and ideological nature of literary criticism in both late Imperial and then Soviet Russia led to largely humorless approaches through a grim or weighty lens: politics and ideology (Mikhailovsky, Engel'gardt, Lunacharsky), religion (Merezhkovsky, Rozanov, Shestov), and philosophy of language (Ivanov, Bakhtin).⁶ When Bakhtin returned to Dostoevsky decades after his

---

³ PSS, 15: 77; Fyodor Dostoevsky, *The Brothers Karamazov*. Translated by Richard Pevear and Larissa Volokhonsky (New York: Farrar, Straus and Giroux, 2002), 642.

⁴ In her essay for this volume on the evolution of Bakhtin's thought on comedy and carnival, Caryl Emerson notes: "Finally, among Bakhtin's more curious surviving fragments are several plans for a history of the 'seriousification' of the world [*oser'eznenie mira*], the unavoidable result of the disintegration of Europe's primordial carnival mind." Emerson, "Bakhtin and Laughing Genres on the Brink of Total War," 36.

⁵ Joseph Frank, *The Seeds of Revolt, 1821–1849* (Princeton, NJ: Princeton University Press, 1976), 174, 313. See also Yuri Tynianov's groundbreaking essay on Dostoevsky's parody of Gogol as a means of overcoming Gogol. See Yuri Tynianov, "Dostoevsky and Gogol (Toward a Theory of Parody) (1919/1921)," in *Permanent Evolution: Selected Essays on Literature, Theory, and Film*. Translated and Edited by Ainsley Morse and Philip Redko (Boston, MA: Academic Studies Press, 2019), 27–63.

⁶ Nikolai Mikhailovsky, *Zhestokii talant* (A Cruel Talent) (1882); V. V. Rozanov, "Legenda o velikom inkvizitore F. M. Dostoevskogo" [F. M. Dostoevsky's "Legend of the Grand Inquisitor"] (1894); D. S. Merezhkovsky, *L. Tolstoi i Dostoevskii* (1900–1901); Lev Shestov, *Dostoevskii i Nitshe: filosofiia tragedii* [*Dostoevsky and Nietzsche: the Philosophy of Tragedy*] (1903); A. V. Lunacharsky, "Dostoevskii kak khudozhnik i myslitel'" [Dostoevsky as an artist and thinker] (Stenogramma rechi proiznesennoi A. V. Lunacharskim na torzhestve v chest' stoletiia so dnia rozhdeniia F. M. Dostoevskogo)" Krasnaia nov', 1921, no. 4, p. 204–11; B. M. Engel'gardt, "Ideologicheskii roman Dostoevskogo" in *F. M. Dostoevskii, Stat'i i materialy*, II, ed. A. S. Dolinin (Moscow-Leningrad: Mysl', 1924 [1925]). Viacheslav Ivanov began writing a series of essays about Dostoevsky in 1911, and these were ultimately published in book form as *Dostojewskij: Tragödie—Mythos—Mystik* (1932).

groundbreaking *Problems of Dostoevsky's Poetics* was published, his sprawling chapter on Menippea as the historical origins of the serio-comic paid only passing attention to the actual *comic*. His interest lay elsewhere, with historical poetics and a "carnival sense of the world" as a metaphysical idea.

Meanwhile, Western readers and critics have seemed deeply invested in a particular image of Dostoevsky. The study that introduced Russian literature to the West, Eugene Melchior De Vogüé's *Le Roman Russe* (1886), presented Dostoevsky as "a phenomenon of another world, an abnormal and mighty monster," not as a humorist to rival Mark Twain.[7] More recently, the American comedian Woody Allen (whose early short story "Notes from the Overfed" was inspired by reading *Notes from Underground* and a *Weight Watchers* magazine on the same airplane flight) had a character in his 1992 film *Husbands and Wives* sum up a Dostoevsky novel "as a full meal with a vitamin pill and extra wheat germ"—in other words, as mirthlessly and sanctimoniously nutritious.[8] As Bakhtin began to make inroads into Western scholarship, R. L. Busch undertook a blow-by-blow account of *Humor in the Major Novels of Dostoevsky* in his 1987 monograph.[9] Since then, there have been scattered articles in Russian, English, and other languages, but no study that concentratedly shines a light on Dostoevsky's light side. While this collection makes no claims to offer an all-encompassing theory of Dostoevskian comedy, it does provide wide-ranging, provocative new perspectives. Some of them draw on the efflorescence in comedy studies over the last two decades; others tap into more traditional approaches to capturing and understanding one of humankind's most universal and elusive sensibilities.

---

[7] Eugène-Melchior de Vogüé, *Le Roman Russse* (*The Russian Novelists*). Translated by Jane Loring Edmands (Boston: D. Lothrop Co, 1887), 197.

[8] Allen confessed in an interview that "like everybody else, I would have liked to have written the Russian novels." See Zachary T. Ingle, "A Full Meal with a Vitamin Pill and Extra Wheatgerm: Woody Allen, Dostoevsky, and Existential Morality," in *Referentiality and the Films of Woody Allen*. Edited by Klara Stephanie Szlezák and D. E. Wynter (London: Palgrave Macmillan, 2015), 119.

[9] R. L. Busch, *Humor in the Major Novels of Dostoevsky* (Columbus, OH: Slavica Publishers, 1987). Other more recent contributions to the study of Dostoevsky and humor include, Sarah Hudspith, "Why We Must Laugh at the Underground Man," *Studies in Slavic Literature and Poetics*, Leiden, vol. 57 (2012): 67–79; T. S. Martakova, "Antropologiia smekha v proizvedeniiakh Dostoevskogo (1846–1859): K voprosu o 'smekhovom portrete'" [Anthropology of Laughter in Dostoevsky's Works (1846–1859): Toward a "Laughter Portrait"], *Vestnik Cheliabinskogo gosudarstvennogo universiteta* [*Chelyabinsk State University Bulletin*], no. 15 (2007): 89–94; Robin Miller-Gulland and Olga Soboleva, "'Excellent Material, I See': What Happens in Bobok?," *Studies in Slavic Literature and Poetics*, Leiden, vol. 57 (2012): 135–47; John Givens, "A Narrow Escape into Faith? Dostoevsky's *Idiot* and the Christology of Comedy," *The Russian Review*, vol. 70, no. 1 (2011): 95–117; and L. M. Rozenblium, "Iumor Dostoevskogo" ["Dostoevsky's Humor"], *Voprosy literatury* (*Literary Issues*), no. 1 (1999): 141–89.

The Funny Thing about Theories of Humor

The cardinal problem with theories of comedy is that comedy and theory are two human projects that should never get anywhere near each other. Anthony Ludovici put his finger on the fundamental incompatibility (dare we say "incongruity"?), although as a philosopher, he understandably defaulted to faulting the comedians "because the humorous mind shirks the heavy task of solving thorny problems and prefers to make people laugh about them."[10] By contrast, the theoretical mind (we may presume as per Ludovici) is too often self-important and humorless. We have therefore sought a "theory of comedy" that outwits this apparent incompatibility. Comedy is by its very nature too irreverent and irregular for theory, and theory is too serious and limited for comedy. This much ought to be clear at the outset. The funny thing is, despite the seeming obviousness of this proposition, very serious thinkers have sought for millennia to advance their theories of humor and comedy. Among them are Aristotle, Thomas Hobbes, Arthur Schopenhauer, Immanuel Kant, Sigmund Freud, Henri Bergson—a veritable Who's Who from the Western canon, some of whom seemed to lack a single funny bone in their bodies. But the comic domain was too important not to be taken seriously. Although their efforts have yielded striking insights about humor, nothing like a consensus has ever been achieved, no "unified theory" of humor has presented itself as unifying.

The first issue requiring clarification is a very basic one: what are they—and we—talking about? Laughter, comedy, jokes, humor all seem to fall within the sphere of comic amusement, although they have referred to different things at different times, and in other times and places have not been differentiated at all. Broadly speaking, "comedy" is "the art devoted to making us laugh;" jokes are generally understood as verbal genres designed for this purpose, whereas "laughter" until the Renaissance referred not merely to the vocal expression of mirth but to all humor and amusement.[11] Humor, by contrast, didn't mean funniness until the end of the seventeenth century when it came to denote what was amusing, funny, and comic.[12] In general, the attitude toward mirth in all

---

[10] Anthony Ludovici, *The Secret of Laughter* (New York: Viking, 1933), 12–13. Quoted in John Morreall, *Comic Relief: A Comprehensive Philosophy of Humor* (Malden, MA: John Wiley and Sons, 2009), 93.

[11] Morreall, *Comic Relief*, 66–8.

[12] Ibid., 28.

its manifestations during the Christian era was negative (although striking examples of clerical and Christian humor did exist) with the exception of the restricted sphere carved out for carnival festivities, and laughter was regarded as the handmaiden of sin. Women's laughter especially was closely associated with sexual license.

In this, though, medieval Christendom was not significantly more dour than its classical predecessors. The Greco-Roman world viewed laughter and comedy as "lower" and always suspect when it came to the serious business of upholding the social and moral order through more edifying arts, such as tragedy. As something of a safety valve, the satyr plays of antiquity formed the uproarious tail end of tragedies before being incorporated into Apollonian ritual or attaining generic autonomy in Aristophanes' comedies.[13] Even with this degree of integration, comedy was appropriate solely for inferior or ridiculous subjects. From Aristotle and Cicero to Hobbes and Descartes, laughter was synonymous with ridicule, scorn, and mockery at the expense of its target and evinced the "sudden glory" of the manifestly superior laughing subject. What in retrospect appears quite a cruel theory of humor (if we were to sit in moral judgment), known as the "superiority theory" and grounded in humiliation, prevailed for almost two millennia while the social hierarchy remained largely unchallenged. More physiological and cognitive theories of humor were proposed in step with the Enlightenment and scientific revolution, and Immanuel Kant transcended Descartes's mind/body dualism by elaborating a theory in which humor's gratification of the mind pleasures the body. Or rather, the stimulation of the mind, like a tease, stops short of complete gratification and has a salubrious effect on the body, which then redounds upon the mind in a beneficial feedback loop. Since Kant's theory of humor is often reduced to a single premise ("Laughter is an affectation arising from the sudden transformation of strained expectation into nothing") and simplified beyond recognition, it is worth recalling his holistic theory of laughter.

> In everything that is to excite a lively convulsive laugh there must be something absurd (in which the understanding, therefore, can find no satisfaction). Laughter is an affection arising from the sudden transformation of strained expectation into nothing. This transformation, which is certainly not enjoyable

---

[13] Peter Berger, *Redeeming Laughter: The Comic Dimension of the Human Experience* (New York: Walter de Gruyter, 1997), 16–17.

to the understanding, yet indirectly gives it very active enjoyment for a moment. Therefore, its cause must consist in the influence of the representation upon the body, and the reflex effect of this upon the mind; not indeed, through the representation being objectively an object of gratification (for how could a delusive expectation gratify?), but simply through it as mere play of representations bringing about an equilibrium of the vital powers in the body.[14]

Indeed, for Kant it is not the disappointment of expectation itself, but the "play of representations" that induces and relieves tension first in the body and then in the mind, as humor's effects ping-pong between the two. The "incongruity theory of humor" attributed to Kant has proved the most durable in modern times. As a concept, incongruity is remarkably elastic and applies to anything that confounds expectations: a departure from the form or the norm of our conceptual or social patterns that occasions a pleasurable reorientation rather than distressing disorientation. With its strong physiological emphasis, Kant's cognitive theory anticipates the "relief theory" of laughter, which was worked out in assiduous detail by Herbert Spencer, who explained laughter's "half-convulsive actions" as the organism's liberation of surplus nervous excitement. In keeping with the spirit of his age, Spencer's paradigm is cruder and more mechanical than Kant's. It seems even to anticipate, ironically, Henri Bergson's famous observation in *Le Rire* that laughter is evoked by our perception of "something mechanical encrusted upon the living," a metaphor that revises incongruity theory in light of industrial modernity.[15] Laughter provided relief or temporary reprieve from the physiological strain imposed by "modern times'" technologies and tempo. In the early twentieth century, Sigmund Freud outfitted Spencer's purely physiological relief theory with a psychoanalytical twist whereby the joke (mostly conceived as sexist or racist) provided an escape valve and thus reduced the psychic expenditure necessary for repression. Implicitly, then, jokes for Freud were psychically and economically efficient means to vent civilization's discontents in a socially admissible and, no less importantly, pleasurable way.[16]

---

[14] Immanuel Kant, *Critique of Judgement*. Translated by Nicholas Walker (Oxford: Oxford University Press, 2007), 161.

[15] Henri Bergson, *Laughter: An Essay on the Meaning of the Comic*. Translated by Brereton Cloudesley and Fred Rothwell (Project Gutenberg, 2003) https://www.gutenberg.org/cache/epub/4352/pg4352-images.html

[16] Sigmund Freud, *The Joke's Relation to the Unconscious*. Translated by Joyce Crick with an Introduction by John Carey (New York: Penguin Classics, 2003), 114–15.

Both incongruity and relief theory are premised on what Sianne Ngai and Lauren Berlant refer to as humor's "scalar shifts," which capture its unexpected cognitive and physiological jolts: "comedic events take place with such rapidity or illogicity that we can't believe for a moment what we've seen or what we've heard."[17] The "shift" figures prominently in Mikhail Bakhtin's discussion of carnival, too, where its meaning is ultimately metaphysical, for the "very core of the carnival sense of the world [is] the pathos of shifts and changes, of death and renewal ... carnival celebrates the shift itself, the very process of replaceability, and not the precise item that is replaced."[18] Carnival, explains Bakhtin, is not substance but function, and the same may be said for comedy and humor (too many theorists have become fixated on *what* is funny). For Bakhtin, these shifts are the province of "cheerful relativity," which seems to refer to a cognitive-affective state combining what is frequently referred to as "comic distance" with merriment. Bakhtin's interest in carnival borders on humor and comedy, but his primary focus is the language of carnival, composed of its forms and intimate practices, and how this language shaped modern literature (the "carnivalization of literature"). Nevertheless, Bakhtin's conception of carnival as a "big tent" of ritualized fun is probably capacious enough to accommodate all theories and species of humor: the superiority theory, whereby carnival forces the renewal of authority through ridicule and carnival decrowning; the incongruity theory, because carnival is rife with "eccentricity" and "the violation of the usual and generally accepted"; and most obviously, the relief theory, since carnival provides ritualized relief from the stifling seriousness of officialdom.[19] Bakhtin's carnival is something between a historical institution and a mythical topos. In its essence, carnival is where everyone has license to play, to ignore orders and commands, to be "an active participant ... Carnival is not contemplated, and strictly speaking, not even performed; its participants live in it, they live by its laws as long as those laws are in effect."[20] Bakhtin's formulation soberly reminds us that carnival's "laws" are as transient as the "shift" that it reifies—and that play, pleasure, and eccentricity are life's exceptional states of being, even if the renewal they foster is the rule.

---

[17] Sianne Ngai and Lauren Berlant, "Comedy Has Issues," *Critical Theory*, (Winter 2017): 234.
[18] Mikhail Bakhtin, *Problems of Dostoevsky's Poetics*. Edited and Translated by Caryl Emerson (Minneapolis and London: University of Minnesota Press, 1984), 125. Hereafter abbreviated as *PDP*.
[19] Bakhtin, *PDP*, 126.
[20] Ibid., 122.

Dostoevsky at Play

Dostoevsky was far from what the Greeks conceived as an *eutropelos*, a pleasant person with a happy cast of mind who gives his words and deeds a cheerful turn—anything but. But he did like to play, and not only (as an inveterate gambler) at cards. His brother Andrei recalled Dostoevsky as a "real ball of fire" and the leader and inventor of their childhood games; his wife, Anna, preserved in her memoirs Dostoevsky entertaining their daughter Luba for long stretches while she was indisposed and recalls him gleefully playing practical April Fools' jokes. Even more notably, as Irina Erman shows in the last chapter of this volume, there is ample evidence that playing in the most literal sense fueled Dostoevsky's novelistic creativity.[21] At the same time as Bakhtin was turning his attention to the carnival roots of the Rabelaisan novel, Johan Huizinga published his *Homo Ludens* (1938), which identified play "as the direct opposite of seriousness," and the necessary but insufficient origins of all human culture. Play, as defined by Huizinga, has key points of contact with carnival: it is a sphere of freedom, although structured by rules that create its own order; it is distinct from real "lived" life, both in locality and duration; and it is disinterested and non-utilitarian.[22] In play, human creativity is unbowed by the conditions and structures of "ordinary life" (although play recognizes its inferiority to seriousness) and given free rein. Even though Huizinga himself distinguished between play and laughter or humor, the philosopher of humor John Morreall emphasizes that since all humor is created by someone, amusing people is a way of playing with them.[23]

But how are we let in on the joke, cued to that shift from seriousness and "ordinary life" to jocular play known as humor? The traditional line in the philosophy of humor is that Homo Sapiens is the only species that indulges in comic laughter, and that laughter and humor requires the faculty of abstraction acquired through language. For Huizinga, language forms the very basis of the cognitive shift, since in language the "spirit is continually 'sparking' between matter and mind, as it were, playing with this wondrous nominative faculty."[24]

---

[21] Joseph Frank, *The Seeds of Revolt, 1821–1849* (Princeton: Princeton University Press, 1976), 23; *Vospominaniia A. G. Dostoevskoi*. Edited by A. P. Grossman (Moscow, Leningrad: Gosudarstvennoe izdatel'stvo, 1925), 203–4.

[22] Huizinga, *Homo Ludens*, 8–10.

[23] Morreall, *Comic Relief*, 34.

[24] Huizinga, *Homo Ludens*, 4.

But humans and animals share reliable ways to convey the shift and invite others to share in the fun of play prior to and without language. These include vocalizations and facial expressions, or what is known among evolutionary biologists as "the play pant" (in humans, laughter) and the "open-mouthed play face" (in humans, smiling).[25] Common to human beings and certain mammal species, these signal not only a friendly rather than an aggressive attitude, but the shift from potential fight to boisterous fun. Brian Boyd locates the connection between the fun of mammalian play and the funniness of humor in the surprise and unexpectedness of both, which "catch us off guard … simulate risk and stimulate recovery."[26] We and other mammals are play-seeking creatures not only to tune up our predatory hunting or stalking skills but because, within the delimited space/time of "play faces" and "play pants," we experience incomparable pleasure at surprises, destabilizations, and inversions that allow for risk and recovery, the disruption of expectation followed by the reaffirmation of a more stable meaning.[27]

Morreall and Boyd subscribe to a model of humor that derives from play and so is non-utilitarian and aesthetic, though not in the narrow sense of the beautiful and the ugly.

> Humor is aesthetic to the extent that the cognitive shift is enjoyed for its own sake and not for any boon that it signals or advantage that it achieves. Humor is only one of the modes in which we enjoy cognitive shifts: the aesthetic categories of the tragic, grotesque, macabre, horrible, bizarre, and fantastic. Of these, only humor evokes laughter, the others tend to evoke a negative emotional state.[28]

Both play and the play of humor cue a suspension of seriousness of purpose and disbelief. While the literary arts from drama to the novel cue mimesis or make-believe, only comedy and the humor cue laughter, and these cues, or so Bakhtin would argue, are preserved in the genre memory and so readily accessible to creators of humor and their beneficiaries.

---

[25] Brian Boyd, "Laughter and Literature: A Play Theory of Humor," *Philosophy and Literature*, vol 28, no. 1 (April 2004): 6. Boyd is drawing upon the work of Dutch primatologist, Jan van Hooff, as well as the psychologist Robert Provine, the evolutionary psycholinguist Steven Pinker, and the neuroscientist Terrence Deacon.

[26] Brian Boyd, "Laughter and Literature: A Play Theory of Humor," 10.

[27] Berger notes that such cues or signals are also culturally specific, that there are comic cultures *en miniature* (in families or friend groups), within subcultures, and cultures which extend to entire societies. Berger, *Redeeming Laughter*, 68.

[28] Morreal, *Comic Relief*, 74.

When we imagine Dostoevsky at work on his novelistic creations, we would do well to imagine him as an inveterate playboy, seeking and finding numerous ways to play. The surfeit of "suddenlys," raucous "collective scenes," and buffoonish performances along with the less overtly comically inflected structures that Bakhtin identified as central to Dostoevsky's creation (polyphony, heteroglossia, doubled or layered voicing) create the comic texture intrinsic to his novels. For Bakhtin, of course, the novel itself was a carnivalized genre seeded by the fairground voices and performances of the rogue, the fool, and the clown. In "Discourse and the Novel" Bakhtin locates the origins of the novel itself in funniness, "in the social depths, on fairground stages and popular stages, [where] clowning heteroglossia, the mimicry of all 'languages' and dialects could be heard."[29] Dostoevsky's comic texture is certainly woven from the threads of language, as Tatyana Kovalevskaya observes in her chapter in this volume on the difficulties of translating Dostoevsky's humor. The individualized, idiosyncratic (eccentric) discourse of characters which Bakhtin referred to as heteroglossia serves as one of Dostoevsky's most pervasive comic devices by creating the constant comic irony that everyone is speaking their own language (a language often rife with incongruities) and thus being at least partially, if not entirely, misunderstood. In *The Brothers Karamazov*, Dmitry's response to Grigory's testimony at his trial for his father's murder provides a prime example:

> "Except for the door, it's all true as he said," cried Mitya loudly. "For combing
> the lice out of my hair, I thank him; for forgiving me my blows, I thank him;
> the old man has been honest all his life, and was as faithful to my father
> as seven hundred poodles."
> "Watch your words, defendant," the judge said sternly.
> "I am not a poodle," Grigory also grumbled.
> "Then I am, I am a poodle!" cried Mitya. "If he's offended, I take it upon myself and
> ask his forgiveness: I was a beast and cruel to him! I was cruel to Aesop, too."
> "What Aesop?" the judge again picked up sternly.
> "That Pierrot ... my father, Fyodor Pavlovich."
> The presiding judge repeated once again to Mitya, imposingly and most sternly
> now, that he should watch his words more carefully.
> "You are harming yourself in the opinion of your judges."[30]

---

[29] Mikhail Bakhtin, "Discourse and the Novel: On Issues in the Stylistics of the Novel," in *The Dialogic Imagination: Four Essays*. Edited and Translated by Michael Holquist and Caryl Emerson (Austin, TX: University of Texas Press, 1982), 273.

[30] Dostoevsky *PSS*, 15: 98–9; Dostoevsky, *The Brothers Karamazov*, 666.

The judge reproaches Dmitry as if his rogue use of language (his comic tropes of exaggeration and metaphor) were highly inappropriate in this most serious and official of venues. As the reader well knows, however, this is Dmitry's characteristically eccentric means of sincere self-expression; he has no other. Like his father, Dmitry is a "Pierrot" (a clown) in both love and language, but this linguistic clownishness, which affords the courtroom audience and the reader some amusement, ultimately condemns Dmitry to be tragically misjudged. Dmitry's insistence that "I am, I am a poodle!" is also dialogically directed at the novel's most spiritual teaching: that we are most of all guilty for all and everything. Here, the novel superbly fulfills its carnivalizing function. Dmitry's version parodically chimes with Zosima's "We are all guilty, and I most of all," hilariously rendering it as "we are all poodles, and I am the most poodle-y of all."

Our conception of language must include the body and its languages as well and the prodigious comic capacity of both. While some theorists of humor consider laughter primarily a bodily matter, others recognize that laughter itself is incongruity par excellence, as it brings the opposites of body and soul (mind) together in one ecstatically vibrating mortal coil. Although "physical humor" or "slapstick" is often regarded as humor's lowest form (the crudest fairground fare), in Dostoevsky's art the physical expression of an idea is inseparable from the idea itself, and the absurd gesture throws a comic wrench into the entire endeavor. It is easy, however, to underestimate the complexity of the language of physical humor, which depends on a host of kinesthetic and contextual factors. Both physical and verbal humor can be base and basic (think the oldest tool in the toolbox of jesters and schoolboys: farts) but also exceedingly subtle. "Given that a simple joke can utilize language skills, theory of mind, symbolism, abstract thinking and social perception, humour may arguably be humankind's most complex cognitive attribute."[31] While this may be the self-justifying conclusion of a scholar of comedy, comedy and humor in Dostoevsky is as complex as the linguistic texture and structural polyphony of his novels. In the Dostoevskian novel, ironic incongruity rises like steam at the intersection of different perspectives, or a different perspective illuminates the humorous side of an otherwise appalling situation.

---

[31] Joseph Polimeni and Jeffrey P. Reiss, "'The First Joke: Exploring the Evolutionary Origins of Humor,'" *Evolutionary Psychology*, vol. 4 (2006): 348.

In *Crime and Punishment*, not only the maid Nastasya, but Porfiry Petrovich and Svidrigailov find Raskolnikov sincerely amusing, and their perspectives illuminate the humorous incongruity of Raskolnikov: he is a moralistic murderer and a lay about "man of action." But comic incongruity assumes truly global and ontological proportions in Dostoevsky's thematics of "the ontological jest," first articulated as the Underground Man's premise that "Man is comically arranged" and "a frivolous and unseemly being;" in short, man himself is incongruous. In her chapter devoted to "the ontological jest" in this volume, Alina Wyman examines its profoundly tragic implications for those who sadly cannot take a joke. The irony is that laughter itself confirms human beings' "eccentric" position in the universe, as creatures who perceive the gap between their immediate experience and their reflections on it, between the "physical and psychical"—an absolutely unique position which gives rise to both laughter and despair.[32]

Play Nice

That is not to say that laughter and humor don't have their dark sides. In fact, as noted above, the "dark/diabolical side" was all most medieval Christian writers perceived until Thomas Aquinas infused classical reason into Christianity's view of humor. Nonetheless, contemporary theorists of humor continue to hold humor ethically suspect. If humor is perpetually "freshly dangerous" and exhibits a "propensity to get in trouble" as Ngai and Berlant remark, this is because "the funny is always tripping over the non-funny, sometimes appearing identical to it."[33] Humor is indeed social, exhilarating, and liberating, but it licenses and liberates noxious sentiments, too. As much as it may temporarily diminish self-control, it can facilitate social control by ridiculing, shaming, denigrating, and marginalizing, or simply by reinforcing consensus that is congenial to some and oppressive to others. Within or between social groups, the freewheeling play of humor can be transformed into competition for and shows of dominance, and in such instances Hobbes' superiority theory seems remarkably on the

---

[32] Simon Critchley, *On Humour* (Abingdon: Routledge, 2002), 29–30. Here Critchley draws upon the German anthropologist, Helmuth Plessner, and his seminal work, *Lachen und Weinen* (1941). It is notable how much foundational work on play and laughter was produced prior to or during the Second World War.
[33] Ngai and Berlant, "Comedy Has Issues," 223–4.

mark.³⁴ Several scholars have burst Bakhtin's egalitarian carnival bubble by demonstrating the cruelty of carnival laughter, which "punched down" and targeted disadvantaged groups through brutal and demeaning practices, while others have exposed the state-sponsored gaiety and sinister role of collective ridicule in authoritarian regimes.³⁵

Our intention is not to idealize humor in general or Dostoevsky's humor more specifically. It goes without saying that Dostoevsky doesn't always "play nice"; he often weaponizes humor, especially in his hilarious but blisteringly satirical takedowns of ideological opponents. The weaponization of humor and humorous play are directly opposed in that the former uses humor instrumentally for the purposes of dominance. "Superiority theory" is still alive, well, and eminently applicable here, even though these ridicule fests often perform a social service by exposing the incongruity of hypocritical social posing and ideological positions. Dostoevsky's array of holy fools and buffoons are frequently deployed for the purpose of provocation and exposure within the diegetic worlds of the novels, rather than for their comic properties or humorous play.³⁶ The fool's mask and its cultural authorization simply serve as a comic diversion from the ulterior purposes of his or her activity.

Unarguably, there are genres and uses of humor which sociologists like Peter Berger characterize as "socionegative," including racist, ethnic, and sexist humor.³⁷ As we have seen, Dostoevsky uses ethnic accents, malapropisms, and stereotypes with seeming abandon as comic devices. Yet in calling out Dostoevsky's ethnic humor at the expense of Germans, Poles, or Jews, there is

---

³⁴ David Gillota, *Ethnic Humor in Multiethnic America* (New Brunswick, New York, and London: Rutgers University Press, 2013), 5. Gillota affirms that Hobbes' superiority theory is the most obvious suspect, with Freud's "relief theory" also known as "aggression theory" following close on its heels. Gillota also cites Werner Sollors to remind us that ethnic humor is a form of "boundary construction ... ethnic humorists go to great lengths to build ethnic boundaries and then use their comic skills to defend them, often ingeniously, against real or imagined invaders" (p. 19). In this regard, Dostoevsky's ethnic humor with its aggressive superiority and defense of boundaries works at cross-purposes with carnival laughter as Bakhtin conceives it. Christie Davies, on the other hand, argues that ethnic jokes merely "play with superiority and disparagement," but that unlike games or contests which are processes for deciding actual superiority, a joke's outcome is already given. In this sense, ethnic jokes are "the creation of an illusion, a form of temporary deception by agreement that does not involve a seeking of advantage." Davies, *The Mirth of Nations* (New Brunswick, NJ, and London, UK: Transaction Publishers, 2002), 13–14.

³⁵ Ken Hirschkop, *The Cambridge Introduction to Mikhail Bakhtin* (Cambridge: Cambridge University Press, 2021), 138–9.

³⁶ See my chapter on *Notes from Underground* as comedic provocation. Lynn Ellen Patyk, *Dostoevsky's Provocateurs* (Evanston, IL: Northwestern University Press, 2023), 46–63.

³⁷ Berger, *Redeeming Laughter*, 59.

the danger of feeling ethically (not ethnically) superior to Dostoevsky and of not copping to the fact that we laugh heartily at the scene at the police station in *Crime and Punishment*, when Louisa Ivanovna coaxes Officer Gunpowder out of his explosive pique by laying on thick her heavily German-accented flattery and obsequiousness. An argument could be made for the applicability of every theory of humor to this scene: superiority (on Dostoevsky and the Russian reader's part), incongruity (the honey-tongued whorehouse madam insisting on the "nobility" of her establishment), relief (the strung-out Raskolnikov certainly feels it!), and carnival (the inversion of authority—the prostitute bests the police). But what is most striking is the utter lack of necessity or utilitarian purpose within the plot and novelistic structure, as if Dostoevsky as writer just went off on a romp in the middle of the workday. In this he resembles the painters Mikolka and Mitka in an earlier scene of the novel, who launch into boisterous rough-and-tumble oblivious to the murderer lurking behind the door.

The counterpoint between terror/death and laughter/life could not be more evident than in this seemingly gratuitous scene which juxtaposes Raskolnikov's deadly serious game of hide-and-seek after committing a double murder with the painters' oblivious frolic. Play is life at its most care-free and effusive. Although play and humor are not the same nor do they serve the same adaptive or social-psychological function, humor and comedy originate in the impulse to play, to cast off seriousness and utilitarian purposefulness.[38] Of the philosophers of humor, Robin Tapley follows Huizinga in seeking to distinguish between humor and play: "Humor requires comic distance and a pleasant cognitive shift ... comedy, in all its guises, is a complicated cognitive adventure."[39] Whereas play, according to Tapley, is completely immersive; the cognitive-emotional distance necessary for humor would destroy the utter absorption necessary for play. Tapley's mantra for this distinction is that play is fun, whereas humor is funny.[40] But this, we believe, is a false dichotomy. If we bother to create humor at all, it's precisely because it's fun and requires *both* immersion and distance ("cheerful relativity"). How else could we "lose ourselves" in laughter except through immersion? In our estimation, Homo Sapiens, Homo Ludens, and Homo Ridens are one and the same: knowing, playing, and laughing are inseparable and intrinsic to our being. We're funny,

[38] Ibid., 16.
[39] Robin Tapley, "On Morreall: A Failure to Distinguish between Play and Humor," *The Journal of Value Inquiry*, vol 47, no. 1–2 (2013): 152.
[40] Ibid., 158.

and we know it. Huizinga's concept of play lends support to the Underground Man's hyperconscious sense of man's irrationality, as when Huizinga writes: "Play only becomes possible, thinkable, and understandable when an influx of *mind* breaks down the absolute determinism of the cosmos. The very existence of play continually confirms the supralogical nature of the cosmos. We play and know that we play, so we must be more than rational beings, for play is irrational."[41] Thomas Aquinas clearly perceived the connection between play and humor, deed and word, necessity and pleasure, and laughter and the soul. In Question 168 of *Summa Theologiae*, he described playfulness and humor as virtually one and the same and prescribed them as a necessary elixir: "Those words and deeds in which nothing is sought beyond the soul's pleasure are called playful and humorous, and it is necessary to make use of them at times for solace of the soul."[42] This "solace" or "rest" was to be taken in accord with reason and moderation, and "only when we have done our duty by grave and serious matters."

No one can fault Dostoevsky for not doing his "duty by grave and serious matters"; in fact, we submit that Dostoevsky is readable and *survivable* only because he is both fun and funny. Some Dostoevsky scholars might balk at the notion that play or comic amusement has a central place in Dostoevsky's novels, and it is certainly fair to argue that laughter in Dostoevsky is often mean-spirited if not demonic.[43] In that case, though, the demonic in Dostoevsky exhibits a duality or schism not unlike Dostoevsky's anti-heroes and may be maliciously destructive on the one hand and playfully redeeming on the other. Perhaps our ears are more attuned to the former due to what psychologists call the "negativity bias," which has its literary corollary in the tragedy bias. Peter Berger makes a strong case for "redeeming laughter," which seems at least as applicable—if not more so—to Dostoevsky's art than Bakhtin's "carnival laughter" where "cheerful relativity" indeed often displays cruel undertones. Berger proposes a different paradox than Dostoevsky's devil: that the "comic is the most serious

---

[41] Huizinga, *Homo Ludens*, 4.

[42] Quoted in Morreall, *Comic Relief*, 71.

[43] Adam Weiner unfurls the "Russian tradition of comic literary deviltry" and locates it in the semantic distinction between *demon* and *bes*, the latter being a minor or petty devil which cut a rather mischievous and shabby figure, compared to the formidable *demon*. This folk tradition of comic deviltry resonates with Bakhtin's description of the devil of medieval lore as a "gay ambivalent figure expressing the unofficial point of view" which was superseded by the Romantics' "terrifying, melancholy and tragic" demon whose "infernal laughter was somber and sarcastic." According to Weiner, the Russian novel reflects both traditions by incorporating the "seductive craftiness and insolent derision" of the petty demon and demonic irony. Weiner's reading of Dostoevsky's *The Devils*, however, does not engage the overtly comic aspects. See Weiner, *By Authors Possessed, The Demonic Novel in Russia* (Evanston, IL: Northwestern University Press, 1998), 48–56.

perception of the world there is."⁴⁴ For Berger, humor offers two possibilities for transcendence. The first is the subjective, momentary transcendence of a pedestrian perspective thanks to the estranging and pleasurable "jolt" or "shift" that humor effects. This "lower" form of transcendence is nonetheless both mind- and mood-altering. The second is metaphysical and profoundly resonates with Dostoevsky's Christian worldview. The experience of the comic, according to Berger, is supremely counterfactual, in that it "presents a world in which pain does not exist … Generally, any comedy turns into tragedy as soon as real suffering, real pain are allowed to enter into it."⁴⁵ The promise of redemption through Christ's crucifixion and resurrection offers the vision of just such a painless, comic world, and Christianity's cardinal symbol of the risen Christ, according to Berger, receives its comic incarnation in the jack-in-the-box or the slapstick pratfall, where the fallen spring backs up (as do Raskolnikov, Stepan Verkhovensky, and Dmitry, but not Stavrogin, Prince Myshkin, or Ivan). Both Bakhtin and Berger advance a comic paradigm of the inevitable rebound, although Bakhtin's is founded on cyclical death and renewal, whereas Berger's Christian framework makes the comic vision a fundamentally eschatological one, which faith renders receptive to "signals of transcendence, or if you will, glimpses of Him who is playing the game of cosmic hide-and-seek with us."⁴⁶

A pithier distillation of the Dostoevkian post-Siberian novel as a cosmic/comic game of hide-and-seek is hard to find. Both Berger and Simon Critchley emphasize that humor and play, while woven into the very fabric of life, are still the "exception," the "intrusion," the fleeting "signal of transcendence" that flashes but ultimately enables us to see our flawed world in a new light. Critchley offers a more secular spin on comic revelation. "The consolations of humour come from acknowledging that this is the only world and, imperfect as it is and we are, it is only here that we can make a difference … Humour is not noumenal, but phenomenal, not theological, but anthropological, not numinous, but simply luminous."⁴⁷ Comic laughter is not otherworldly, but this worldly. To paraphrase Ivan Karamazov, humor offers redemption "not somewhere and sometime in infinity, but here and now, on earth, so [we] can see it ourselves."⁴⁸

---

⁴⁴ Berger, *Redeeming Laughter*, 6.
⁴⁵ Ibid., 194–5.
⁴⁶ Ibid., 198.
⁴⁷ Critchley, *On Humour*, 17.
⁴⁸ Dostoevsky, *PSS*, 14: 220; Dostoevsky, *The Brothers Karamazov*, 244.

The most redeemingly comic characters in Dostoevsky's fiction (for this honor we nominate Razumikhin, Madame Epanchina, Ivan's devil) are precisely phenomenal, anthropological, and luminous. They possess an acute awareness of the world's imperfections without forsaking or attempting to destroy it (or themselves). Humor as a "signal of transcendence" that accomplishes momentary reorientation can occur completely unexpectedly even in situations that epitomize irreconcilable antagonism to the world, such as Kirillov's suicide note, when he adds the flourish of a face sticking out its tongue. Out at whom? At his "handler," Peter Verkhovensky, at the whole world, at God, at death? But the *incongruity* of the gesture that expresses Kirillov's sense of *superiority* in this darkest scene of the novel is simply funny—dark, but funny—and offers the flash of *relief* from the tension of the scene as well as from the killing seriousness still to come in the novel. In a similar but far more redemptive vein, Ivan's devil is not a chthonic figure from the Underworld but can be read as more of a Lucifer and an *eutrepolos*, bringing witty and lighthearted illumination to Ivan's deadly serious delusions.

"Für die Frauen": Finding Dostoevsky Funny

The project of finding Dostoevsky funny seems at first a bit audacious and uncouth, like the Englishwoman inadvertently bursting in on "die Männer," where nature's endowments were on full display. Indeed, the contributors to this volume are all women who have "burst in" on an unduly "seriousified" author, begging the question of whether a focus on the lost or marginalized comedy of Dostoevsky may in some respects be a gendered project. Are only women willing to openly laugh at Dostoevsky, to find him funny, just as the maid Nastasya in *Crime and Punishment* dissolves into irrepressible laughter at a man (Raskolnikov) who takes his thinking so lethally seriously?[49] Several of the

---

[49] There is a tradition, originating in antiquity, of maids' (women's) mirth at their masters' serious preoccupations. In *Theaetetus*, Plato has Socrates launch his inquiry with the following anecdote: "[The] jest which the clever witty Thracian handmaid is said to have made about Thales, when he fell into a well while looking up at the stars. She said that he was so eager to know what was going on in heaven that he could not see what was before his feet." Plato added that this applies to anyone who gets involved with philosophy. Cited in Berger, 15. And in Erasmus's *In Praise of Folly*, Folly is personified as a female divinity who claims herself the "fountain and nursery of life" and "[debunks] the pretensions of academics and other intellectuals." Berger, *Redeeming Laughter*, 20. Berger offers a number of anecdotes featuring the humorous/comic debunking of a serious male "thinker" by a feminized being but does not himself recognize the gendered aspect of the enterprise.

chapters in this volume address gender and/or the marginalization of comedy, and all intrepidly reveal the comedy and humor that have been in plain view all along. Perhaps like Erasmus's female divinity Folly, female subjectivity embodies the comic experience based on its "foolish estrangement" from patriarchal seriousness and is therefore more attuned to the underlying truths of the comic worldview.

Caryl Emerson's chapter "Bakhtin and the Laughing Genres on the Brink of War" addresses the elephant in the room (Bakhtin) and his interest (or lack thereof) in comedy and humor. Despite being the theorist of the renewing laughter of carnival, Bakhtin published surprisingly little on comedy as such, and even less in the context of his work on Dostoevsky. Emerson traces and elucidates Bakhtin's thoughts on the laughing genres and identifies his work on satire at the bleak end of the 1930s as a "tipping point" in his evolving "metaphysics of laughter." For Bakhtin, the most ancient and productive form of satire was not ridicule but an open-ended, good-natured negation of the present. Its purpose was to "refresh" and "renew," but not with any specific replacement filler or forms in mind; satire simply feels good the way an unplanned vacation or playing hooky feels good. Insofar as the Dostoevskian novel goes, Emerson finds that Bakhtin's metaphysics of the carnival mask of the rogue, clown, or fool illuminates how the wily Dostoevskian narrator with his comic tonality and shiftiness emerges as a key element in the novel's carnivalization, or for our purposes, its "funniness."

The translation of Dostoevsky's comedy and humor, as Tatyana Kovalevskaya shows in her chapter, is far from fun and games, however: it's intensely demanding work. Kovalevskaya deftly demonstrates the difficulties of translating Dostoevsky's humor into English by comparing different translators' accomplishments in rendering key comic moments from his darkest (and funniest) works. In highlighting Dostoevsky's favored comic devices, Kovalevskaya identifies his penchant for "heuristic irony" and layered voicing, wherein the comic effect is achieved by mixing stylistic registers and/or using unexpected shifts in meanings of commonly used words. While this type of humor poses extra difficulties for the translator, Kovalevskaya's analysis emphasizes the importance of recognizing that Dostoevsky's humor not only plays an important tonal role but also is intrinsic to the ideational aspects of his works.

Of the volume's chapters, Fiona Bell's reading of Raskolnikov as a murderous clown (or clownish murderer) is the most audacious in finding Dostoevsky's anti-heroes funny. Bell offers a deeply original reading of *The Double* and *Crime and Punishment* through the prism of the slapstick genre. Like Dostoevsky himself, slapstick comedy sits at the nexus of social critique and spirituality. It is a performance genre deeply concerned with the absurdity of work under capitalism and the self-victimization of capitalism's clownish drones. Simultaneously, like Orthodox theology, slapstick emphasizes the fallibility of the body and the fallacy of human authority. Bell reveals the slapstick mode, with its ontological and spiritual implications, at the heart of Dostoevsky's most "serious" works.

If, after Bell's chapter, we find this both funny and deeply disturbing, Melissa Frazier drills down to discover why in her chapter on "Sensations of Laughter." Dostoevsky was a master of sensation in more ways than one, with a reputation for provoking strong physiological reactions in his readers. Laughter, argues Frazier, was one of the more benign of these reactions, and the materialism of his nihilist ideological opponents was a frequent butt of his jokes. Frazier argues that Dostoevsky's many comic riffs on (im)materiality, above all in *The Brothers Karamazov*, make the same point on two levels at once. Firstly, they expose and mock the hypocrisy of Chernyshevsky-style "vulgar materialists," who claim the primacy of the material world only to deny their bodies in service of their ideological quest. Secondly, drawing upon Alenka Zupančič's theory of comedy, Frazier shows how Dostoevsky's jokes advocate a different relationship with the material world in which mind and body, spirit and matter are intertwined.

Which is not always a good thing. As Alina Wyman argues, Dostoevsky's heroes are acutely aware that "man is comically arranged," a mortal creature striving for eternity. This "ontological jest" is the source of deep existential suffering for Dostoevsky's *ressentiment*-afflicted heroes and metaphysical rebels, and whether they "get the joke" depends on what Wyman refers to as their "comedy coefficient": their ability to achieve the freedom intrinsic to humor (as might Vladimir Soloviev) and perspective or comic distance (as does Lev Pumpiansky) to find it funny. Unfortunately, only the Underground Man has the comic chops to give as good as he gets, whereas the tubercular young Ippolit in *The Idiot*, an especially painful case, manifests the bathos of metaphysical rebellion. His attempt to preempt the cosmic comedian ends only in a humiliating farce.

Arguably, Ippolit's youthfulness (the dying boy is only nineteen) prompts him to rush to meet death head on—which results in his farcical suicide attempt. In her chapter the "Impatience of Youth in *Demons*," Chloe Papadopoulos demonstrates how youth plus impatience equals a very successful comic formula not only in *The Idiot*, but in Dostoevsky's novel about revolutionary violence and terror, *Demons*. The comic tension between the intimidating but completely indifferent "leaders" (Stavrogin and Verkhovensky) of the revolutionary cell and the ridiculous and rushed younger cohort is fundamental to Dostoevsky's *Demons*, which represents one of the author's strongest critiques of sudden, sweeping social upheaval. Combining unyielding temporality with the cognitive-affective state of expectation, Dostoevsky renders revolutionary impatience a prime target of comic incongruity as formulated by Kant, where strained expectation resolves into nothing—or alternately, into something disastrously unexpected. *Demons*' critical stance vis-à-vis revolutionary social movements hinges on its rendering of its radical youths (especially the female nihilist who exhibits a thirst for change that manifests as boisterous impatience) as both menacing and downright hilarious.

Dostoevsky's darkest novel, *Demons*, may in fact also be his funniest, but Susanne Fusso illuminates a different kind of parody, one in which adversarial humor is not key to its power to renew. Parody need not be funny, and Fusso demonstrates how *Demons*, or *Devils* (1869), and Lin-Manuel Miranda's *Hamilton* (2015) employ what she identifies as "restorative parody." Hinging on an in-depth reading of the Shatov family nativity scene with Maria as an edgy, nihilist Madonna in *Devils* and the rapping revolutionary fathers in *Hamilton*, this chapter demonstrates the provocative parallels in both authors' use of the double-edged word of parody to radically renew petrified values and symbols: motherhood and the Sistine Madonna in Dostoevsky's case and the Founding Fathers in Miranda's.

Our volume's final chapter confronts the issue of gender and comedy head-on. It is a commonplace of Dostoevsky criticism when it does focus on gender to identify the victimization of women at the core of his narratives and to then contend with whether this manifests the misogyny of his "cruel talent" or the proto-feminism of his social critique. Irina Erman, in her chapter "The Funny and the Furious: Laughter and Gender in Dostoevsky," takes a different approach and begins by demonstrating that humor and play were intrinsic to Dostoevsky's creative process and his staging of an emphatically feminized comic counterpoint to misogynist violence in his 1866 novel *Crime and Punishment*. The chapter then turns to earlier texts, namely, "The Husband under the Bed" and "Uncle's Dream" to trace the evolution of Dostoevsky's feminine/feminist comic type: a wily, unruly, and profoundly hilarious heroine. This heroine is fully realized in *The Idiot*'s Madame Epanchina, where her phenomenal capacity for taking on problematic gender relations through dimensions of laughter and thereby defying patriarchy's objectifying, abusive power structures is on luminous display.

Dostoevsky's novels have, among other things, made us laugh a lot. Until *Funny Dostoevsky*, we thought that perhaps we were laughing alone, mistaking the "unfunny" for the funny or out of some twisted sense of humor that Dostoevsky's Underground types would fully share. The contributions to this volume, however, offer what Bakhtin refers to as affirming "choral support" for our laughter. More than that, our bid to illuminate Dostoevsky's light side, his penchant for humorous play, reveals the more profound comic sensibility that inflects his tragic vision and buoys his faith.

Bibliography

Bakhtin, Mikhail. "Discourse and the Novel: On Issues in the Stylistics of the Novel," in *The Dialogic Imagination: Four Essays*. Edited and Translated by Michael Holquist and Caryl Emerson, 259–422. Austin, TX: University of Texas Press, 1981.

Bakhtin, Mikhail. *Problems of Dostoevsky's Poetics*. Edited and Translated by Caryl Emerson. Minneapolis and London: University of Minnesota Press, 1984.

Berger, Peter. *Redeeming Laughter: The Comic Dimension of the Human Experience*. New York: Walter de Gruyter, 1997.

Bergson, Henri. *Laughter: An Essay on the Meaning of the Comic*. Translated by Brereton Cloudesley and Fred Rothwell. Project Gutenberg, 2003, https://www.gutenberg.org/cache/epub/4352/pg4352-images.html.

Boyd, Brian. "Laughter and Literature: A Play Theory of Humor," *Philosophy and Literature*, vol. 28, no. 1 (April 2004): 1–22.

Busch, R. L. *Humor in the Major Novels of Dostoevsky*. Columbus, OH: Slavica Publishers, 1987.

Critchley, Simon. *On Humour*. Abingdon: Routledge, 2002.

Davies, Christie. *The Mirth of Nations*. New Brunswick, NJ and London: Transaction Publishers, 2002.

de Vogüé, Eugène-Melchior. *Le Roman Russse* [The Russian Novelists]. Translated by Jane Loring Edmands. Boston: D. Lothrop Co, 1887.

Dostoevskaia, Anna. *Vospominaniia A. G. Dostoevskoi*. Edited by L. P. Grossman. Moscow and Leningrad: Gosudarstvennoe izdatel'stvo, 1925.

Dostoevsky, Fyodor. *The Brothers Karamazov*. Translated by Richard Pevear and Larissa Volokhonsky. New York: Farrar, Straus and Giroux, 2002.

Dostoevsky, Fyodor. *Fyodor Dostoevsky, Complete Letters*, vol. 4, 1872–7. Edited and Translated by David Lowe. Ann Arbor, MI: Ardis, 1991.

Dostoevsky, Fyodor. *Polnoe sobranie sochinenii i pisem v tridtsati tomakh*. Ed. by V. G. Bazanov, et al. Leningrad: Nauka, 1972–1990.

Frank, Joseph. *The Seeds of Revolt, 1821–1849*. Princeton, NJ: Princeton University Press, 1976.

Freud, Sigmund. *The Joke's Relation to the Unconscious*. Translated by Joyce Crick with an Introduction by John Carey. New York: Penguin Classics, 2003.

Gillota, David. *Ethnic Humor in Multiethnic America*. New Brunswick, New York, and London: Rutgers University Press, 2013.

Givens, John. "A Narrow Escape into Faith? Dostoevsky's *Idiot* and the Christology of Comedy," *The Russian Review*, vol. 70, no. 1 (2011): 95–117.

Hirschkop, Ken. *The Cambridge Introduction to Mikhail Bakhtin*. Cambridge: Cambridge University Press, 2021.

Hudspith, Sarah. "Why We Must Laugh at the Underground Man," *Studies in Slavic Literature and Poetics*, Leiden, vol. 57 (2012): 67–79.

Huizinga, Johan. *Homo Ludens: A Study of the Play Element in Culture*. London: Routledge, 2002.

Ingle, Zachary T. "A Full Meal with a Vitamin Pill and Extra Wheatgerm: Woody Allen, Dostoevsky, and Existential Morality," in *Referentiality and the Films of Woody Allen*. Edited by Klara Stephanie Szlezák and Dianah E. Wynter, 119–36. London: Palgrave Macmillan, 2015.

Kant, Immanuel. *Critique of Judgement*. Translated by Nicholas Walker. Oxford: Oxford University Press, 2007.

Martakova, T. S. "Antropologiia smekha v proizvedeniiakh Dostoevskogo (1846–1859): K voprosu o 'smekhovom portrete' [Anthropology of Laughter in Dostoevsky's Works (1846–1859): Toward a 'Laughter Portrait']," *Vestnik Cheliabinskogo gosudarstvennogo universiteta* [*Chelyabinsk State University Bulletin*], vol. 15 (2007): 89–94.

Miller-Gulland, Robin and Olga Soboleva. "'Excellent Material, I See:' What Happens in Bobok?," *Studies in Slavic Literature and Poetics*, Leiden, vol. 57 (2012): 135–47.

Morreall, John. *Comic Relief: A Comprehensive Philosophy of Humor*. Malden, MA: John Wiley and Sons, 2009.

Ngai, Sianne and Lauren Berlant. "Comedy Has Issues," *Critical Theory*, vol. 43, no. 2 (Winter 2017): 230–42.

Polimeni, Joseph and Jeffrey P. Reiss. "The First Joke: Exploring the Evolutionary Origins of Humor," *Evolutionary Psychology*, vol. 4 (2006): 347–66.

Rozenblium, L. M. "Iumor Dostoevskogo ['Dostoevsky's Humor']," *Voprosy literatury* (*Literary Questions*), vol. 1 (1999): 141–89.

Tapley, Robin. "On Morreall: A Failure to Distinguish between Play and Humor," *The Journal of Value Inquiry*, vol. 47 (2013): 147–62.

Tynianov, Yuri. "Dostoevsky and Gogol (Toward a Theory of Parody) (1919/1921)," in *Permanent Evolution: Selected Essays on Literature, Theory, and Film*. Translated and Edited by Ainsley Morse and Philip Redko, 27–63. Boston, MA: Academic Studies Press, 2019.

Weiner, Adam. *By Authors Possessed, The Demonic Novel in Russia*. Evanston, IL: Northwestern University Press, 1998.

1

Bakhtin and the Laughing Genres on the Brink of Total War

Caryl Emerson

Late in 1940, Mikhail Bakhtin was commissioned to write an entry on "Satire" for the Soviet *Literary Encyclopedia*. Hoping to avoid re-arrest, he and his wife were sitting out the latest wave of Stalinist terror in the town of Savelevo, north of Moscow. Despite the inconvenience of internal exile and his worsening osteomyelitis (resolved by the amputation of his right leg in 1938), Bakhtin had been exceptionally productive throughout the 1930s. As Ken Hirschkop demonstrates in his recent excellent book on Bakhtin's life and works, during this decade Bakhtin produced drafts of several studies on the European novel as well as a thousand pages of handwritten notes that morphed into three huge projects, none of them definitively completed.[1] The first was a treatise on the Bildungsroman. The second was a history of Western literary forms through a meta-concept Bakhtin called the chronotope. The third, featuring François Rabelais, was a massive study of popular-festive forms, the folkloric grotesque, and cultures of laughter.

The first two projects, Hirschkop argues, were compatible with the norms of Soviet literary scholarship during the 1930s and designed to fit in to its current debates.[2] However, the study of Rabelais, eventually submitted as a doctoral dissertation, did not fit in; its defense was even something of a scandal. As for Bakhtin's entry on satire, it never appeared. Page proofs of the *Encyclopedia*'s

---

[1] Ken Hirschkop, *The Cambridge Introduction to Mikhail Bakhtin* (Cambridge: Cambridge University Press, 2021), 106–15.

[2] Ibid., 90. One of Hirschkop's aims is to dispel the myth that Bakhtin was some solitary genius "intellectually stranded" in a Stalinist wasteland. Regretfully, the English translations of Bakhtin's work from the 1930s were made from heavily edited versions published in the 1970s, cleansed of many references.

final volume disappeared in the chaos of the German invasion, and Bakhtin's contribution was later reconstructed from his drafts.[3]

This 1940 exercise on satire, one of many attempts by Bakhtin to tie comedic energy to the history of the novel, is a useful focus for what Robert Bird (who translated the entry) calls Bakhtin's "metaphysics of laughter."[4] Its account of the laughing genres is not as ecstatic as his later global bestseller, *Rabelais and His World*. Here Bakhtin writes according to template; he is obliged to move fast over many years and national traditions, cramming in names and categories from Hellenistic times up to the Soviet present. But one senses a certain excitement. Nothing by Bakhtin had been published since his book on Dostoevsky in 1929, and a decade's worth of new ideas seemed to find enthusiastic release in this last-minute commission. As with so many of Bakhtin's now-famous concepts—dialogue, polyphony, heteroglossia, the ambivalent grotesque—his theory of satire, Bird argues, should be read neither as "empirical generalization" of data, nor as a description of any actually existing mode or genre. It is, rather, an "active intervention" in cultural awareness, a *model* of how Bakhtin wanted the world to behave.[5] The encyclopedia entry and a brief note from the same period, "On the Question of a Theory of Laughter" [*K voprosam teorii smekha*],[6] are visionary statements. Both complain that the wrong scholarly work has been done and the truth of laughter overlooked.

These two texts also provide a backstory to the huge new chapter 4 that Bakhtin, two decades later, would add to his revised edition of the Dostoevsky book (1963). Its hero is the omnivorous but spectral genre of Menippean satire. The first half of this chapter, announced by Bakhtin as a "historical digression" that would oblige him to "take leave of Dostoevsky for a time" so as to visit "the most remote antiquity," has been much criticized.[7] It is not organic to arguments

---

[3] M. M. Bakhtin, "Satira" in *Sobranie sochinenii v semi tomakh*. (Moscow: Russkie slovari, 1996), 5: 11–38. (The Collected Works henceforth noted as *Ss*). For a translation, see M. M. Bakhtin, "Satire," Translated and Annotated by Robert Bird, in *Persistent Forms. Explorations in Historical Poetics*. Edited by Ilya Kliger and Boris Maslov (New York: Fordham University Press, 2016), 369–91.

[4] Robert Bird, "Schematics and Models of Genre. Bakhtin and Soviet Satire," in *Persistent Forms*. 429–57, here 433.

[5] Ibid., 431–2.

[6] M. M. Bakhtin, "K voprosam teorii smekha," *Ss*, 5: 49–50. This single page of text was found together with Bakhtin's further notes toward a theory of the novel and segues into comments on the poet Mayakovsky, all jottings from the early 1940s.

[7] M. M. Bakhtin, "Zhanrovye i siuzhetno-kompozitsionnye osobennosti proizvedenii Dostoevskogo," *Ss*, t. 6: *Problemy poetiki Dostoevskogo*, 120. In English, Mikhail Bakhtin, *Problems of Dostoevsky's Poetics*. Translated by Caryl Emerson (Minneapolis: University of Minnesota Press, 1984), chapter 4. "Characteristics of Genre and Plot Composition in Dostoevsky's Works," 106–37. Further in text referred to as: PPD *Ss* 6 (for Russian); PDP (for English).

in the other more formal text- and word-centered chapters. Its generalizations are too broad; their tone is more rapturous than scholarly. What is more, Bakhtin claims that Dostoevsky accessed this ancient laughing tradition not through knowledge of any founding texts (of which almost none survive) but by a curious vehicle Bakhtin calls "genre memory"—not Dostoevsky's "subjective memory," but the "objective memory of the very genre in which he worked."[8] Granting these reservations, the expansive, euphoric chapter 4 also accomplishes more modest and necessary literary tasks. It contains subtle close readings of crisis time and threshold space that integrate into a single persuasive worldview Dostoevsky's love of public scandal, his quest for an antinomic sense of truth that mandates the coexistence and reconciliation of opposites, and his elaboration, largely successful, of a non-biographical model for personal maturation. But most importantly for us here, in his new chapter 4 Bakhtin connects, at the root, virtues that have often been presented as opposed: a "carnival sense of the world" permeated by laughter, and the more sober, responsible arts of dialogue and polyphony.[9]

Do these virtues justify the anthropomorphizing move to give genre itself a memory? Ilya Kliger has argued on Bakhtin's behalf that it does; for genre memory does not function as a repository for personal, concretely framed past events. Rather, it is an energy, generous and ephemeral, feeding into a domain that Bakhtin calls Great (i.e., nonlinear) Time [*bol'shoe vremia*] and Great (i.e., supra-personal) Experience [*bol'shoi opyt*]. Accessing this force enables a writer to grasp an entire worldview, sometimes hitherto unbeknownst to him, via contact with the thinnest slice of a genre, at times only an intuition of its driving spirit.[10] "Does this mean that Dostoevsky proceeded *directly* and *consciously* from the ancient menippea?" Bakhtin asks. "Of course not!"[11] But Dostoevsky was certainly familiar with works that had been carrying this energy for millennia.

---

[8] Bakhtin, PPD, *Ss*, 6: 137; PDP, 121.

[9] In this regard, this chapter is something of a milestone for its author. My initial distaste for carnival was intense, as reflected in an early co-authored speculative study, Gary Saul Morson and Caryl Emerson, *Mikhail Bakhtin: Creation of a Prosaics* (Stanford: Stanford University Press, 1990), Part III, ch. 10, "Laughter and the Carnivalesque," 433–70. As more of Bakhtin was published and annotated in the emerging Russian Collected Works, I began to modify my view; see Caryl Emerson, "Coming to Terms with Bakhtin's Carnival: Ancient, Modern, Sub Specie Aeternitatis," in *Bakhtin and the Classics*. Edited by R. Bracht Branham (Evanston: Northwestern University Press, 2002), 5–26. Now, two decades later, I think I appreciate Bakhtin's position.

[10] Ilya Kliger, "On 'Genre Memory' in Bakhtin," in *Persistent Forms*. Edited by Kliger and Maslov (New York: Fordham University Press, 2016), 227–51.

[11] Bakhtin, PPD, *Ss*, 6: 137; PDP, 121.

The heady concepts of Great Time, Great Experience, and Great Memory first appear in Bakhtin's fragmentary writings in the early-to-mid 1940s. They reflect the continuing evolution in his thought away from classical notions of the subject and toward a more trans-personal concept of genre, understood as categories of value and energy to which I can contribute creatively, but which do not depend upon me and need not remember me. Galin Tihanov has suggested that during these years Bakhtin evolves from a language-centered personalist into a philosopher of culture, perhaps even one "who would have liked to write a history of literature without names." The philosophical footprint becomes a "humanism without subjectivity," an "odd, decentered Bakhtinian humanism, seeking and celebrating alterity rather than otherness, and revolving not around the individual but around the generic abilities of the human species to resist and endure in the face of natural cataclysms or an ideological monopoly on truth."[12] Bakhtin's "greatest breakthrough as a thinker," Tihanov contends, comes during the 1930s, with texts that "continue to teach proximity without empathy, optimism without promise or closure." For Bakhtin, these values of non-empathetic proximity and promise-free optimism found their warmest welcome in the laughing genres.

This chapter considers Bakhtin's metaphysics of laughter as it came together at this mid-career tipping point, in between his two versions of the Dostoevsky book (1929/1963). Alternately despairing and inspirational, Bakhtin's patchy, enigmatic writings from the war period fill volume 5 of his Collected Works. Thanks to the meticulous labors of Irina Denischenko and Alexander Spektor (and in an earlier pioneering excerpt, Sergeiy Sandler), these fragments are now moving into English.[13] It is always a delicate enterprise to work with scraps of writing that were never prepared, or even intended, for publication. A lapidary phrase that was a mere placeholder for its author can become, for later readers, too easy to remember, like an aphorism or a limerick, and thus too authoritative. Bakhtin's legacy is heavy in such rough drafts. In his recent book on Bakhtin, Hirschkop foregrounds the fact that only one scholarly project was published "on

---

[12] Galin Tihanov, *The Birth and Death of Literary Theory: Regimes of Relevance in Russia and Beyond* (Stanford: Stanford University Press, 2019), ch. 3, "Toward a Philosophy of Culture: Bakhtin beyond Literary Theory," 106–8.

[13] See M. M. Bakhtin, "Bakhtin on Shakespeare: Excerpt from 'Additions and Changes to *Rabelais*'," Translated by Sergeiy Sandler, *PMLA*, vol. 129, no. 3 (May 2014): 522–37. Three additional texts were translated by Denischenko and Spektor for their forum, "The Dark and Radiant Bakhtin. Wartime Notes," in *Slavic and East European Journal* 61.2 (Summer 2017). A volume of these and other texts from the 1940s is forthcoming 2024 under their editorship with the title *Bakhtin at the Mirror. Notebooks and Fragments*.

time" (i.e., soon after it was written): the initial 1929 edition of the Dostoevsky book. Bakhtin's other writings—working notebooks, outlines, finished and unfinished monographs—were censored, shaped, and edited by others, often decades later, all of them "in some way deformed and distorted."[14] From these uncertain texts, most of the English translations were made.

More significant for the Russian context, however, is that Bakhtin's developing thought did not enter public circulation. From 1930 through the 1950s, his ideas were not formally aired or reviewed in print and did not provoke debate and feedback. Perhaps, given capricious Soviet censorship and Russia's increasingly unfree academic discourse, this non-dialogic, self-enclosed state of affairs was a blessing to the integrity of Bakhtin's ideas. Such a hypothesis legitimates somewhat our focus in this chapter on two unpublished texts. For the first, the "Satire" entry, Bakhtin is known to have revised it twice in accordance with the editor's comments. (By nature not polemical, Bakhtin was also no coward in public forums. Here, at least, he was the one making the revisions; since the essay's final paragraph is pure Stalinist boilerplate, contradicting everything said prior to it, it is best read as itself satiric.) The second text, "On the Question of a Theory of Laughter," is a brief polemic against then-regnant theories of laughter, primarily Henri Bergson's. Bakhtin appears to have written this note solely to, and for, himself. Together, these two texts provide a guide to Bakhtin's metaphysics of laughter that is arguably more compact, transparent, and universal than either of the arguments attached to novelists: the Menippean satire appended to Dostoevsky in 1963, or the earlier, extravagantly annotated socio-ethnic study of laughing cultures in Rabelais.

By Saying No, Laughter Opens the Way to Yes

Bakhtin begins his 1940 encyclopedia essay by defining three types of satire. Two of them are literary genres (Roman and Greek); the other is an attitude that an author can apply to any genre—namely, a negating intent toward a concrete object. Common to all three is that the satirist is harsh on the present.

---

[14] Hirschkop, *The Cambridge Introduction to Mikhail Bakhtin*, 59. Since Bakhtin kept circling around the same subject matter, little of which entered the public domain, Hirschkop helpfully provides a "List of Bakhtin's published works" organized not chronologically but topically. The laughing genres are subsumed under "Works on Rabelais (popular-festive culture and the novel): 1938 onwards" (pp. 65–6).

But crucially, although satire negates what it sees, this negation is not one-way or single-voiced; ridicule and profanity occur in the context of some new or better thing glimpsed on the horizon. (Early on, we sense that satire is run by the same dynamics that govern the other polarly fused, socially addressed emotions in Bakhtin, such as the praise–blame rituals in carnival.) Satire is rooted in ancient "popular-festive forms"—this phrase is something of a godterm for Bakhtin—and such images, being cyclical and supra-personal, cannot be nihilistic. Nothing disappears that is not immediately replaced; indeed, those processes are simultaneous. "Laughter fixes, as it were, the very moment of this change," Bakhtin writes; it is change itself that is celebrated, rather than the qualities adhering to before or after.[15] Such is the overarching principle of his metaphysics of laughter: its energy works not primarily along the axes of superiority, unexpectedness, or incongruity (as in most classical theories of laughter), or even along the axis of ethics (for laughter can be joyous or cruel). Satire is dependent not on emotions but on the more neutral axis of time. Being old and dying are always laughable and negated; being born and being young are unequivocally affirmative. Such nonnegotiable generational negation is beyond judgment and supremely healthy, Bakhtin avers; it is a natural result of the "spontaneous dialectical nature of ridicule."

It is important to grasp how Bakhtin uses the term "negation" [*otritsanie*] when speaking of the laughing genres and a dialectics of ridicule. It is not the linear, progressive Hegelian "overcoming" of thesis by antithesis resulting in new synthesis. Everything coexists. In 2010, Ksana Blank explored Dostoevsky's idea of antinomies—the coexistence of contrary truths and the interdependence of opposites—in the context of Lao Tzu, Heraclitus, Aristotle, Kant, and several Russian religious philosophers, concluding her book on Mikhail Bakhtin.[16] Contrasting Ivan Karamazov's rationalistic "Euclidian mind" and the Elder Zosima's "alternative approach to contradiction," Blank shows how characters' truths in Dostoevsky "are not just conflicting but also mutually fulfilling," since "thesis and antithesis are inseparable."[17] More recently Denis Zhernokleyev, in an illuminating study of Bakhtin's 1944 fragment "On Flaubert," assigns the

---

[15] Bakhtin, "Satire," 375.
[16] Ksana Blank, *Dostoevsky's Dialectics and the Problem of Sin* (Evanston: Northwestern University Press, 2010), ch. 7, "Antinomic Truth (*Istina*)," 111–20. Blank draws parallels between Bakhtin's dialogism and Pavel Florensky, Sergii Bulgakov, Nicholas Berdyaev, and Semyon Frank.
[17] Ibid., 118–19.

"negating image" a spiritually ambitious role.[18] It does not resolve in a higher synthesis. It does not serve disintegration, degradation, decay—all gloomy processes obsessed with the fate of individual bodies and texts. Nor does this image feed our sentimental fascination with things gothic or grotesque. Optimally for Bakhtin, negation is larger than that; it is apophatic, inclusive, liberating. We do not laugh down a thing out of fear, anger, grief, or denial. Laughing is done from a position of strength, and thus always refreshes and renews the entire surrounding world. Here we might recall Viktor Shklovsky conceiving his idea of defamiliarization, *ostranenie*, in the trenches of the First World War: make even what is awful wondrous and strange. Now, one Total War later, Bakhtin, a respectful opponent of Russian Formalism in the 1920s, deploys the positive energy of negating laughter not to renew the aesthetic pleasure of individual perception but to urge on us a medieval cosmology of supra-individual wholes. The laughter of ridicule is outside of time; it cannot be reduced to an epic shaming contest or a "lyric of indignation." Folkloric laughter works like a faith system. It confirms that no person is ever alone, and that there is no death. Robert Bird is correct to call Bakhtin's theory of laughter precisely a metaphysics—not a physics, an empirical practice, a politics, or even a personal therapy.

This optimistic archaic worldview is further reinforced in our second text: Bakhtin's brief, undated, thoroughly dissatisfied note on theories of laughter from the early 1940s.[19] Its targets are Kant, Spencer, and above all Henri Bergson, whose *Le Rire* (1900) was well-known in Russian circles.[20] According to Bergson, laughter is overall a blank, mean-spirited reflex. We laugh at physical awkwardness, rigidity, or whenever we sense "something mechanical encrusted on the living," that is, when "a person gives us the impression of being a thing."[21] Essential to the spontaneous laughter-reflex, Bergson insists, is an "absence of

---

[18] Denis A. Zhernokleev, "Bakhtin o Flobere: poetika 'otritsaiushchego obraza'," *Literaturovedcheskii zhurnal*, vol. 54, no. 4 (2021): 166–78. Here as with Rabelais and Dostoevsky, Zhernokleyev assures us, Bakhtin does not approach Flaubert with "formal philological interest" as much as "submerge him in the vortexing movement of his own thought." For all that Flaubert has been associated with Decadence and fin-de-siècle naturalism, Bakhtin focuses on *La Tentation de Saint Antoine* as his central text. Bakhtin's fragment appears as "<O Flobere>" in Bakhtin, *Ss*, 5: 130–7, and is included in Denischenko and Spektor, eds., *Bakhtin at the Mirror*.

[19] "K voprosam teorii smekha," in Bakhtin, *Ss*, 5: 49–50.

[20] Henri Bergson's *Le Rire* was translated into Russian as *Smekh v zhizni i na stsene* [*Laughter in life and on stage*, 1900]; Bakhtin in Savelevo appears to have consulted a later translation, from 1914.

[21] Quotes are from Henri Bergson, *Laughter. An Essay on the Meaning of the Comic*. Authorized translation by Cloudesley Brereton and Fred Rothwell (New York: Macmillan, 1911), 37, 58.

feeling." "Indifference is its natural environment, for laughter has no greater foe than emotion."[22] Unsurprisingly, Bergson's argument draws heavily on Molière and on traditions of commedia dell'arte in its presupposition that "every comic character is a type," doomed to repetition and unable to react to the world in an unexpected way.[23] Near the end of his essay, Bergson provides a dour summary of his thesis that clearly caught Bakhtin's eye, because he quotes a phrase from it verbatim in his own brief note. "Laughter is, above all, a corrective," Bergson writes. "Being intended to humiliate, it must make a painful impression on the person against whom it is directed. [...] Laughter punishes certain failings somewhat as disease punishes certain forms of excess, striking down some who are innocent and sparing some who are guilty [...] In this sense, laughter cannot be absolutely just. Nor should it be kind-hearted either."[24]

Bakhtin's rebuttal of this ascetic, punitive theory is straightforward, foregrounding his preference, as a classicist, for the more affirmative mocking genres of antiquity.[25] Bakhtin opens his note on a paraphrase of Kant: "Laughter is caused by an expectation that suddenly resolves into nothing."[26] Next cited is Herbert Spencer, who is also deflating; we laugh, says Spencer, when our efforts "lead us to a barren spot." Both definitions endorse what Bakhtin everywhere resists: the notion that we laugh because we are disappointed. This ignores the "moment of joy and merriment that is present in all living, sincere laughter."[27] Here as elsewhere, Bakhtin the classicist appears to work with a concept of hope that was current in the ancient pagan world, namely, that to hope for a positive thing is a weakness and a set-up for failure—distracting, irrational, self-destructive, and offensive to the gods.[28] The most we should do is to hope

---

[22] Bergson, *Laughter*, 4.

[23] Ibid., 148.

[24] Ibid., 197–8.

[25] Bakhtin's refutation of Bergson closely follows the argument in *Geschichte der groteksen satyre*, 1894, by the German classicist Heinrich Schneegans (1863–1914). Cf. Bakhtin, *Ss*, 5: 434–6.

[26] "K voprosam teorii smekha," in Bakhtin, *Ss*, 5: 49. The definition occurs at the end of Kant's *Critique of the Power of Judgment*, section 54, placing Kant in the "incongruity" school of laughter theory. See Patrick T. Giamario, "'Making Reason Think More': Laughter in Kant's Aesthetic Philosophy," *Angelaki. Journal of the theoretical humanities*, vol. 22, no. 4 (December 2017): 161–76.

[27] Bakhtin, *Ss*, 5: 49.

[28] For more on the limits of hope in the ancient world—and the reformulation of hope into a potentially positive virtue (and thus into a vehicle of disappointment), beginning with Christianity and moving through the Romantic and Modern eras, see Adam Potkay, *Hope: A Literary History* (Cambridge: Cambridge University Press, 2022).

that *the worst does not happen*. Then an expectation that comes to naught, that "resolves into nothing," is indeed cause for joyous laughter, or at least for a sigh (and grin) of relief. But there is more at stake than joy and merriment. Bakhtin goes on to insist that laughter is not only liberation from "gloomy seriousness" (a constant refrain of the Rabelais book), but also from expectation and effort more generally. Effort is inevitably a serious official thing, but laughter is always unofficial, the freedom of taking time off, of not turning up, of picking a fight, of cursing out a close friend. This is the playful and affirmative zone of the unplanned vacation, of life among the unsupervised young. This truth, Bakhtin notes, is not grasped by Bergson. His scarecrows, puppets, and toys are funny not because they are mechanical but because they are creaky, graceless, worn out, and worst of all faked, "old age pretending to be alive."[29] Bergson, a moralist, knows only the negative pole of the comic. He never gets beyond laughter as a "corrective measure," as "that which ought *not to be*." And such judgments are permeated by juridical categories and norms, which are hostile—as the "official" always is—to ambiguity and antinomy. "In comic phenomena," Bakhtin writes, "the negative and positive are fused inseparably."[30]

This contretemps with famous laughter theorists reinforces the virtues of the comic catalogued in the earlier "Satire" entry, and airs many of the same grievances. Behind both we sense an abstract, cosmic metaphysics of laughter, one that is inevitably constrained and impoverished every time its energy is localized in an individual author. The bedrock concept here is *narodnaia smekhovaia kul'tura*, a communal "folk culture of laughter," which Bakhtin had been devising (partly with footnoted research, partly with inspired imagination) for a decade. By the end of the 1930s, the *Rabelais* study, in over five hundred pages, was complete. Bakhtin would defend its final draft as a dissertation in 1946, but several years earlier he had already begun negotiations with the State Literary Publishing House (Goslitizdat) to bring it out as a book. Toward that end, he was making copious notes toward its revision during the final years of the war, 1944–5. The times were tumultuous and sacrificial. In the official sphere, on public squares and over radio broadcasts, war trauma was being overlaid with the euphoria of an anticipated victory. As Tihanov notes, around this time Bakhtin was shifting ground as a theorist, eager to illumine his work of the 1930s (all still unpublished) with the rejuvenating resources of the novel as a genre.

[29] Bakhtin, *Ss*, 5: 50.
[30] Ibid.

Among the complaints that will be lodged against his carnival monograph is its indifference to the person of François Rabelais as author, ironist, and man of the Church. Now, equipped with "genre memory," Bakhtin appears poised to go even further along this de-personalizing road. Perhaps carnival energy could be made yet more ambitious, extended still further back in time? Laughter, which needs a mouth but not necessarily a name, could serve as the lubricant and the glue.

This restless, faceless strand of Bakhtin's thought surfaces again in the 1960s, in the new chapter 4 of the revised Dostoevsky book. As noted earlier, Bakhtin adds to his prior study a "historical digression" (in thirty pages) celebrating the indestructible vitality of archaic cultural forms and worldviews. The catch-all categories now are Menippean satire and the "serio-comical," two genres endowed with phenomenal scope and memory, which permit Bakhtin to assert that the roots of Dostoevsky's creativity "reach back into the most remote antiquity." Fourteen tell-tale traits are attributed to Menippean satire—a list so broad that almost any narrative plot would qualify for inclusion. But in one important respect, Bakhtin's extension of the carnival idea to Dostoevsky echoes the 1940 encyclopedia entry on Satire. True to his claim in the original 1929 Preface (repeated in 1963), Bakhtin concerns himself solely with the formal tool-kit, the "poetics," that governs Dostoevsky's polyphonic novel. He will not engage matters of "content," that is, philosophy, psychology, social justice, or body count. He will not rank things in a hierarchy, or pass judgment on institutions or ideas. He starts with what is self-evident: for there to be a decrowning, the world needs kings. Through every decrowning, there already glints a new coronation. Thus the laughing genres are not an ethics, but closer to a portal and (even better) a hinge. "Carnival celebrates the shift itself, the very process of replaceability, and not the precise item that is replaced"—thus does Bakhtin caution the reader who might be looking for judgments of right and wrong. "Carnival is, so to speak, functional and not substantive."[31] Or as he had stated the matter back in his 1940 entry on Satire, "Laughter fixes, as it were, the very moment of this change."

Just as carnival in Bakhtin's world is a social practice as well as a state of mind, so laughter is not only a physical reflex but also an orientation—or a function. It attacks the very idea of permanence. If a person dies, she is giving birth at the same time. If an insult is received, it is instantly returned and instantly forgotten. Since such bodies-in-transition have neither memory nor pain, their laughter

---

[31] Bakhtin, PPD, Ss, 6: 141; PDP, 125.

cannot support a normative or deontological ethics. So far, we have seen this functional laughter play out among persons, either as emotional affect or (in Bakhtin's phrase) as "concretely sensuous form": profanity, ridicule, merriment, relief. But Bakhtin never strayed far from a poetics. Accordingly, he had an additional task: to show how a comedic persona could be utilized by the novel to solve purely technical narrative problems. Solutions began to take shape at the end of the 1930s, in chapter 6 of his essay on the chronotope, and also in his ever-shifting notebooks for the Rabelais revisions. For this story, we turn to another cluster of themes that emerge during the prewar and war period: the problem of seriousness, the loss of carnival wholeness, the possibility of keeping oneself and the world open, and (somewhat surprisingly) the virtues of the mask.

Getting Serious, Masking Up

To begin with seriousness. Overall, Bakhtin is unforgivingly harsh on it. He tends to simplify and homogenize "the serious," to fuse it with governmental power [*vlast'*] and terror [*strakh*]. Officialdom and serious (unlaughing) authority never seem to bring any goods or benefits. For all the dazzling detail of his research base, Bakhtin avoids placing power structures in concrete historical or political context. The "culture of laughter" in the Rabelais book, for example, ostensibly set in sixteenth-century France, is grounded in a vague timeless folklore, too distanced and exotic to be easily identified with any period and suspiciously universal in its appetites (the assumption seems to be that since we all have bodies, all of them function and signify in much the same way). Discussing *Gargantua and Pantagruel*, Bakhtin largely ignores the value-system of its author François Rabelais, one of the great Renaissance humanists.[32] And a rigid binary rules the whole: Power (whether of Church or State) is always frowning, oppressive, punitive, monologic; the common people on the public square are intuitively joyous, playful, uninsultable, and dialogic. Nowhere does

---

[32] Although she appreciated the "freshness and force" of this Russian effort to celebrate a complex French writer, the eminent British historian Frances Yates reviewed *Rabelais and His World* upon its publication (long before the Bakhtin cult and boom), concluding: "Anyone who knows anything about the Renaissance, and about Rabelais, will know that the Bakhtin method has come up with the totally wrong answers." Frances A. Yates, "The Last Laugh," *The New York Review of Books*, October 9, 1969. For a sampling of domestic disapproval in the 1960s–90s (Aleksei Losev, Victor Shklovsky, Sergei Averintsev, and Mikhail Gasparov), see Caryl Emerson, *The First Hundred Years of Mikhail Bakhtin* (Princeton, NJ: Princeton University Press, 1997), 93–107 and later in the same volume, ch. 4 on Carnival, 163–206.

Bakhtin acknowledge vicious or death-dealing laughter—say, Ivan the Terrible's grinning executioners, or any other well-documented carnivalized tortures. (Bakhtin could not allude, of course, to the carnivalesque atmosphere of the purge trials or the vicious anti-God campaigns.) Nor does Bakhtin entertain the possibility that official governmental power, *vlast'*, might co-opt this popular energy through media censorship and persuade an entire population that it was living in the happiest of times, that joyous laughter was its birthright, and that satirical laughter of a destructive sort was legitimate solely against domestic traitors or enemies from the outside.[33]

These caveats about Bakhtin's "utopia of laughter" cannot be ignored. But we might place them in a more generous perspective by considering Bakhtin's own efforts at re-balancing his enthusiasms. Although he never lost his idealism about laughter, a self-critical remark in his working notebook for 1938 suggests that he feared he might have gone too far, "drawing out too many threads from Rabelais in all directions," allowing himself too many juxtapositions and analogies and thus "weakening the bridle [*uzda*] of scholarly method."[34] What is more, in the early 1940s, Bakhtin loosened up his binary of the official (serious) versus the unofficial (laughing). In his notes for revising *Rabelais*, he toyed with the idea of non-exploitative types of seriousness that, being powerless, deserve our pity and respect. These include the "unofficial seriousness of suffering, of fear, of being frightened, of weakness, the seriousness of the slave and the seriousness of the sacrificial victim (as separate from the sacrificing priest)."[35] Finally, among Bakhtin's more curious surviving fragments are several plans for a history of the "seriousification" of the world [*oser'eznenie mira*], the unavoidable result of the disintegration of Europe's primordial carnival mind.[36] Only scattered

---

[33] Such is the thesis of Evgeny Dobrenko and Natalia Jonsson-Skradol in their *State Laughter. Stalinism, Populism, and Origins of Soviet Culture* (Oxford: Oxford University Press, 2022). The authors challenge "the stereotypical (Bakhtinian) perception of the social function of collective laughter as always anti-totalitarian" (p. 3). The opposite, they claim, was true. Official Stalinist culture was soaked in laughter. Out of archaic folklore sources, the image of a joyous laughing people was programmed by the state to appeal to the quasi-urbanized Russian peasant. "The laughter of the authorities is so radical that it is practically impossible to separate it from that of the laughing masses" (pp. 392–3). A Russian edition of this book was published in 2022 under the title *Gossmekh: Stalinizm i komicheskoe*.

[34] Commentary to "Istoriia 'Rable': 1930–1950-e gody," *Ss*, 4(1): 890.

[35] M. M. Bakhtin, "Dopolneniia i izmeneniia k 'Rable' (1944)," in *Ss* t. 4(1), (Moscow: Iazyki slavianskikh kul'tur, 2008), 682. See the translation by Sergeiy Sandler of M. M. Bakhtin, "Bakhtin on Shakespeare: Excerpt from 'Additions and Changes to *Rabelais*'," *PMLA*, vol. 129, no. 3 (2014): 522–37, here 524–5.

[36] The neologism "seriousification" (p. 682) is rendered by Sandler as "seriousening" (524).

guidelines exist for this unrealized history, which has been pieced together in several variants by the editors of the Collected Works.[37] Two of Bakhtin's variant guidelines for this project culminate in Dostoevsky.

One historical line begins with Sophocles (*Oedipus the King*), moves through Shakespeare's tragedies (*Hamlet* and *Macbeth*), and ends on *The Brothers Karamazov*.[38] Here the focus is on the emergence of a tragic "I" out of the decaying ancient chorus, which always sang of more than a single isolated fate. Shakespeare's tragic kings have lost this choral wholeness; they chart an unsuccessful external quest to justify the individual life (without succession or descendants). In contrast to both, Dostoevsky opens up the rich, fertile inner person. In another portion of his notebooks, Bakhtin provides an alternative line, this time beginning with Rabelais (the individual as breakaway part of the *rodovoe narodnoe telo*, the ancestral folk body) but also passing through Shakespeare's externalized regal struggles to conclude on the "deepest possible innerness in the novels of Dostoevsky" (892). Dostoevsky, it seems, although saturated with Menippean satire and delight in public scandal, is also the maximal endpoint of internalization, the soul.

But up to this point Bakhtin, during his wartime rethinkings, appears indifferent to what this book has identified as "Funny Dostoevsky." Polyphony, dialogue, innerness, testing the "person of the idea": this is serious intellectual material. What about the outrageous jokes, the buffoons, the slapstick, the fact that we so often laugh out loud during the grimmest parts of Dostoevsky's novels? Lest we lose our way and fail to appreciate the close bond between our innermost soul and carnival laughter, at the end of the new chapter 4 Bakhtin makes an eloquent case for a "carnival sense of the world" as the indispensable enabler of the polyphonic novel. It is carnivalization, we read, that "made possible the creation of the *open* structure of the great dialogue," helping Dostoevsky "overcome epistemological and ethical solipsism" by showing that "a single person, alone with himself, cannot make ends meet even in the deepest and most intimate spheres of his own spiritual life."[39] But carnivalization, Menippean satire, and the serio-comical are still insufficient to explain why Dostoevsky is so funny. To understand how the polyphonic novel endured the decay of laughter,

---

[37] See the discussion in Kommentarii [Commentary] to "Dopolneniia i izmeneniia k <Rable>," in Bakhtin, *Ss*, 4(1): 887–93.

[38] "Kommentarii," *Ss*, 4(1): 888–9.

[39] Bakhtin, PPD, *Ss*, 6: 201; PDP, 177.

the "seriousification" of the world, unrelieved tragedy and injustice, and still make us laugh like no other genre, we must consider the mask.

What does Bakhtin think a mask can do? Masks are artificial, not organic. Without violence or deceit we can play with them, detach them, layer them, swap them; a mask is a persona, not a personality. But the primary function of a mask remains fascinatingly unclear. Is it to mimic, to conceal, to negate, to liberate, perhaps even to create? Since masks can be so recklessly played with, we might ask: are they compatible with ethical behavior—that is, with personal actions that add up and that we agree to answer for? Despite Bakhtin's efforts, there has long been a tension between those who love him for his dialogism, and those who love his (masked) carnival. Dialogue involves not inner essences but outer edges and interactions—but still, over time, it creates an identity. Dialogue entails speaking, answering, remembering, and it also requires that I commit to my own place in the world, what Bakhtin calls "putting my signature" on events. There is a distinct ethical flavor to dialogic processes. Carnival would seem to embrace the opposite. It is all about orifices—tunnels teeming with multiple bodies, all in transit—and not about the accumulation of an individual self. Under carnival conditions, grunts, guffaws, verbal abuse and curses are more prized than conversations built up out of responsible words. Everything in carnival is loud, ambivalent, and present-tense, like laughter itself.

But Bakhtin, significantly, saw no contradiction between the "double-voiced word" of dialogue and the "double-bodied image" of carnival. Both are shapeshifters—and both, he would insist, utilize masks. Each inserts a protective layer on the border between inside and outside that permits a person some privacy, playfulness, re-negotiation of identity, and symbolization. In his Introduction to the Rabelais book, Bakhtin wrote:

> The mask is the most complex theme in folk culture, linked with the joy of succession and re-embodiment, ... with the cheerful negation of all uniform identity and singularity of meaning .... Parody, caricature, grimace, eccentric posturing and comic gesture are in their essence all derivatives of the mask ... The mask never becomes just one thing among other things.[40]

---

[40] M. M. Bakhtin, "Tvorchestvo Fransua Rable i narodnaia kul'tura srednevekov'ia i Renessansa [1965]," *Ss*, 4(2): 50–1; in English, Mikhail Bakhtin, *Rabelais and His World*. Translated by Hélène Iswolsky (Bloomington: Indiana University Press, 1984), 39–40 (translation amended). In these same pages, Bakhtin regrets the Romantic re-accentuation of masks, where gothic horror strips away all regenerating, renewing, ambivalent laughter: "A terrible vacuum, a nothingness lurks behind it" (51/40).

This protective intermediate layer, or mask, permitting the play of "inside versus outside" and always on a boundary, is one of the two basic parameters that govern Bakhtin's universe. Similar to laughter and related to it, the mask is also a metaphysics. "Inside" (myself, my body) versus "outside" (your self, your body) are incommensurate; I can never experience you as you experience yourself, and you can never experience me as I experience myself. But happily, human beings do manage to communicate their experiences to one another, because of a second parameter: open versus closed. "Open" is as much an attitude as it is a spatial or volumetric property. Open means laughing, unfinished, mobile, alive: what Bakhtin calls personality. Closed means serious, completed, static, dead: what he calls a thing. These two options are not absolutes but conditions of possibility. All human acts or orientations partake of both tendencies and move between two extremes: either we treat an outside entity like a person, or like a thing.[41] The information hub for these acts is the face, and that face can be manipulated by a mask, which is "never just one thing among other things." Bakhtin believed in the reality of masks, in their virtue as cultural as well as spiritual commodities. He regretted their disappearance from the theatrical stage, and rejoiced at their survival in carnival. Masks not only allow us to try on new, transitory identities and thus negate what we thought was fixed and final. Human beings, Bakhtin believed, have always been hungry to connect with the symbolic order—which masks always facilitate.

Of course human beings react to the world throughout their bodies, and with their whole bodies. But for Bakhtin, humanness is centered on speaking, laughing, hearing, and seeing, so the face is the essential focal point. It is also pleasingly archaic. As the matter has been put by Daniel McNeill, historian of this crucial region of the body, although a face isn't strictly necessary to animals, it is surprisingly common in biology: "A true face bundles mouth and sense organs, and it may be older than shell or bone."[42] So why cover it up? Perhaps the face is too responsive, too vulnerable, too nude. Here masks help us: they can stylize a face (heighten it), or protect it. What is more, a ritual mask (on the border between a thing and a personality) can come alive, but only when we wish it to and when we believe in it, as during a ritual act. And art more generally? Any

---

[41] For a lucid explication of these limits, see Irina M. Denischenko, "Beyond Reification: Mikhail Bakhtin's Critique of Violence in Cognition and Representation," in "Bakhtin Forum. The Dark and Radiant Bakhtin. Wartime Notes." *Slavic and East European Journal* 61.2 (Summer 2017): 255–77.

[42] Daniel McNeill, *The Face. A Natural History* (Boston, MA: Little, Brown and Company, 1998), 13.

actor will confirm that the key to mastering the art of performance is to *show* an emotion, not to feel it on stage in an unmediated way. To this end all theaters in the world used to be masked, McNeill notes. In Europe, "medieval mystery plays required masks, as did *commedia dell'arte* ... But as verisimilitude rose in popular esteem, cosmetics came to replace masks. By the time of Shakespeare, they were gone."[43] All this recalls Bakhtin's unwritten three-tiered histories of seriousification, which we will now revisit and deepen through the lens of the mask.

Recall Bakhtin's sequence of events. Slowly, the tragic hero emerges out of the deterioration of the ancient carnival worldview, which was always masked and always ambivalent. Masks remain for a while in ritual and in artistic practice, but the meaning of the mask changes. It narrows and stabilizes. It begins to mean only one thing. Bakhtin conceptualized this degeneration of "carnival wholeness" in three phases. Phase one was the Oedipus plays of Sophocles. Although tragic masked heroes speak their own word, ancient Greek tragedy retained a trace of communal carnival in the (also masked) Chorus, a wiser, more powerful voice than any possessed by an individual hero. The second phase in this dissipation of carnival is Shakespearean tragedy. The mask has now been lost; we see the naked face of King Lear, of Macbeth. These naked-faced kings symbolize the "tragedy of individuation," the breaking-out of a singular, one-way body that resists its own aging and resents its own mortality. There is nothing fertile about these royal trajectories, no cosmic laughter, no confidence that death is pregnant with new life, nothing is shared or passed on to a younger generation; the only tools are power and terror. The Chorus is nowhere to be found. True to this frozen trapped temporality, gestures on the tragic stage should be exaggerated, stylized, deep, and violent. Up is heaven, down is hell; in between is nothing but misery, confusion, and witchcraft. Bakhtin calls Shakespearean parameters "topographical," modeled as they are on miracle and mystery plays—and surprisingly, he seems to care very little about words. Everything is in the absence of the mask.

Bakhtin held out little hope that the modern "post-Ibsen" stage could learn from these rich classical and medieval models. Surprisingly, avant-garde theater of the 1920s, with its astonishing devices for comedy and its creative use of the

---

[43] Ibid., 265.

grotesque, apparently held little theoretical interest for Bakhtin, although at the end of his life he recalled with pleasure seeing Meyerhold's plays.[44] For a century or so, Bakhtin notes, European neoclassical drama preserved a stylized grandeur. But then the stage took a wrong turn. In pursuing the realistic, both tragic and comic theater became trivial, "merely personal." Like the progressive enfeeblement of laughter he laments in the Rabelais book, dramatic art too became flatter, emptier, thinner, more cluttered, and diluted with petty detail. When the stage lost its philosophical height and depth, it forgot how to transmit both true tragedy and true life-affirming comedy. Bakhtin, with his premodern preferences, thirsts after immortal wholes, the fitting of a human being into the symbolic order. Once the Chorus is lost, and once we lose the sense of the two-tiered, two-layered face, matters inevitably get serious and frightening. This is the reality of an unmasked, mortal world.

When the theatrical stage defaulted to realism, however, height, depth, and the majesty of a cosmic topography did not disappear from art. These virtues merely shifted to another genre—to Dostoevsky's polyphonic novel. Bakhtin's exemplar is *The Brothers Karamazov*. This is the third phase and culminating benchmark in the crumbling carnival legacy. Ill-labeled "novel-tragedies," Dostoevsky's works are shot through with comedy, even though not performed; they have no theatrical masks at their disposal. But they reproduce the grandeur of the masked mystery plays—only now, miraculously, the cosmic coordinates are all writ on the inside. Recall Dostoevsky's "discovery and justification of the inner person, of the soul, in the intensive coordinates of the 'deepest possible innerness.'"[45] The solipsistic despair that accompanies this innerness is forever a temptation, from the Underground Man to his later Ridiculous descendent. There is, however, another cast of characters to balance the tragically serious. In the spirit of his 1873 cemetery farce "Bobok," Dostoevsky is careful to create, as primary narrators and as secondary storytellers in his novels, his own ambivalent chorus of carnival fools.

---

[44] See Interview Five, March 22, 1973, in *Mikhail Bakhtin. The Duvakin Interviews, 1973*. Edited by Slav N. Gratchev and Margarita Marinova, Translated by Margarita Marinova (Lewisburg, PA: Bucknell University Press, 2019), 183.

[45] See the reconstructions in the Kommentarii to "Dopolneniia k 'Rable' (1944–45)," in *Ss*, 4(1): 888–9 and 891–2, quote on 891–2.

There is a minor industry in American Slavic Studies devoted to the complexity, irregularity, and unreliability of Dostoevsky's narrators.[46] Most attention has been paid to *The Idiot* and *Devils*, but also closely scrutinized is *The Brothers Karamazov*, with its more congenial and benignly embodied storytelling voice. These narrators gossip, invent, claim to have witnessed what they cannot possibly know, drop out of the story at crucial junctures, and slyly mislead the reader. Their antics and intonations are a major source of Dostoevsky's humor. In Bakhtin's world, however, narrators are something of a neglected category. Early in his career he concentrated on "authors" and "heroes"—that is, on writers and their fictive characters—at the expense of more nuanced or mediating forms of storytelling authority.

Bakhtin did have something to say about narrative technique. His best insights come not in the Dostoevsky book, however, but in the writings discussed in this chapter, where Bakhtin argues as a classicist, a committed premodern. The ancient tragic mask and the carnival masks of Rabelais had to make the transition to the Dostoevskian face, but without losing "topographical grandeur," which is to say, without sacrificing the symbolic order. In European literary history, as we have seen, this was an outside-to-inside project of enormous seriousness. To be "unmasked" means to accept that your flesh is mortal. It means that your natural face is all you have. Does there exist a vehicle for ambivalent carnival laughter in an unmasked world? A vehicle that could function as a force for renewal in a world that had undergone "seriousification"—and what is more, a world that practiced the lonely, inner experience of private reading? Bakhtin thought that there was. It no longer had to be tied to cyclical seasons of carnival and Lent, monitored by official Church or state authorities. A character with the proper behavioral profile could transfer this energy (largely a comic energy) into the novel, available at any time to any reader.

This "foolish" precondition for Dostoevsky's narrative art is addressed by Bakhtin in Part 6 of his huge historical study of the chronotope, completed in

---

[46] Its founding text is Robin Feuer Miller's now classic *Dostoevsky and The Idiot: Author, Narrator, and Reader* (Cambridge MA: Harvard University Press, 1981). In 2004, Sarah J. Young extended the ethical implications of narration with her concept of character "scripting" (*Dostoevsky's The Idiot and the Ethical Foundations of Narrative: Reading, Narrating, Scripting* [London: Anthem Press]). The chronicler-narrator of *Demons*, Anton Lavrentievich G-v, is so inscrutably virtuosic that he himself has often been associated with the unclean force (see, for example, Ch. 3, "Narrative Possession in *The Devils*," in Adam Weiner, *By Authors Possessed. The Demonic Novel in Russia* [Evanston: Northwestern University Press, 1998], 92–137).

the late 1930s and subtitled "Notes toward a historical poetics."[47] Earlier parts of the study deal with Greek and Roman adventure-time, ancient biography and autobiography, chivalric romance, and "folkloric inversion"—the act of flipping optimal future goodness and virtue back into the past. This backward flip of value Bakhtin considered an "epic" move, one that tended to distance, ossify, and "seriousify" human relations. Part 6 redirects all energy back in the "novelistic" direction, toward more intimacy, flexibility, and comic gesture. The section is titled "The functions of the rogue, the clown, and the fool in the novel." In Russian it's almost a limerick: *ploot* [rogue or rascal], *shoot* [jester or clown], *durak* [simpleton or fool]. Why these three disobedient, provocative outliers? They are all funny, of course, and they act in a way designed to make us laugh. But they are also crucial generic enablers, and what they enable is the multivoiced, forward-looking modern novel.

Rogues, clowns, and fools, Bakhtin says, are the right sort of speaking persons for this complex narrative task. They carry with them into written literature the "theatrical trappings of the public square" and the "mask of the public spectacle."[48] A rogue is not necessarily a scoundrel or a crook, nor need he be morally compromised—just as Lear's Fool, the King's official jester, is not foolish, and clowns are not always trivial. As Bakhtin explains, these figures cannot be taken literally, for "they are not what they seem .... Their existence is a reflection of some other's mode of being—and even then, not a direct reflection. They are life's maskers [*litsedei zhizni*]; their being coincides with their role, and outside this role they do not exist."[49] This "fused-to-the-face" aspect of the mask lasts only as long as the scripted role. But novels are arenas of freedom (unlike the more stable, singularly authored voices of epic, lyric, and drama) and thus readers of novels have the right to expect a surprise.

To this end, Bakhtin immediately qualifies the relation between persona and personality, between the artificially assumed mask and the natural face. What he

---

[47] "VI. Funktsii pluta, shuta, duraka v romane," in "Formy vremeni i khronotopa v romane," Bakhtin, *Ss*, 3: 411–12. In English, see "Forms of Time and of the Chronotope in the Novel," in M. M. Bakhtin, *The Dialogic Imagination*. Translated by Caryl Emerson and Michael Holquist (Austin, TX: University of Texas Press, 1982), 158–67. The order of parts in the English translation differs from the Collected Works, where a section on the chivalric romance precedes Part 6 on the rogue, jester, and fool (pp. 411–18).
[48] Bakhtin, *The Dialogic Imagination*, 15.
[49] Bakhtin, *Ss*, 3: 412; Bakhtin, *The Dialogic Imagination*, 159.

adds is an element of resistance and reciprocity. The result is a metaphysics of the mask that overlaps with his metaphysics of laughter:

> Essential to these three figures is a distinctive feature that is also a privilege, the right to be "other" in this world, the right not to make common cause with any single one of the existing categories that life makes available; none of these categories quite suits them, they see the underside and falseness of every situation. Thus they can exploit any position they choose, but only as a mask. The rogue still has some ties that bind him to real life; the clown and the fool, however, are "not of this world," and therefore possess their own special rights and privileges. These figures are laughed at by others, and laugh back as well.[50]

When these "public-square maskers" enter the novel, Bakhtin contends, they are transformed and assume vital new communicative functions. They must do so, because novels have a problem that the older canonical genres—epic, lyric, and drama—do not have. Unlike their communal and performative predecessors, anchored in folklore or myth, novels must position their authors and narrators. Storytellers in a novel must justify their access to the material. "Personal authorship is complicated by the need to have some substantive, 'uninvented' mask that would have the capacity both to fix the position of the author vis-à-vis the life portrayed (*how* and *from what angle* all this private life can be seen and exposed) and also to fix the author's position vis-à-vis the readers, the public."[51] Such narrators must also acknowledge their limited human dimension. Monologic novels can assume omniscient narration or a God's-eye view. Bakhtin is more interested in the dialogic tradition, however, where the modesty of delimited human perspective is most efficiently relayed by a willingness to be *laughed at* by others. We are now fully in the realm of the clown and the fool. They provide a point of view on the world that is a-social, outsiderly, indifferent to the smooth invisible running of things, but still unthreatening—a person "in life, but not of it; life's perpetual spy and reflector."[52] Since their masks are native to them, as it were "uninvented," they offer a flexible, trans-personal, largely pain-free refuge for all layers of authorship. With Dostoevsky in mind, however, we must wonder: how far can these comic figures be trusted?

---

[50] Bakhtin, *Ss*, 3: 412; Bakhtin, *The Dialogic Imagination*, 159. Translation modified.
[51] Bakhtin, *Ss*, 3: 412; Bakhtin, *The Dialogic Imagination*, 160.
[52] Bakhtin, *The Dialogic Imagination*, 161.

Perhaps, however, Bakhtin would insist that trust—at least in our everyday interpersonal sense of the term—is not an appropriate criterion. What matters is multiplicity of perspective, potential access to other worlds, and (more than we know) simple relief. In closing, we marshal some contrasting opinions.

A Coda on the Funniness and Coherence of Carnival

In his work on Soviet-era tricksters, Mark Lipovetsky pays tribute to the section on rogues, clowns, and fools from Bakhtin's chronotope essay.[53] In Russian culture, Lipovetsky writes, the trickster (rogue, scoundrel, rascal, clown, fool, pretender, and imposter) is universally beloved. Nineteenth-century writers tended to be embarrassed by this love (although Dostoevsky was among the more ambivalent); they depicted such characters "with an obvious note of moral condemnation."[54] Not so, however, in twentieth-century Soviet literature, when tricksters "became true cult heroes, depicted with sympathy by their authors and adored by readers." The government chimed in and laughed along, co-opting these illegals and misfits for its own purposes (scapegoat or safety valve), just as it had co-opted folk laughter. Lipovetsky identifies three types of trickster-masks—the carnivalesque, the ironic messiah, and the noxiously hilarious hyper-collaborator who turns himself into a grotesque stylization of conformity and obedience to official norms.[55] All these tricksters, in their subversion of authority as well as in their fawning subservience to it, are cynics. And all radiate to the Soviet public a sense of freedom and individual agency that is otherwise unobtainable. In this context, Bakhtin's theoretical exaltation of rogues, clowns, and fools appears quite mainstream for the 1930s, another example of Bakhtin, marginalized literary scholar, cannily "fitting in."

Concepts fit in with a cost. In the heady glasnost period, the eminent classicist Sergei Averintsev expressed his reservations about festive folk laughter, both as a

---

[53] Mark Lipovetsky, "The Trickster and Soviet Subjectivity: Narratives and Counter-Narratives of Soviet Modernity," *Ab Imperio*, vol. 4 (2020): 1–26. Bakhtin is discussed on pp. 7–9.

[54] Ibid., 5.

[55] The "hyperperformativity" of the trickster, Lipovetsky (2020) writes, contains "the embryo of a metaposition" that is central to Bakhtin's concept of outsideness and also formative for the novel (9). And here the unsettling limits of every "meta" come into view: metaphysics (whether of laughter or of the mask), metaposition, now metaverse. First its world feels real, then it competes with the real, then (with the proper equipment and addiction) it replaces the real.

sociohistorical fact and as a universal concept. He then added: "I have absolutely no doubts about the irreproachable purity of Bakhtin's philosophical intentions, especially in view of the fact that all his efforts were devoted ... to defending the freedom of the spirit in a time when such an undertaking appeared to be hopeless."[56] Nevertheless, Averintsev insists, Bakhtin's glorification of laughter was unseemly and incorrect. Neither civil society nor responsible human agency could be secured in this way—only, perhaps, personal transcendence. Robert Bird raised the same issue when considering Bakhtin's "law of satire," laid out in that encyclopedia essay of 1940. "The question remains to what degree Bakhtin was serious in his model-making," Bird writes, "[A]nd to what degree he was engaged in simple play, seeking an inward self-consistency among parts of the models he built, while remaining mindful of being a plaything of the gods."[57] Would Bakhtin have had an answer to this, on the brink of total war and during its darkest years?

Nikolai Pan'kov, archival researcher and specialist in Bakhtin's Rabelais project, devoted a lengthy essay to the Bakhtin-Averintsev "agon" over laughter, offering two variants on a response.[58] The first is the more personal. "I think Bakhtin most likely would have shrugged his shoulders and simply called Averintsev an *agelast*, 'a person who doesn't laugh,'" Pan'kov remarked.[59] But then he mounts a methodological defense. Why do readers so often assume that Bakhtin liked carnival and found its laughter reassuring? Throughout the dissertation defense in 1946, and then in his working notebooks during the 1960s to early 1970s, Bakhtin repeatedly remarked that personally, as a modern intellectual, he was not just alien to folk-festive culture but suspicious of it, even hostile to it and repelled by it.[60] But "overcoming our sense of the alien [*chuzhdost'*] (and the

---

[56] Averintsev's critique of Bakhtin's carnival utopia, "Bakhtin, smekh, khristianskaia kul'tura," appears in *M. M. Bakhtin kak filosof* (Moscow: Nauka, 1992): 7–19, quote on this page 15. In English see "Bakhtin, Laughter, and Christian Culture," in *Bakhtin and Religion. A Feeling for Faith*, Edited by Susan M. Felch and Paul J. Contino, (Evanston: Northwestern University Press, 2001), 79–95, quote on this page 87. Averintsev was deeply sympathetic to Bakhtin's person and to aspects of his thought (especially the early philosophical manuscripts, which he co-edited for publication in 1979), but Russian history, he avers, contains "more than enough examples of a direct connection between laughter and violence, carnival and authoritarianism" (87).

[57] Bird, "Schematics and Models of Genre: Bakhtin and Soviet Satire," 451.

[58] "M. M. Bakhtin i S. S. Averintsev: Dva vzgliada na teoriiu smekha," in N. A. Pan'kov, *Voprosy biografii i nauchnogo tvorchestva M. M. Bakhtina* (Moscow: Izd. Moskovskogo universiteta, 2010), 400–17.

[59] Pan'kov, *Voprosy*, 402.

[60] Ibid., 406.

hostile) is the first step to understanding."⁶¹ If scholars do not approach their object of study with "heuristic love," it will not be seen.⁶² And Pan'kov concludes: "As far as we can tell, Bakhtin in no way saw Rabelais or Dostoevsky as 'apostles' [*glashatai*] of carnival; he did not think that they fully shared the view of the public-square crowd regarding the problems of existence."⁶³ But carnival images provide an "aesthetic instrument" that literary genius recognizes and uses, a "second language" separate from the language of subjective individual consciousness. Evidently, Averintsev and Bakhtin meant different things by laughter. For Bakhtin it was (in addition to the energy that Kliger senses) a universal language; for Averintsev, it was the easily corruptible response of a single organism. Temperamentally, Averintsev took the side of Henri Bergson.

This multiplicity of meanings is also a response to Robert Bird. Most likely Bakhtin did not fret overmuch the internal inconsistency of his models. The models were themselves antinomic, designed to contain contradictions. He would have insisted that "not coinciding with oneself" was always more hopeful than it was irresponsible, since the verbal and material mask enjoys enormous narrative advantages when delivering a polyphonic (non-essentialist) truth. In the world Bakhtin knew, only the laughing genres could permit us to be serious in a sustainable way.

Bibliography

Averintsev, Sergei. "Bakhtin, Laughter, and Christian Culture," in *Bakhtin and Religion. A Feeling for Faith*. Edited by Susan M. Felch and Paul J. Contino, 79–95. Evanston: Northwestern University Press, 2001.

Averintsev, S. "Bakhtin, smekh, khristianskaia kul'tura," in *M. M. Bakhtin как filosof*. Edited by S. Averintsev, et al., 7–19. Moscow: Nauka, 1992.

Bakhtin, M. M. "Bakhtin on Shakespeare: Excerpt from 'Additions and Changes to Rabelais,'" Translated by Sergeiy Sandler, *PMLA*, vol. 129, no. 3 (2014): 522–37.

---

[61] On the huge role that *chuzhdost'* has played in the history of culture, see "Rabochie zapisi 60-x—nachala 70-x godov," in Bakhtin, *Ss*, 6: 409. "Power [*vlast'*] (both state and church) makes use of it for their own aims (fanning the flames of hostility for everything that is other)." This half-page of commentary was not included in the selected English translation of these working notebooks in M. M. Bakhtin, *Speech Genres and Other Late Essays*, a selection that now reads as naively carnival-friendly.

[62] Pan'kov, *Voprosy*, 406.

[63] Ibid., 409.

Bakhtin, M. M. "Dopolneniia i izmeneniia k 'Rable,'" [1944] in *Sobranie sochinenii v semi tomakh*, vol. 4(1): 681–732. Moscow: Iazyki slavianskikh kul'tur, 2008.

Bakhtin, M. M. *The Duvakin Interviews, 1973*. Edited by Slav N. Gratchev and Margarita Marinova, Translated by Margarita Marinova. Lewisburg, PA: Bucknell University Press, 2019.

Bakhtin, M. M. "Forms of Time and of the Chronotope in the Novel," in M. M. Bakhtin, *The Dialogic Imagination*. Translated by Caryl Emerson and Michael Holquist, 158–67. Austin, TX: University of Texas Press, 1982.

Bakhtin, M. M. *Formy vremeni i khronotopa v romane*, in *Sobranie sochinenii v semi tomakh*, V. 3: 340–512. Moscow: Iazyki slavianskikh kul'tur, 2012.

Bakhtin, M. M. *Problems of Dostoevsky's Poetics*. Translated by Caryl Emerson. Minneapolis: University of Minnesota Press, 1984.

Bakhtin, M. M. *Problemy poetiki Dostoevskogo*, *Sobranie sochinenii v semi tomakh*, V. 6. Moscow: Russkie slovari, 2002.

Bakhtin, M. M. *Rabelais and His World*. Translated by Hélène Iswolsky. Bloomington: Indiana University Press, 1984.

Bakhtin, M. M. "Satira," in *Sobranie sochinenii v semi tomakh*, Edited by S. G. Bocharov and L. A. Gogotishvili, vol. 5, 11–38. Moscow: Russkie slovari, 1996.

Bakhtin, M. M. "Satire," in *Persistent Forms. Explorations in Historical Poetics*. Edited by Ilya Kliger and Boris Maslov, Translated and Annotated by Robert Bird, 369–91. New York: Fordham University Press, 2016.

Bakhtin, M. M. "Tvorchestvo Fransua Rable i narodnaia kul'tura srednevekov'ia i Renessansa" [1965], *Sobranie sochinenii v semi tomakh*, Vol. 4(2): 7–516. Moscow: Iazyki slavianskikh kul'tur, 2010.

Bergson, Henri. *Laughter. An Essay on the Meaning of the Comic*. Authorized translation by Cloudesley Brereton and Fred Rothwell. New York: Macmillan, 1911.

Blank, Ksana. *Dostoevsky's Dialectics and the Problem of Sin*. Evanston: Northwestern University Press, 2010.

Denischenko, Irina M. "Beyond Reification: Mikhail Bakhtin's Critique of Violence in Cognition and Representation," in "Bakhtin Forum. The Dark and Radiant Bakhtin. Wartime Notes." *Slavic and East European Journal*, vol. 61, no. 2 (Summer 2017): 255–77.

Denischenko, Irina and Alexander Spektor. "Forum Introduction: Bakhtin Forum. The Dark and Radiant Bakhtin. Wartime Notes," *Slavic and East European Journal*, vol. 61, no. 2 (Summer 2017): 189–200.

Dobrenko, Evgeny and Natalia Jonsson-Skradol. *State Laughter. Stalinism, Populism, and Origins of Soviet Culture*. Oxford: Oxford University Press, 2022.

Emerson, Caryl. "Coming to Terms with Bakhtin's Carnival: Ancient, Modern, Sub Specie Aeternitatis," in *Bakhtin and the Classics*. Edited by R. Bracht Branham, 5–26. Evanston: Northwestern University Press, 2002.

Emerson, Caryl. *The First Hundred Years of Mikhail Bakhtin*. Princeton, NJ: Princeton University Press, 1997.

Giamario, Patrick T. "'Making Reason Think More': Laughter in Kant's Aesthetic Philosophy," *Angelaki. Journal of the Theoretical Humanities*, vol. 22, no. 4 (December 2017): 161–76.

Hirschkop, Ken. *The Cambridge Introduction to Mikhail Bakhtin*. Cambridge: Cambridge University Press, 2021.

Kliger, Ilya. "On 'Genre Memory' in Bakhtin," in *Persistent Forms. Explorations in Historical Poetics*. Edited by Ilya Kliger and Boris Maslov, 227–51. New York: Fordham University Press, 2016.

Lipovetsky, Mark. "The Trickster and Soviet Subjectivity: Narratives and Counter-Narratives of Soviet Modernity," *Ab Imperio*, vol. 4 (2020): 1–26.

McNeill, Daniel. *The Face. A Natural History*. Boston, MA: Little, Brown and Company, 1998.

Miller, Robin Feuer. *Dostoevsky and* The Idiot: *Author, Narrator, and Reader*. Cambridge, MA: Harvard University Press, 1981.

Morson, Gary Saul and Caryl Emerson. *Mikhail Bakhtin: Creation of a Prosaics*. Stanford: Stanford University Press, 1990.

Pan'kov, N. A. "M. M. Bakhtin i S. S. Averintsev: Dva vzgliada na teoriiu smekha," in *Voprosy biografii i nauchnogo tvorchestva M. M. Bakhtina*, 400–17. Moscow: Izd. Moskovskogo universiteta, 2010.

Potkay, Adam. *Hope: A Literary History*. Cambridge: Cambridge University Press, 2022.

Tihanov, Galin. *The Birth and Death of Literary Theory: Regimes of Relevance in Russia and Beyond*. Stanford: Stanford University Press, 2019.

Weiner, Adam. *By Authors Possessed. The Demonic Novel in Russia*. Evanston: Northwestern University Press, 1998.

Yates, Frances A. "The Last Laugh," *The New York Review of Books* (October 9, 1969).

Young, Sarah. *Dostoevsky's* The Idiot *and the Ethical Foundations of Narrative: Reading, Narrating, Scripting*. London: Anthem Press, 2004.

Zhernokleev, Denis A. "Bakhtin o Flobere: Poetika 'otritsayushchego obraza,'" *Literaturovedcheskii zhurnal*, vol. 54, no. 4 (2021): 166–78.

2

Funny Dostoevsky in Translation: How Funny Is He?

Tatyana Kovalevskaya

In her 2017 book *The Anna Karenina Fix*, Viv Groskop, a British writer, journalist, and stand-up comedian with a master's degree in Russian literature from Cambridge, aptly sums up the widespread popular view of Russian classical literature. "The Russian classics are, admittedly, not the most obvious place to look for tips for a happier life," Groskop acknowledges, given the perception that "Russian literature is full of gloomy people wondering how on earth they have ended up in the appalling predicament in which they find themselves, looking around desperately for someone else to blame and then realizing that, in fact, they were right in the first place: life really is extremely inconvenient and annoying, and we are all just waiting to die."[1] Soviet and Russian scholars also noted this particular perception as a feature of readers' attitude specifically to Fyodor Dostoevsky: "In the minds of a large number of readers, the image of a tragic writer usually blocks out Dostoevsky's comic talents."[2]

Nonetheless, the comic element in Dostoevsky's works has long been researched in Russian scholarship, although the scholars' conclusions, as it has often happened with Dostoevsky studies, could be almost diametrically opposed. As E. Ponkratova observes, "Laughter is a means of communication, characterology, axiology, psychology. The comical often structures the plot, permeates the very fabric of narration, determines its multiaspectual nature, and eliminates the unequivocality of conclusions. Taken together, all the categories

---

[1] Viv Groskop. *The Anna Karenina Fix: Life Lessons from Russian Literature* (New York: Penguin Books Ltd., 2017), 15, Kindle.
[2] Liia M. Rozenblium, "Iumor Dostoevskogo," *Voprosy literatury*, no. 1 (1999): 142–88, https://voplit.ru/article/yumor-dostoevskogo/?ysclid=lpvkr0y1hy636895537. Unless otherwise specified, translations from Russian are mine—T.K.

in Dostoevsky's comic elements beget the incomplete, contradictory, dynamic, polyphonic world of his novels."[3] In this interpretation, Bakhtin's notion of polyphony is taken to its relativistic extreme, and the comical element is seen as the crucial structural element of this incompleteness. Other scholars, also largely following Bakhtin, stress the corporeal element in Dostoevsky's humor writing that "the characters' humor is pointedly, emphatically corporeal, and such is that humor's specific feature."[4] Such notions of "incompleteness," "contradictoriness," and "polyphony" that apparently do not allow for a single and unequivocal understanding of Dostoevsky appear to contradict Dostoevsky's own views of poetics.

Although Dostoevsky did not put forward a clearly formulated poetic theory, he did present his readers with some crucial views on the relationship between an author, their text, and a reader. This "theory" of Dostoevsky, in contravention of the theoretical staples of today, envisions readers as being fully able to understand a *good* work of art; in fact, readers understanding the meaning of the work as the author intended are the ultimate testament to a given writer's artistic ability. In his programmatic 1861 article "Mr.–bov and the Question of Art," Dostoevsky claims that "artistry … in a novelist is the ability to express their thought so clearly in the persons and images of the novel that a reader, upon reading the novel, understands the writer's thought exactly as the writer himself understood it when creating the work. … in simple words, artistry in a writer is the ability to write well."[5] Consequently, "incompleteness" and "contradictoriness" would be seen as hallmarks of insufficient talent and artistic failure, not of success or poetic intention. Note that in Gary Saul Morson's opinion, Bakhtin elevated his polyphonic principle to "a general theory of language, literature, and ethics."[6] Morson believes that this principle emerged in the works of Herzen, found its fullest embodiment in Tolstoy and Chekhov, while Dostoevsky and Turgenev experimented with it, yet ultimately rejected it.[7] It would, therefore, be doing a

---

[3] E. Ponkratova, "Smekh i komicheskoe v tvorchestve F. M. Dostoevskogo: o nekotorykh osobennostiakh estetiki pisatelia," *Vestnik Tomskogo gosudarstvennogo universiteta*, no. 349 (2011): 19–22, http://journals.tsu.ru/vestnik/&journal_page=archive&id=862&article_id=5835.

[4] T. S. Martakova, "Antropologiia smekha v proizvedeniiakh Dostoevskogo (1846–1859): K voprosu o 'smekhovom portrete,'" *Vestnik Cheliabinskogo gosudarstvennogo universiteta*, no. 15 (2007): 89.

[5] Fyodor Dostoevsky, *PSS*, 18: 80.

[6] Gary Saul Morson, "Gogol's Parables of Explanation: Nonsense and Prosaics," in *Essays on Gogol: Logos and the Russian Word*. Edited by Susanne Fusso and Priscilla Meyer (Evanston, IL: Northwestern University Press, 1992), 203.

[7] Ibid.

disservice to Dostoevsky's artistic intentions to ascribe to him poetic principles that he would see as a poetic failure.

Consequently, it is Liia Rozenblium's view of Dostoevsky's humor that appears to be the most insightful and true to Dostoevsky's intentions:

> The key notions for Dostoevsky's entire *oeuvre* are "fantastic" realism, the "moral center," the Christian ideal, even the image of Christ ("Christ sees it all from above ...") and ... humor. ... "... humor is the wittiness of a profound emotion, and I like this definition a lot. With a keen emotion and mind, an artist can achieve a lot merely by shuffling the roles of all these destitute objects and utensils in a poor house, and to use this funny reshuffle to claw at your heart" (25, p. 91). Stressing the epithet "funny" in his description of a picture that should "claw" at your heart, Dostoevsky once again lays bare his intention to openly combine the tragic and the comical. If, in Dostoevsky's view, "satire should always be lined with tragedy" (24, p. 305), then we can say that we feel Dostoevsky's "humor being lined" with an attempt to morally overcome tragedy.[8]

Humor in this view is not merely another polyphonic device, but a deeply moral and edifying poetic element that, in an almost Dickensian manner, is intended to produce an emotional transformation in a reader's soul.

Yet, however readers assess these essentially polar views of Dostoevsky's humor, the important takeaway is their authors' consensus that the comical element is central to the writer's poetic method. Native speakers of Russian, even if separated from Dostoevsky's era by a gap of over 150 years, are nonetheless presumably "trained" in identifying, processing, and appreciating humor within their language and culture by the very course of gaining mastery of their native means of communication. Dostoevsky, however, is part of the world culture as much as that of his native land.[9] How much of his humor is conveyed to non-Russian readers? How do English audiences of his work fare as regards his humor? Is it preserved or lost in translation? These questions will be the focus of this chapter.

The above quotations also point to the fact that what is termed "humor" as applied to Dostoevsky is a complex phenomenon that does more than merely

---

[8] Rozenblium, "Iumor Dostoevskogo," 152.
[9] In 1995 British claymation short "Wallace and Gromit: A Close Shave," the dog Gromit finds himself in prison and reads *Crime and Punishment* published by Penguin Classics and penned by Fido Dogstoevsky. This sweet little joke is an excellent testimony to the degree to which Dostoevsky has been incorporated into cultures outside Russia.

provide comic relief amid tragedy. My contention in this chapter is that even though Dostoevsky uses a range of comic devices, his preferred mode is irony, specifically what D. C. Muecke termed "heuristic irony," "a heuristic device to lead one's readers to see that things are not so simple or certain as they seem, or perhaps not so complex or doubtful as they seem."[10] This preference for irony is not merely Dostoevsky's personal taste in humor, but a perfect way of using his crucial poetic device I term "layered voicing" and consider in detail below. "Heuristic irony" serves as the ideal form for this specifically Dostoevskian content.

Humor of all kinds poses a notoriously difficult translation problem.[11] As Raymond Chakhachiro rightly notes, "[S]ituations are infinitely variable, difficult to classify and changeable with speech acts."[12] That would appear to make any attempts at generalizing translation as a process extremely hard, if not virtually impossible. However, as Chakhachiro continues:

> [T]he text-type can provide a backdrop against which linguistic devices play identifiable roles. … irony can be inferred from its rhetorical, grammatical, lexical and, occasionally, paralinguistic manifestation. Having said that, rhetorical devices … require the identification of the formal constituents of irony above the theory of meaning in context to decode the irony in the original and encode it in translation. The question then rests on whether a translation shift is required to the formal proponents of irony … and the question structure, to deliver the message.[13]

I shall not consider changes in structure since they are largely determined by language patterns and inevitable in any translation (for instance, English grammatically cannot preserve the structure of Russian impersonal sentences, such as "Вечерело," necessarily transforming them into sentences with a subject, be it real or nominal: "The night was falling" or "It was getting dark"; such examples will not concern me). I will focus on semantic shifts and transformations because they pose a double challenge in translating Dostoevsky. Rendering such philosophically and metaphysically charged works of fiction as

---

[10] Cit. after Raymond Chakhachiro, *Translating Irony between English and Arabic* (Newcastle upon Tyne: Cambridge Scholars Publishing, 2018), 9.

[11] See, for instance, Jeroen Vandaele, "Humor in Translation," in *Handbook of Translation Studies. Volume 1.* Edited by Yves Gambier and Luc van Doorslaer (Amsterdam: John Benjamins Publishing Company, 2010), 147–51.

[12] Chakhachiro, *Translating Irony*, 92.

[13] Ibid.

Dostoevsky's *oeuvre* into another language, translators face the additional burden of constantly keeping in mind the complexity of the texts they are working on. Consequently, while working on a particularly hilarious fragment in the text, the translator has to remain constantly aware of said text being tightly interwoven into the overall semantic fabric of the work. And sometimes, discarding humor in favor of supposed ideas in fact undermines the ideational thrust of a work, as we will see happening below in translations of *Crime and Punishment*. My choice of passages for examination is determined by the considerations outlined above. I will consider an example of a pun from *The Brothers Karamazov* that translators handle with different degrees of success, a darkly funny "axiological metaphor"[14] from *Crime and Punishment*, and several examples of "layered voicing" taken from *The Devils* and *Notes from Underground*, as well as a deliberately satiric poem from *The Devils*.

Of the multiplicity of devices for creating humor, puns and wordplays are particularly problematic for translators. One such instance appears in *The Brothers Karamazov*, when Fyodor Pavlovich uses a pun on the police rank of an *ispravnik* and the last name of the composer and conductor *Napravnik*:

> Идем к исправнику… <…> «Господин **исправник**, будьте, говорю, нашим, так сказать, Направником!»—«Каким это, говорит, **Направником**?» <…> «Я, говорю, пошутить желал, <…> так как господин **Направник** известный наш русский капельмейстер, а нам именно нужно для гармонии нашего предприятия вроде как бы тоже капельмейстера…» <…> «Извините, говорит, я **исправник** и каламбуров из звания моего строить не позволю»[15]
>
> We went to the captain of police… 'Mr. **Ispravnik**,' said I, 'be our **Napravnik**.' 'What do you mean by **Napravnik**?' said he.… 'I wanted to make a joke,' said I, ' … as Mr. **Napravnik** is our well-known Russian orchestra conductor and what we need for the harmony of our undertaking is some one of that sort.' … 'Excuse me,' said he, 'I am an **Ispravnik**, and I do not allow puns to be made on my calling.'[16]
>
> We went to see the *ispravnik*, the district chief of police … "Now then, Mr *ispravnik*, we should like you to be, so to speak, our **Napravnik**!" "What's all this about **Napravnik**?" he said. … "Oh," I said, "I was just trying to make a

---

[14] In such metaphors, the typically metaphoric shift in the meaning of a word endows it with axiological connotations, as I will demonstrate below.

[15] Dostoevsky, *PSS*, 14: 38. Hereafter, boldface in quotations is mine—T.K.

[16] Fyodor Dostoevsky, *The Brothers Karamazov*. Translated by Constance Garnett (New York: Vintage Books, 1955), 44.

joke ... Mr **Napravnik** is actually one of our most renowned orchestral conductors, and that is exactly what we require for the harmony of our enterprise: a sort of conductor ..." ... "I'm sorry," he said, "I am the chief of police, the *ispravnik*, and I will not tolerate people making puns about my rank."[17]

So we called on the police commissioner, the *ispravnik* ... 'Mr. **Ispravnik**,' I said to him, 'be, so to speak, our **Napravnik**!' 'What do you mean, your **Napravnik**?' ... 'I wanted,' I say, 'to make a joke ... Mr. **Napravnik** is our famous Russian *Kapellmeister*, and we, for the harmony of our enterprise, also precisely need a sort of *Kapellmeister*, as it were ...' ... 'I beg your pardon,' he says, 'I am an *ispravnik*, and I will not allow you to use my title for your puns.'[18]

Garnett's translation is fairly incomprehensible as it does not spell out the link between a captain of police and an *ispravnik*. McDuff and Pevear and Volokhonsky provide comments that essentially repeat what is already clear from their translations. Pevear and Volokhonsky add a comment explaining who Napravnik was. Surprisingly, no one comments on the root—прав- with its many meanings, on the original meaning of *ispravnik* "to discharge justice" and its connection with исправлять, to correct, while Napravnik, a Czech name, is associated in Russian with the word "направлять," "to guide," "to conduct." These associations add a wealth of layers and meanings to the pun that are utterly lost on English speakers. The handling of this pun demonstrates the pitfalls that await translators in rendering both the humor and the deeper philosophical meaning of Dostoevsky's laughter-inducing passages.

As I have said, however, Dostoevsky does not use puns often. His preferred mode of comic expression is irony, and the comic effect is achieved by mixing stylistic registers and/or using unexpected shifts in meanings of commonly used words. Here is one example from *Crime and Punishment*:

Если же убеждены, что у дверей нельзя подслушивать, **а старушонок можно лущить чем попало**, в свое удовольствие, так уезжайте куда-нибудь поскорее в Америку![19]

This is brilliant gallows humor that goes deep into the heart of the novel's thematics. The word лущить applies to foods and can be used for nuts, peas,

---

[17] Fyodor Dostoevsky, *The Brothers Karamazov*. Translated by David McDuff (London: Penguin Books, 2003), 58–9.

[18] Fyodor Dostoevsky, *The Brothers Karamazov*. Translated by Richard Pevear and Larissa Volokhonsky (New York: Farrar, Straus and Giroux, 2002), 40–1.

[19] Dostoevsky, *Crime and Punishment*, PSS, 6: 373.

seeds, and everything else that has a hard shell that needs to be removed. Svidrigailov takes the word and applies it to murdering the old woman whom he refers to by using the word *"старушонка"* with its suffix that denotes small size and lack of respect. (Russian suffixes, of course, are the plague of English translations, and need to be handled through an additional array of words.) Svidrigailov uncannily latches onto the underlying philosophy of Raskolnikov's crime: the dehumanization of his victim. Thus, his metaphoric use of the word *"лущить"* becomes axiologically charged.

Translators predictably offer different renditions of this excerpt:

But if you are convinced that one mustn't listen at doors, but **one may murder old women at one's pleasure**, you'd better be off to America and make haste.[20]

If you're convinced one mustn't listen in at doors, but it's all right **to bash old hags with whatever comes to hand**, whenever the mood takes you, then you'd better get yourself off to America or somewhere![21]

But if you're convinced that one cannot eavesdrop at doors, but can go around **whacking old crones with whatever comes to hand**, to your heart's content, then leave quickly for America somewhere![22]

If you're convinced that one shouldn't eavesdrop, but that you can **crack open the skulls of old ladies with anything at hand** for your own enjoyment, then you'd best be off to America as soon as possible![23]

Garnett simply replaces the very expressive verb *"лущить"* with "to murder," a neutral English verb describing premeditated killing. For *"старушонка"*, she settles on "old woman," also a neutral expression. Oliver Ready introduces the somewhat slangy "bash" and uses "old hag" for *"старушонка,"* which appears a bit too strong in this context. Pevear and Volokhonsky use the same strategy, even if a different set of words. Michael Katz reverts to a variation on "old women" with his "old ladies" and expands the word *"лущить"* into "crack open the skulls." This is a rather unique case of English being longer and wordier than Russian. Two

---

[20] Fyodor Dostoyevsky, *Crime and Punishment*. Translated by Constance Garnett (London: Bantam Books, 1981), 418.
[21] Fyodor Dostoyevsky, *Crime and Punishment*. Translated by Oliver Ready (New York: Penguin Books, 2015), 456.
[22] Fyodor Dostoyevsky, *Crime and Punishment*. Translated by Richard Pevear and Larissa Volokhonsky (New York: Alfred Knopf, 1993), 484–5.
[23] Fyodor Dostoyevsky, *Crime and Punishment: A New Translation*. Translated by Michael Katz (New York: Liveright, 2019), 534.

words "*чем попало*" are translated with at least four words in English. Although English has a reputation for being a pithy and laconic language, in sheer word count it is usually "wordier" than Russian, but that wordiness comes from articles, auxiliary verbs, and more prepositions than in Russian. Here, however, English is genuinely more verbose since the laconic Russian "*чем попало*" has to be rendered with four or five English words. Wordiness often takes away from humor that needs to be pithy and concise to have its desired effect.

Most of these translations seem to be problematic, each in its own way. First, none actually renders the uniqueness of Dostoevsky's expression. Regardless of a domesticating or a defamiliarizing strategy a translator chooses, here we have an expression that is defamiliarized in the original. Consequently, a standardized translation creates a familiarizing effect where there was none in the original. Second, by using words such as "whack" or "bash" translators omit the crucial point of the novel: the utter dehumanization of the pawnbroker. She is not a human being, she is foodstuffs. She is not murdered, or whacked, or bashed. She is shucked like a nut or a seed. So, this is one instance where keeping the humor is essential for staying on point with the novel's principal message of universal humanity. Murder is only possible if you dehumanize your victim, and Svidrigailov artfully emphasizes this fact with his word choice. Michael Katz is the only translator who tries to stick to that meaning by using the words "crack open the skulls of old ladies." The question is whether "skulls" somewhat removes that defamiliarizing and dehumanizing effect by adding a definitely humanizing reminder that what gets cracked is a skull, and an "old lady" is not a cultivar of nuts, peas, or seeds, but a human being. But then again, without the words "the skulls" the phrase would likely be unintelligible to an English reader.[24]

Translations of such instances where humor arises from unexpected shifts in usage and, consequently, in meaning seem to present a bigger challenge for translators than Dostoevsky's poetic device of choice I term "layered voicing." An example of this device can be found in the beginning of *The Devils*. Challenges that await a translator of Dostoevsky begin with the very title of the novel. Constance Garnett rendered it as *The Possessed* shifting the accent from an active agency to a passive and even unwilling receptacle of evil. It was also translated as *Demons*, and that translation eliminated the opposition between the "lofty" and seductive evil represented by demons ("*демон*") in Russian literary tradition

---

[24] In the process of preparing this article for publication, the collection's editors suggested "that you can crack open an old lady's nut for your pleasure," which is a perfect version of Dostoevsky's phrase.

(starting with Mikhail Lermontov) on the one hand, and petty, repulsive evil ("*бесы*") on the other. This opposition is spelled out in the text, and this is where translators run into trouble. Dasha tells Stavrogin that she is praying for him and encourages him to turn to her for help, and Stavrogin responds by taking her ideas of lofty and beautiful evil down a few notches into the realm of the disgusting:

> —Да сохранит вас бог от вашего **демона** и … позовите, позовите меня скорей!
> —О, какой мой **демон**! Это просто маленький, гаденький, золотушный **бесенок** с насморком, из неудавшихся.²⁵

> God save you from your **demon**, and … call me, call me quickly!
> "Oh! a fine **demon**! It's simply a little nasty, scrofulous **imp**, with a cold in his head, one of the unsuccessful ones."²⁶

> "May God preserve you from your **dark spirit**, and … call me, call me soon!"
> "Oh, he's no **dark spirit**! He's simply a nasty, scrofulous little **demon** with a runny nose, a failure."²⁷

> "May God preserve you from your **demon** and … call me, do call me as soon as possible!"
> 'Oh, it's quite a **demon** I have! He's simply a small, nasty, scrofulous **little demon** with a head cold, one of life's failures.'²⁸

Without the use of the word "devil," translations simply cannot win. Garnett's "imp" today reads more like a "mischievous creature" without connoting something particularly evil, but at least it leaves the readers in no doubts as to the implied opposition. Pevear and Volokhonsky lose all connection with Russian literary tradition and leave the readers scratching their heads at the implication that a demon is not a dark spirit, while Maguire just uses the same word modified by "little," which to a large degree omits the opposition inherent in the Russian original.

---

[25] Dostoevsky, *The Devils*, *PSS*, 10: 231.

[26] Fyodor Dostoevsky, *The Possessed*. Translated by Constance Garnett (London: William Heinemann LTD, 1956), 266.

[27] Fyodor Dostoyevsky, *Demons*. Translated by Richard Pevear and Larissa Volokhonsky (New York: Vintage Books, 1995), 293.

[28] Fyodor Dostoyevsky, *Demons*. Translated by Robert A. Maguire, edited by Ronald Meyer (New York: Penguin Books, 2008), 326.

The Devils is a hilariously funny novel at places. At the beginning, the narrator retells a poem Stepan Verkhovensky wrote many years ago; it is a pompous and rather silly allegory. The narrator's retelling of the poem represents an example of what I have termed layered voicing. This is not Bakhtin's polyphony that posits a multitude of equal voices coexisting within the space of his works. It is a combination of different voices and points of view *within a single statement*. One example of such layered voicing is a quote from Nikolay Nekrasov's poem in *Notes from Underground* that is cut off abruptly with the rest of the poem replaced with "etc., etc., etc." Robert L. Jackson in his analysis of the story noted that the voice in the text of the poem is Nekrasov's, but the "etc.'s" belong to the Underground Man.[29] In *The Devils*, this layered voicing is used with remarkable consistency, and it is this voicing that creates the ironic tone of the text.

> Сцена открывается хором женщин, потом хором мужчин, потом каких-то сил, и в конце всего хором душ, еще не живших, **но которым очень бы хотелось пожить.** <…> … поют даже насекомые, является черепаха с какими-то латинскими сакраментальными словами, и даже, если припомню, пропел о чем-то один минерал,—**то есть предмет уже вовсе неодушевленный.** <…> … между утесами бродит один цивилизованный молодой человек, который срывает и сосет какие-то травы, и на вопрос феи: зачем он сосет эти травы? отвечает, что он, чувствуя в себе избыток жизни, ищет забвения и находит его в соке этих трав; но что главное желание его – поскорее потерять ум (**желание, может быть, и излишнее**).[30]

> The scene opens with a chorus of women, followed by a chorus of men, then a chorus of incorporeal powers of some sort, and at the end of all a chorus of spirits not yet living but **very eager to come to life**. … even insects sing, a tortoise comes on the scene with certain sacramental Latin words, and even, if I remember aright, a mineral sings about something **that is a quite inanimate object**. … among the rocks there wanders a civilized young man who picks and sucks certain herbs. Asked by a fairy why he sucks these herbs, he answers that, conscious of a superfluity of life in himself, he seeks forgetfulness, and finds it in the juice of these herbs, but that his great desire is to lose his reason at once **(a desire possibly superfluous)**.[31]

---

[29] Robert Louis Jackson, *The Art of Dostoevsky. Deliriums and Nocturnes* (Princeton: Princeton University Press, 1981), 180–3.
[30] Dostoevsky, *The Devils*, *PSS*, 10: 9–10.
[31] Dostoevsky, *The Possessed*. trans. Constance Garnett, 4.

The first scene opens with a chorus of women, then a chorus of men, then a chorus of spirits of some kind, and at the very end, a chorus of souls, which have never yet been alive, but **would very much like to come to life**. ... even insects sing, a tortoise appears with some sacramental words in Latin, and even, if I remember rightly, a certain mineral—**that is, an entirely inanimate object**—bursts into song about something. ... a civilized young man wanders among crags, plucking and sucking herbs of some sort, and when a fairy asks him why he is sucking these herbs, he replies that since he feels an overabundance of life within himself, he seeks oblivion and finds it in the juices of these herbs, but that what he desires most of all is to lose his mind as quickly as possible (**a desire that is perhaps superfluous**).³²

The scene opens with a chorus of women, then a chorus of men, then of some powers, and it all ends with a chorus of **souls** that have not lived yet but **would very much like to live a little**. ... even insects sing, a turtle appears with some sort of sacramental Latin words, and, if I remember, a mineral—**that is, an altogether inanimate object**—also gets to sing about something. ... a civilized young man wanders among the rocks picking and sucking at some wild herbs, and when a fairy asks him why he is sucking these herbs, he responds that he feels an overabundance of life in himself, is seeking oblivion, and finds it in the juice of these herbs, but that his greatest desire is to lose his reason as quickly as possible (**a perhaps superfluous desire**).³³

In this passage, the narrator's voice constantly intercuts with the voice of the poem's author, Stepan Verkhovensky, and adds his own sarcastic quips. Phrases in boldface indicate the narrator's comments on the poem. Constance Garnett here has the greatest trouble with the humor. Both she and Robert Maguire do not render the ironic overtones of "*пожить*" brought out by the words "*очень бы хотелось*." Pevear and Volokhonsky note that shade of meaning and render it as "would very much like to live **a little**." Garnett also detached the comment about the mineral from its immediate denotatum thereby failing to make the mineral part funny. The part where every translator does well is the sarcastic implication that the young man (and, by extension, the younger self of Stepan Verkhovensky) has already lost his mind and so wishing for any further progress in that department is quite unnecessary. Note, however, how Pevear and

---

³² Dostoevsky, *Demons*, trans. Maguire, 10–11.
³³ Dostoevsky, *Demons*, trans. Pevear, Volokhonsky, 10.

Volokhonsky change the word order in "*желание, может быть, и излишнее*" to "a perhaps superfluous desire." Every other translator takes care to place the word "superfluous" in the end where it is logically stressed. It needs to be there precisely for the comedic effect. Pevear and Volokhonsky place it in an adverbial position thus diminishing the sarcastic impact of the narrator's voice. Once again, translations are markedly uneven in their renditions of the funny elements, succeeding in some places and failing in others.

The Devils also has verses in it, which is rather atypical for Dostoevsky. These verses are intentionally bad, comical, and rhymed. Contemporary English poetry is mostly unrhymed, so rhymes help reinforce the bad and comical aspects of the verses in *The Devils*. Let us quote the relevant poems and their English versions:

Жил на свете таракан,	Lived a cockroach in the world
Таракан от детства,	Such was his condition,
И потом попал в стакан	In a glass he chanced to fall
Полный мухоедства … <…>	Full of fly-perdition. …
/ _/_ _ _ /	/ _/_ _ _ /
_ _/_/_	(/) _ _ _/_
(/) _/_/_ /	_ _/_/_ /
/ _ _ _/_	/ _/_/_
Место занял таракан,	But he squeezed against the flies,
Мухи возроптали,	They woke up and cursed him,
Полон очень наш стакан,	Raised to Jove their angry cries;
К Юпитеру закричали.	'The glass is full to bursting!'
Но пока у них шел крик,	In the middle of the din
Подошел Никифор,	Came along Nikifor,
Бла-го-роднейший старик … <…>	Fine old man, and looking in … …
Тут у меня еще не докончено, но все равно, словами!—трещал капитан,—Никифор берет стакан и, несмотря на крик, выплескивает в лохань всю комедию, и мух и таракана, что давно надо было сделать.[34]	"I haven't quite finished it. But no matter, I'll tell it in words," the captain rattled on. "Nikifor takes the glass, and in spite of their outcry empties away the whole stew, flies, and beetles and all, into the pig pail, which ought to have been done long ago."[35]

---

[34] Dostoevsky, *The Devils*, PSS, 10: 141–2.

[35] Dostoevsky, *The Possessed*. trans. Constance Garnett, 159.

In this world a roach did dwell,	'Tis of a cockroach I will tell,
From birth a cockroach, proud and wise,	And a fine cockroach was he,
One day into a glass he fell	But then into a glass he fell
All chockablock with cannibal flies. …	Full of fly-phagy … …
_ _ ⌣/ _⌣/ _ /	(/) _ _⌣/ _ _ _ /
⌣/⌣/⌣/ _ /	_ _//_ _ _ /
(/)/_ _ _⌣/ _ /	_ _ _ _⌣/ _ /
⌣/ _ (/) _⌣/ _ _ /	/ _⌣/ _ /

The cockroach took his rightful place,	The cockroach took up so much room
The flies, they buzzed and clamoured,	It made the flies murmur.
"Our glass is full, there's no more space"	'A crowded glass, is this our doom?'
To Jupiter they yammered.	They cried to Jupiter.

Before the shouts and screams abated	But as the flies did make their moan
Up came Nikifor, old and grizzled,	Along came Nikifor,
A worthy soul, much venerated … …	A kind, old, no-o-oble man … …

"This part's not yet finished, but it doesn't matter, I'll tell it in plain words!" the captain jabbered. "Nikifor picks up the glass, and despite the shouting, he pours the entire comedy out into a bucket, flies and cockroach both, which should have been done long ago."[36]	"I haven't quite finished here, but anyway, in plain words!" the captain rattled on. "Nikifor takes the glass and, in spite of their crying, dumps the whole comedy into the tub, both flies and cockroach, which should have been done long ago."[37]

Здравствуй, здравствуй, гувернантка!	Governess! I kiss your hand,
Веселись и торжествуй.	Joy to you, we're in your debt,
Ретроградка иль Жорж-Зандка,	Reactionary or George Sand.
Все равно теперь ликуй! <…>	It matters not, enjoy this fete. …

Учишь ты детей сопливых	Teaching French to snivelly kids,
По-французски букварю	You'd be glad to take the hand
И подмигивать готова,	Of even a sexton if he rids
Чтобы взял, хоть понмарю! <…>	You of that lethal, boring band. …

---

[36] Dostoevsky, *Demons*, trans. Maguire, Meyer, 195–6.
[37] Dostoevsky, *Demons*, trans. Pevear, Volokhonsky, 177.

Но в наш век реформ великих Не возьмет и пономарь; Надо, барышня, "толиких", Или снова за букварь. <…>	But in our age of great to-do, Even a sexton won't look your way, Unless you have a rouble or two, Else—back to the primer, day after day! …
Но теперь, когда, пируя, Мы собрали капитал, И приданое, танцуя, Шлем тебе из этих зал,—	But now that our gala's power Has yielded us such capital, We're sending each of you a dower From this festive, jubilant hall.
Ретроградка иль Жорж-Зандка, Все равно, теперь ликуй! Ты с приданым гувернантка, Плюй на все и торжествуй!³⁸ _ _/_ _ _/_ (/) _/_/_ / _ _/_ _ _/_ / _ (/) _ _ _ /	Reactionary or George Sand It matters not, enjoy this fete. Now that you're dowered, as we've planned, Spit in triumph on all you've met.³⁹ _/_ _ _ // _/_/_/_ / _ _ _/_ _ _ / / _/_ (/) _ /
Governesses all, good morrow, Triumph on this festive day. Retrograde or vowed George-Sander— Never mind, just frisk away! …	I give you greetings grand and grander, Governess! Be triumphant now, Retrograde or true George-Sander, Be exultant anyhow! …
Teaching French to wet-nosed children, You are glad enough to think You can catch a worn-out sexton— Even he is worth a wink! …	You teach our snot-nosed children French From an alphabetic book, The beadle even, in a pinch, For marriage you won't overlook! …
But in these great days of progress, Ladies, to your sorrow know, You can't even catch a sexton, If you have not got a "dot". …	But now, when great reforms are flowering, Even a beadle's hard to hook: Unless, young miss, you've got a 'dowering,' It's back to the alphabetic book. …

---

³⁸ Dostoevsky, *The Devils*, *PSS*, 10: 362–3.
³⁹ Dostoevsky, *Demons*, trans. Maguire, Meyer, 522–3.

But, henceforth, since through our feasting
Capital has flowed from all,
And we send you forth to conquer
Dancing, dowried from this hall—

Retrograde or vowed George-Sander,
Never mind, rejoice you may,
You're a governess with a dowry,
Spit on all and frisk away![40]
_ _/_///_
/ _/_/_ /
_ _/_ _ _ _/_
/ _ (/) _/_ (/)

Today, however, with our hosting
We have raised much capital,
And while dancing here we're posting
A dowry to you from this hall.

Retrograde or true George-Sander,
Be exultant anyhow!
Governess by dower grander,
Spit on the rest and triumph now![41]
_ _/_///_
_ _/_ _ (/)
/ _ _ _/_/_
/ _ _/_/_ /

These two poems, authored by the same character, Ignat Lebyadkin, exhibit a marked similarity in their trochaic meter. It appears that translators have quite a bit of trouble with the meters, noticeably failing to render the crisp clipping rhythm of the original. They carefully rhyme their verses, although Garnett rhymes only two lines out of four in the governess poem, while other translators rhyme all four lines. However, the metric pattern works best in Garnett's versions of both the cockroach and governess poems. It is appropriately "doggerel-style," while other translations are more cumbersome and rather oddly "serious." Maguire's translation tries for a comic effect by using the traditional Dostoevsky device of combining the incompatible: in this case, a cockroach with the epithets "proud and wise" and "taking his rightful place." However, while that sounds appropriately comical, it undermines the message of the poem, where the cockroach is anything but proud and taking his rightful place. Whatever Lebyadkin's ambitions, he recites the poem to disguise them and to deliberately present his "insect" alter ego as one of the most despicable domestic parasites.

Garnett is also quite on point in the governess poem, aside from her use of the word "frisk" in its oldest meaning of "gamboling, frolicking," which might

---

[40] Dostoevsky, *The Possessed*, trans. Garnett, 427–8.
[41] Dostoevsky, *Demons*, trans. Pevear, Volokhonsky, 472–3.

tax today's readers who are more used to seeing it mean "to pat down, search." Another question emerges from her use of the word "dot" that looks as if Garnett intended it to be pronounced as "dough" to rhyme with "know," or else this stanza remains unrhymed. The examples of Stepan's poem and Ignat Lebyadkin's verses show that translation quality can be quite uneven and vary significantly between different portions of a text. It is particularly noticeable in connection with Garnett's translation. Her rendition of Stepan's poem was not particularly funny, while Lebyadkin's poems are appropriately bad and ridiculous in her translation.

Another darkly funny text is *Notes from Underground*. It posits many problems for translations on the conceptual level, starting with the key words "*злой*" and "*злость*"; these two words are most frequently translated as "spiteful" and "spite" respectively, which entirely loses the meaning of "evil" present in the very first adjective "*злой*" in the Russian text. (Two exceptions of six translations I researched are Boris Jakim who uses "evil"[42] and Jesse Coulson who uses "angry."[43]) The Russian word, of course, combines all three shades of meaning, and English translators are placed in the impossible position of having to choose depending on their predominantly metaphysical (Jakim) or psychological (virtually everyone else) reading.

The Underground Man's signature style features biting sarcasm aimed at everything and everyone around him, including himself. Essentially, Robert L. Jackson's observation about the Underground Man intercutting his own voice with that of Nekrasov's lyrical persona could be extended to all the Underground Man's statements as he constantly double-voices everything, taking other people's implied or imagined words and imbuing them with his own ironic and even sarcastic attitude. The following excerpt is one example of such ironic layering.

> Да осыпьте его всеми земными благами, утопите в счастье совсем с головой, так, чтобы только пузырьки вскакивали на поверхности счастья, как на воде; дайте ему такое экономическое довольство, чтоб ему совсем уж ничего больше не оставалось делать, кроме как спать, кушать пряники и хлопотать о непрекращении всемирной истории,—так он вам

---

[42] Fyodor Dostoevsky, *Notes from Underground*. Translated by Boris Jakim (Grand Rapids, MI: William B. Eerdmans Publishing Co., 2009), 3.

[43] Fyodor Dostoevsky, *Notes from Underground. The Double*. Translated by Jesse Coulson (New York: Penguin Books, 2003), 15.

и тут, человек-то, и тут, из одной неблагодарности, из одного пасквиля мерзость сделает.⁴⁴

Shower upon him every earthly blessing, drown him in a sea of happiness, so that nothing but bubbles of bliss can be seen on the surface; give him economic prosperity, such that he should have nothing else to do but sleep, eat cakes and busy himself with the continuation of his species, and even then out of sheer ingratitude, sheer spite, man would play you some nasty trick.⁴⁵

Indeed, you can shower him with every earthly blessing, drown him in happiness from head to toe so that only bubbles jump about the surface of his happiness, like on water; give him such economic prosperity that he has absolutely nothing left to do except sleep, eat gingerbread, and fuss about the never-ending history of the world—and he's still just a man, and still out of ingratitude alone, out of plain lampoonery will commit abominations.⁴⁶

Shower him with all earthly blessings, immerse him so completely in happiness that the bubbles dance on the surface of his happiness, as though on water; grant him such economic prosperity that he will have absolutely nothing else to do but sleep, eat gingerbread and concern himself with the continuance of world history—and that man, out of sheer ingratitude, out of sheer devilment, will even then do the dirty on you.⁴⁷

Shower him with all earthly blessings; submerge him in happiness over his head, so that only little bubbles pop up on the surface of happiness as if it were water; give him such economic prosperity that he'll have absolutely nothing left to do but sleep, eat cakes, and busy himself with the noncessation of world history—and even then, out of sheer ingratitude, out of sheer perversity, he—man, that is—would still do something vile.⁴⁸

Jane Kentish's translation of the phrase "*непрекращение всемирной истории*" is a little odd as it is not entirely clear whether the man is fussing because he wants history to continue or because he is bothered by its never-ending nature. Kentish, however, was the only translator out of four to latch onto the biblical undertones of the word "*мерзость*" and appropriately translated

---

⁴⁴ Dostoevsky, *Notes from Underground*, PSS, 5: 116.
⁴⁵ Fyodor Dostoyevsky, *Notes from Underground*, trans. Constance Garnett, in *The Short Novels of Dostoevsky* (New York: Dial Press, 1951), 149.
⁴⁶ Fyodor Dostoevsky, *Notes from the Underground* and *The Gambler*. Translated by Jane Kentish (Oxford: Oxford University Press, 1991), 30–1.
⁴⁷ Fyodor Dostoevsky, *Notes from Underground* and *The Double*. Translated by Ronald Wilks (London: Penguin Books, 2009), 28.
⁴⁸ Dostoevsky, *Notes from Underground*, trans. Boris Jakim, 28–9.

it as "abominations." That accords well with the hidden, yet clearly perceived by contemporaries, metaphysical overtones of the work.[49] She also chose an excellent expression "fuss about" for "*хлопотать*" that sounds appropriately out of place in the context of world history. Wilks appears to have compensated for those overtones by using "devilment" for "*пасквиль*." Garnett's translation also takes quite a few liberties with the text as she adds "bubbles of bliss" while removing "as if on water." That makes the text lighter, smoother, more flowing, and, consequently, funnier. Laughter in general is a concise genre that does not like wordiness, so Garnett's omission makes for a funnier reading experience. Jakim—although he appears to stress more the "evil" element in the Underground Man—chooses "something vile" for "*мерзость*" and gives the whole passage more of a sociopolitical slant by using the infamous "eat cakes" popularly ascribed to Marie Antoinette and usually cited to indicate complete lack of awareness of other people's social plight. Once again, no translation probably emerges as a clear favorite on all accounts: humor, precision, and conveying the underlying metaphysical overtones of the excerpt.

***

The preceding was not meant as a criticism of translations. Translation is an arduous, taxing, sometimes impossible, and often ungrateful task, that is, nonetheless, vital for the process of "fussing about" the "noncessation" of world culture. The examples given above from several of Dostoevsky's novels are simply meant to show that the comedic elements present in his works are translated with varying success. Translators fare best when it comes to the overall sarcastic bite of the text and do less successfully in those instances when the dark humor comes from very specific word usage or very specific poetic devices. Even though

---

[49] Mikhail Saltykov-Shchedrin, who cannot be called Dostoevsky's admirer, mocked *Notes from Underground* bitterly in his mini-play "The Swifts" where *Notes* is referred to as *Notes on the Immortality of the Soul*. Saltykov-Shchedrin writes, "It is written in the person of a sick and spiteful swift. First, he speaks about different trifles: that he is sick and spiteful, and everything in the world is fickle, that he has lower back pains, that no one can tell if the coming summer will have an abundance of mushrooms, and, finally, that people are trash, and any person can only become good if he becomes convinced that he is trash, and in the end, he finally moves to the real subject matter of his ruminations. He borrows his arguments primarily from Thomas Aquinas, but since he never mentions the fact, the reader thinks that these thoughts belong to the narrator." See Mikhail Saltykov-Shchedrin, "Literaturnye melochi," in *Sobranie sochinenii v 20 tomakh* (Moscow: Khudozhestvennaya literatura, 1968), 6: 493. Shchedrin's vocabulary is recognizably Dostoevskian, and his reference to Aquinas is intriguing. On what exactly is borrowed from Aquinas see Tatyana Kovalevskaya, "Dostoevsky and Scholastic Theology: Points of Intersection," *Dostoevsky i mirovaya literatura. Filologicheskiy zhurnal*, no. 1(13) (2021): 106–23, https://doi.org/10.22455/2541-7894-2021-1-106-123.

it is in many cases unavoidable owing to the very nature of the English language, it is still regrettable since Dostoevsky's humor is an essential part of his poetics. He uses humor in general and irony in particular to help his readers navigate their way through his works layered with many voices that undercut each other. Authorial irony frequently serves as a guiding light in their complex intertwining to help readers pinpoint the one voice Dostoevsky wants them to hear and listen to. Therefore, translators need to identify the elements of humor in Dostoevsky's works and attempt to render their comical element as faithfully as possible.

Yet in translation, Dostoevsky ideational thrust and his irony often seem to exist in a state of complementary distribution when it is either one or the other. Sometimes, translators try to make up for what is lost by spicing up with humor other elements of their translations. While it helps preserve the comic aspect of Dostoevsky's works, it frequently fails to manifest the integral connection between Dostoevsky's humor and the philosophical and religious content of his works. And while such compensation does help dispel the notion of Dostoevsky as a gloomy and hopeless author, it does not do full justice to the profound ideational role humor plays in the writer's works.

Bibliography

Chakhachiro, Raymond. *Translating Irony between English and Arabic.* Newcastle upon Tyne: Cambridge Scholars Publishing, 2018.

Dostoyevsky, Fyodor. *Crime and Punishment.* Translated by Constance Garnett. London: Bantam Books, 1981.

Dostoyevsky, Fyodor. *Crime and Punishment.* Translated by Oliver Ready. New York: Penguin Books, 2015.

Dostoyevsky, Fyodor. *Crime and Punishment: A New Translation.* Translated by Michael Katz. New York: Liveright, 2019.

Dostoyevsky, Fyodor. *Demons.* Translated by Richard Pevear and Larissa Volokhonsky. New York: Vintage Books, 1995.

Dostoyevsky, Fyodor. *Demons.* Translated by Robert A. Maguire, Edited by Ronald Meyer. New York: Penguin Books, 2008.

Dostoyevsky, Fyodor. *Notes from Underground.* Translated by Boris Jakim. Grand Rapids, MI: William B. Eerdmans Publishing Co., 2009.

Dostoyevsky, Fyodor. *Notes from Underground,* in *The Short Novels of Dostoevsky.* Translated by Constance Garnett, 127–222. New York: Dial Press, 1951.

Dostoyevsky, Fyodor. *Notes from Underground. The Double.* Translated by Jesse Coulson. New York: Penguin Books, 2003.

Dostoevsky, Fyodor. *Notes from Underground and the Double*. Translated by Ronald Wilks. London: Penguin Books, 2009.

Dostoevsky, Fyodor. *Notes from the Underground, and the Gambler*. Translated by Jane Kentish. Oxford: Oxford University Press, 1991.

Dostoevsky, Fyodor. *Polnoe sobranie sochinenii v tridtsati tomakh*. Moscow-Leningrad: Nauka, 1972–1990.

Dostoevsky, Fyodor. *The Brothers Karamazov*. Translated by Constance Garnett. New York: Vintage Books, 1955.

Dostoevsky, Fyodor. *The Brothers Karamazov*. Translated by David McDuff. London: Penguin Books, 2003.

Dostoevsky, Fyodor. *The Brothers Karamazov*. Translated by Richard Pevear and Larissa Volokhonsky. New York: Farrar, Straus and Giroux, 2002.

Dostoevsky, Fyodor. *The Possessed*. Translated by Constance Garnett. London: William Heinemann Ltd, 1956.

Groskop, Viv. *The Anna Karenina Fix*. New York: Penguin Books, 2017. Kindle.

Jackson, Robert Louis. *The Art of Dostoevsky. Deliriums and Nocturnes*. Princeton: Princeton University Press, 1981.

Kovalevskaya, Tatyana. "Dostoevsky and Scholastic Theology: Points of Intersection," *Dostooevsky i mirovaia literatura. Filologicheskiy zhurnal*, vol. 1, no. 13 (2021): 106–23, https://doi.org//10.22455/2541-7894-2021-1-106-123.

Martakova, T. S. "Antropologiia smekha v proizvedeniiakh Dostoevskogo (1846–1859): K voprosu o 'smekhovom portrete'," *Vestnik Cheliabinskogo gosudarstvennogo universiteta*, vol. 15 (2007): 89–94.

Morson, Gary Saul. "Gogol's Parables of Explanation: Nonsense and Prosaics," in *Essays on Gogol: Logos and the Russian Word*. Edited by Susanne Fusso and Priscilla Meyer, 203–39. Evanston, IL: Northwestern University Press, 1992.

Ponkratova, E. "Smekh i komicheskoe v tvorchestve F.M. Dostoevskogo: o nekotorykh osobennostiakh estetiki pisatelia," *Vestnik Tomskogo gosudarstvennogo universiteta*, vol. 349 (2011): 19–22, http://journals.tsu.ru/vestnik/&journal_page=archive&id=862&article_id=5835.

Rozenblium, Liia M. "Iumor Dostoevskogo," *Voprosy literatury*, vol. 1 (1999): 141–88, https://voplit.ru/article/yumor-dostoevskogo/?ysclid=lpvkr0y1hy636895537.

Saltykov-Schedrin, Mikhail. "Literaturnye melochi," in *Sobranie sochinenii v 20 tomakh*, 6: 473–94. Moscow: Khudozhestvennaya literatura, 1968.

Vandaele, Jeroen. "Humor in Translation," in *Handbook of Translation Studies. Volume 1*. Edited by Yves Gambier and Luc van Doorslaer, 147–52. Amsterdam: John Benjamins Publishing Company, 2010.

3

Raskolnikov's Red Nose: The Slapstick Comedy of Dostoevsky's Serious Protagonists

Fiona Bell

What if, when reading *Crime and Punishment*, in your mind's eye you cast the slapstick comedian Buster Keaton as Raskolnikov? This wouldn't be a stretch. Raskolnikov wears ridiculous clothes. He paces and mutters maniacally in public. Like a clown with a gigantic mallet, he uses a comically oversized instrument—an axe, when a knife would do. A cabby whips him in the street, and an old woman, taking him for a beggar, gives him money, which he accepts. Raskolnikov moves in fits and starts: falling over, jumping up, breaking into a run, and collapsing. The novel's setting resembles an early Hollywood film set, whether on the Petersburg streets, with their violence, poverty, and police chases, or in Raskolnikov's comically small garret, with its ever-growing group of visitors.

Readers of *Crime and Punishment* recognize the ridiculousness of Raskolnikov's grand idea from the very first moment they see him move. In fact, Dostoevsky's most serious characters are some of his finest practitioners of slapstick comedy. Their buffoonish gesture signals the comic divide between their extreme intellectual preoccupations and their unruly, vulnerable bodies. This article considers Dostoevsky's cultivation of the slapstick mode in *The Double* to set the stage for a close reading of Raskolnikov in *Crime and Punishment*. Golyadkin and Raskolnikov perform similar slapstick gags: bodies acting like objects, frenzied movement, failure to understand directions, and over-adaptation to social norms. As the first in Dostoevsky's genealogy of wandering, muttering, mentally over-stimulated urban heroes, Golyadkin is a striking forbear of Raskolnikov. To be sure, as we move from *The Double* to *Crime and Punishment*—and the stakes rise from society balls to murder—the designation of "slapstick" may feel less and less comfortable. Raskolnikov's slapstick lineage shines through, however, at a critical moment: the murder scene. As

Raskolnikov's physicality shifts between slapstick and melodramatic modes in this episode, the reader is primed to respond to him with pity and disgust by turns. Dostoevsky's intergeneric movement within this scene accomplishes an essential characterization of Raskolnikov: the "split," which remains salient for the remainder of the novel.

Scholars of Dostoevsky love performance metaphors. And so, just as Mochulsky likened *Crime and Punishment* to a five-act tragedy, and Peter Brooks indicated Dostoevsky's melodramatic imagination, I ask, in turn, what we can uncover when we recognize the slapstick mode at the heart of Dostoevsky's "serious" works. Such a recognition will, among other things, clarify our basic vision of the writer. Like Dostoevsky himself, slapstick comedy sits at the nexus of social critique and spirituality. It is a performance genre deeply concerned with the absurdity of work under capitalism. Simultaneously, like Orthodox theology, slapstick emphasizes the fallibility of the body and the fallacy of human authority. In Dostoevsky's works, the slapstick mode marks the elusive meeting point between the author as critic of capitalist modernity and as champion of Orthodoxy. In *Crime and Punishment*, the slapstick murder scene is both class revolt *and* sin. When we recognize the slapstick in Dostoevsky, we permit these seemingly conflicting sides of his writerly project to coexist.

Of course, every claim about Dostoevsky's genre is a sort of performance, a "playing at" generic coherence where there is none. I now invite the reader to consider Dostoevsky's use of slapstick comedy not as an unfortunate tic, but as an intentional device, much like the clown's artful and controlled fall. Nor is it embarrassing to read these works as comic; scholarship is its own sort of gag, an attempt to disrupt accepted systems that occasionally ends in failure. Most importantly, criticism requires faith that the literary work, like a jack-in-the-box, will spring back up when subjected to various critical apparatuses, that *Crime and Punishment* will still be magnificent if the murder scene is funny. And so, as I present Dostoevsky's "serious" heroes as clowns, I invite readers to imagine Dostoevsky himself as a sort of clown, and the scholar as a tertiary clown. Now let's all get in the car and go.

Genre Trouble in Dostoevsky

Dostoevsky's comic aesthetics have traditionally been dismissed as juvenilia or, in the case of his later novels, relegated to discussions of holy fools and minor characters. One scholar has identified Dostoevsky's 1859 novella *The Village of Stepanchikovo* as "crude slapstick," "egregious farcicality," the aesthetically impoverished work of a writer who had, in exile, become "thoroughly detached from literary life." Describing the author's bathroom humor in the novella, this scholar wonders: "How did Dostoevsky descend to this point?"[1]

This anti-comedy response characterizes a long critical tradition that has imagined Dostoevsky as a novelist-tragedian.[2] According to this tradition, Dostoevsky's works contain comic interludes only in the way that Shakespeare's tragedies do.[3] In figuring the writer as a tragedian, critics have tended to foreground his work's spiritual thematics and, moreover, address an anxiety about the perceived incongruence between these spiritual thematics and the "lowness" of the novel form. In his seminal 1976 work, *The Melodramatic Imagination*, Peter Brooks challenged this critical allergy to "low" forms, arguing that the nineteenth-century novel not only incorporated, but is characterized by, devices from contemporary vaudeville theater. Though Dostoevsky's name peppers the monograph, Brooks does not apply his theorization to the Russian writer's works: "The figure whose absence may most be felt is Dostoevsky," he writes in the preface, "a direct heir of Balzacian melodrama and one of the novelists who puts melodramatic representations to most effective use."[4] Scholars of Dostoevsky have taken up where Brooks left off. Simon Karlinsky observes that the writer regularly drew on vaudeville stock characters when developing characters for his prose works.[5] Susanne Fusso has demonstrated that these vaudevillian conventions characterize not only the writer's early works but also his late style.[6] Irina Erman has indicated Dostoevsky's generic affinity with the cuckold play, locating the trope of the small, enclosed space—so key

---

[1] Lewis Bagby, *First Words: On Dostoevsky's Introductions* (Brighton, MA: Academic Studies Press, 2016), 27–39.

[2] For a discussion of this critical history, see Ilya Kliger, "Dostoevsky and the Novel-Tragedy: Genre and Modernity in Ivanov, Pumpyansky, and Bakhtin," *Modern Language Association*, vol. 126, no. 1 (2011): 73–87.

[3] Viacheslav Ivanov goes so far as to call Dostoevsky the "Russian Shakespeare" in Ivanov, "Dostoevskii. Tragediia—Mif—Mistika," in *Sobranie sochinenii v chetyrekh tomakh* (Briussel': Foyer Oriental Chrétien, 1987), 4: 498.

[4] Peter Brooks, *The Melodramatic Imagination: Balzac, Henry James, Melodrama, and the Mode of Excess* (New Haven: Yale University Press, 1976), xiv.

[5] Simon Karlinsky, *Russian Drama from Its Beginnings to the Age of Pushkin* (Berkeley, CA: University of California Press, 1985), 156.

[6] Susanne Fusso, "Husbands and Lovers: Vaudeville Conventions in 'Another Man's Wife,' 'The Jealous Husband,' and *The Eternal Husband*," in *Before They Were Titans: Essays on the Early Works of Dostoevsky and Tolstoy*. Edited by Elizabeth Cheresh Allen (Brighton, MA: Academic Studies Press, 2015), 62.

to the writer's *oeuvre*—in the vaudevillian tradition.[7] Deborah Martinsen uses the lexicon of clown and *commedia dell'arte* to track the dynamics of shame in Dostoevsky's later novels, and Rima Iakubova has highlighted the author's particular use of *balagan* puppet theater motifs in *Demons*.[8]

Dostoevsky's identities as novelist and as theatergoer were deeply intertwined. The vaudeville variety show reached its zenith in Imperial Russia during the writer's youth: the 1830s and 1840s.[9] In this period, Petersburg's Aleksandrinskii Theater featured a harmonious juxtaposition of low and high, heavy and light genres.[10] Often translated or adapted from French and English models, Russian vaudevilles "reflected the age of Balzac and Dickens," centering on the lives of merchants and poor clerks.[11] Vaudeville was a deeply rooted element of the writer's cultural milieu, and it informed his work significantly. Dostoevsky drafted comic plays throughout the 1840s and 1850s; *The Village of Stepanchikovo* was first conceived as a satirical drama.[12] He also wrote about theater: in his 1861 *Notes from the House of the Dead*, Dostoevsky takes an ethnographic interest in the pantomimes performed by incarcerated people. Even when Dostoevsky is writing neither for the theater nor about theater, these influences are discernable. Following scholars who have commented on Dostoevsky's comic modes, I propose that Dostoevsky enjoys not only a melodramatic imagination, but also a slapstick one.

In the Russian context, slapstick performance can be located in traveling *skomorokhi* troupes, *balagan* street puppetry, and staged vaudeville performances. Dostoevsky represents these traditions in his prose works—*Crime and Punishment* features several street performers, including an organ grinder and, briefly and unsuccessfully, the widowed Katerina Ivanovna. In my use of the term "slapstick," I reference a transhistorical phenomenon, one that existed in

---

[7] Irina Erman, "'Husband under the Bed': Specular Enclosures, Cuckoldry, and Logorrhea in Dostoevsky's Early Works," *The Russian Review*, vol. 76, no. 3 (2017): 312.

[8] Deborah A. Martinsen, *Surprised by Shame: Dostoevsky's Liars and Narrative Explorers* (Columbus: The Ohio State University Press, 2003); Rima Iakubova, "Dostoevsky's Novel *Demons* and Russian *Balagan*," in *The New Russian Dostoevsky: Readings for the Twenty-First Century*. Edited by Carol Apollonio (Bloomington, IN: Slavica, 2010), 217–28.

[9] Monika Katz, *F. A. Koni und das russische Vaudeville: Zur Geschichte des Unterhaltungstheaters in St. Petersburg 1830–1855* (Berlin: Frank & Timme, 2017), 47.

[10] Iurii Lotman, "Theater and Theatricality in the Order of Early Nineteenth Century Culture," in *Semiotics and Structuralism: Readings from the Soviet Union*. Edited by Henryk Baran (White Plains, NY: International Arts and Sciences Press, 1976), 44.

[11] Karlinsky, *Russian Drama*, 274.

[12] George Steiner, *Tolstoy or Dostoevsky: An Essay in Contrast* (London: Faber and Faber, 1980), 136–7.

imperial Russia but, in the critical literature, is more often associated with early modern *commedia dell'arte* troupes and Hollywood silent film comedy. Rather than dismissing film scholarship as anachronistic to the study of Dostoevsky, I draw on these rigorous studies of slapstick's formal elements to further develop a cross-temporal, transnational, and intermedial understanding of the slapstick tradition. After all, Charlie Chaplin first developed his film persona on the British vaudeville stage, which, in turn, supplied plots and gags to the Russian vaudeville theater, whose many attendees included Fyodor Dostoevsky.

The term "slapstick" comes from a prop developed by sixteenth-century *commedia dell'arte* troupes and used by performers ever since: two pieces of wood joined at one end that, when hit together, make a loud slapping noise. Like the prop for which it was named, this genre involves the playacting of violence. Numerous humor theorists have taken up the glaring ethical problem of laughing at others' pain; Muriel Andrin fears that "to laugh at such violent acts [...] reveals our repressed desire to humiliate other human beings." In her eloquent article on empathy and slapstick, Andrin concludes that this performed violence is too hyperbolic to be taken seriously, and too fast-paced to be registered with empathy by viewers.[13] In any case, as slapstick theorist Alex Clayton reminds us, "laughter is not an index of comic achievement," and I would add that it is not even a reliable indicator of an event's status as slapstick.[14] Regardless of its felicitous evocation of laughter, slapstick is a genre with distinctive forms. The smallest unit of slapstick is the gag, which could be a fall, blow, overreaction, or misunderstanding. Gags often operate through some sort of exaggeration. Sometimes clowns endure an exaggerated amount of violence and make little response, and, other times, they respond exaggeratedly to a small stimulus. An impressive tool may yield ridiculously small results, while a puny object may wreak havoc.

Slapstick shares these hyperbolic tendencies with melodrama, but the family resemblance essentially ends there. Brooks characterizes melodrama by its "metaphoricity of gesture," its creation of a system in which physical gestures symbolize essential moral truths.[15] Slapstick, by contrast, rejects any sort of system at all. According to Eileen Bowser, "[A]ll things that the

---

[13] Muriel Andrin, "Back to the 'Slap': Slapstick's Hyperbolic Gesture and the Rhetoric of Violence," in *Slapstick Comedy*. Edited by Tom Paulus and Rob King (New York: Routledge, 2010), 227.
[14] Alex Clayton, *The Body in Hollywood Slapstick* (Jefferson, NC: McFarland & Company, 2007), 14.
[15] Brooks, *The Melodramatic Imagination*, 10.

moral melodrama was meant to suppress appeared again in slapstick comedy: anarchy, amorality, eroticism, vulgarity, fantasy, cruelty, the total disrespect for the forces of organized society."[16] In Tom Gunning's terms, the slapstick gag is "an unexpected undermining of an apparent purpose, a detouring, if not derailing, of a rational system of discourse or action. The gag suddenly interrupts, or radically redefines, the apparent predictability of an action or system, leaving its original goals shattered and in tatters."[17] These preliminary distinctions signal the subgenres' contrasting political tendencies—melodrama is preservationist, while slapstick is anarchic. In slapstick, the "system" under attack, from the nineteenth century to the present, is often capitalism. While slapstick performance exists across historical and geographical contexts, the genre has a special place—and a new set of resonances—in the era of industrial capitalism, enacting concerns about "the disintegration of the self" and "the value of individuation in a mechanical society."[18] On a formal level, the slapstick gag is often structured as a unit of labor in which the clown attempts to "do a good job" and fails spectacularly or, alternately, makes comically little attempt to fulfill expectations. Therefore, even when clowns aren't literally "on the job"—like Tramp in Chaplin's *Modern Times* or Lucy and Ethel at the chocolate factory in *I Love Lucy*—slapstick routines can be read as embodied meditations on working-class precarity. Where melodrama enacts crises of individual morality, slapstick enacts large-scale social critiques.

At its heart, slapstick is concerned with the material world. If melodrama directs attention from the body to the soul, slapstick's directionality is opposite, emphasizing the comic distance between abstract intention and physical ridiculousness. The clown's body is not the faithful representative of the mind or soul, but, rather, a "traitorous" entity that defies rational or spiritual intentions.[19] If melodrama affirms the body's moral signifying power, slapstick denies the body's potential to signify anything beyond its own banality, mortality, and weakness.

While Dostoevsky is certainly concerned with morality, he does not develop a consistent metaphoricity of gesture. Instead, using the slapstick mode, the writer

---

[16] Eileen Bowser, "Subverting the Conventions: Slapstick as Genre," in *The Slapstick Symposium*. Edited by Eileen Bowser (Brussels: FIAF, 1988), 14.

[17] Tom Gunning, "Mechanisms of Laughter: The Devices of Slapstick," in *Slapstick Comedy*. Edited by Tom Paulus and Rob King (New York: Routledge, 2010), 139.

[18] Andrin, "Back to the 'Slap,'" 230.

[19] Alan Dale, *Comedy Is a Man in Trouble: Slapstick in American Movies* (Minneapolis: University of Minnesota Press, 2000), 14.

indicates the illegibility and even semiotic instability of gesture in the human world. When Sonia asks Raskolnikov to kiss the earth and beg forgiveness, she is requesting a melodramatic gesture. However, when Raskolnikov kneels and kisses the earth passers-by jeer at him and call him a drunkard. The hero rises before he can admit to his crime. This scene of *bathos*—one of many in Dostoevsky—exemplifies the illegibility of gesture in the slapstick mode. And yet, for all of slapstick's semiotic anarchism, its cheeky refusal to signify, this type of gesture is not carnivalesque in the Bakhtinian sense. For Golyadkin and Raskolnikov, slapstick physicality is not playful or regenerative, but painful, involuntary, and even objectifying.

A Rag with Feelings: Protagonist as Prop

Buster Keaton was an American film comedian renowned for his deadpan facial expression and incredible physical stunts. From the age of five, Keaton performed in a family vaudeville act, where he was introduced as "The Little Boy Who Can't Be Damaged," and his father made a show of throwing him around.[20] In one bit, "The Human Mop," Keaton's father literally wiped the floor with him. Keaton describes his childhood slapstick role as that of a prop, a "human mop, dishrag, beanbag, or football," on which violence is performed.[21] Although Keaton apparently enjoyed these performances, he quickly learned that the audience laughed only if he appeared "miserable, humiliated, hounded, and haunted, bedeviled, bewildered, and at [his] wit's end."[22] And so his distinctive expression was born.

The protagonist of Dostoevsky's *The Double* also resembles an object. The Petersburg winds push Golyadkin around like a weathervane.[23] When he falls off a droshky and rolls away, the narrator compares him to a sack of flour.[24] Unlike

---

[20] Marion Meade, *Buster Keaton: Cut to the Chase* (New York: Harper Collins Publishers, 1995), 19.

[21] Buster Keaton, *My Wonderful World of Slapstick* (Garden City, NY: Doubleday & Company, 1960), 13.

[22] Ibid.

[23] Fyodor Dostoevsky, "The Double," in *Polnoe sobranie sochinenii v tridtsati tomakh* (Leningrad: Nauka, 1972), 1: 140. Unless otherwise noted, translations of Dostoevsky are from the following editions: Fyodor Dostoevsky, *Notes from the Underground and The Double*. Translated by Ronald Wilks (New York: Penguin, 2009); Fyodor Dostoevsky, *Crime and Punishment*. Translated by Michael Katz (New York: W.W. Norton & Company, 2019). All other translations are my own.

[24] *PSS*, 1: 206.

Keaton, however, Golyadkin is truly miserable in his objectification. Having been publicly humiliated by his double, Golyadkin insists: "But no, I won't let myself be used as a rag [...] I'm not a rag, my dear sir, oh no, I'm not a rag!"[25] Yet, the narrator admits that a person might turn Golyadkin into a rag—that is, subjugate him—

> without meeting any opposition and with impunity [...] and then the result would have been a rag [ветошка] and not a Golyadkin—yes, a rag, a disgusting filthy rag—but not an ordinary rag, though: this rag would have had ambition [амбиция], this rag would have been endowed with animation and feelings, and even though those feelings would have been mute and hidden deep within the filthy folds of that rag, they would nonetheless have been feelings ...[26]

In personifying this hypothetical rag, Golyadkin protests the denial of his subjectivity, his treatment "as something whose experience and feelings ... need not be taken into account," a form of "objectification" as theorized by philosopher Martha Nussbaum.[27] If Golyadkin must be a rag, then at least he is a rag with feelings—precisely the aesthetic of Keaton's slapstick comedy.

The agent of Golyadkin's objectification is indistinct. Vinogradov argues that "[Golyadkin's] movements are mechanized, and he himself has turned into a puppet figure, repeating a certain cycle of movements at the will of the author."[28] Conversely, Mikhail Bakhtin contends that Dostoevsky creates characters who are autonomous and fully equal to their author.[29] I would submit that Dostoevsky is less an author-puppeteer and more of a circus ringleader, with characters acting less like puppets and more like clowns. The clown is a subject who often experiences objectification wrought by the surrounding world. As Keaton's childhood career suggests, slapstick violence is typically enacted by two figures: the active aggressor and objectified victim (father and son). However, slapstick frequently consolidates these identities, so that the clown is both the violent subject and the violated object. The clown who bumps into a wall, slips on a banana peel, or falls down a flight of stairs is the agent of his own harm. In these moments, the slapstick comedian emblematizes the fallacy of human agency and self-control. The essential grammatical mode of self-harming slapstick, then, is

---

[25] *PSS*, 1: 168.

[26] *PSS*, 1: 168–9.

[27] Martha Nussbaum, "Objectification," *Philosophy and Public Affairs*, vol. 24, no. 4 (1995): 257.

[28] V. V. Vinogradov, "Stil' peterburgskoi poemy 'Dvoinik'," in *Stat'i i materialy*. Edited by A. S. Dolinin (Peterburg: Mysl', 1922), 220.

[29] Mikhail Bakhtin, *Problems of Dostoevsky's Poetics*. Translated by Caryl Emerson (Minneapolis, MN: University of Minnesota Press, 1999), 7.

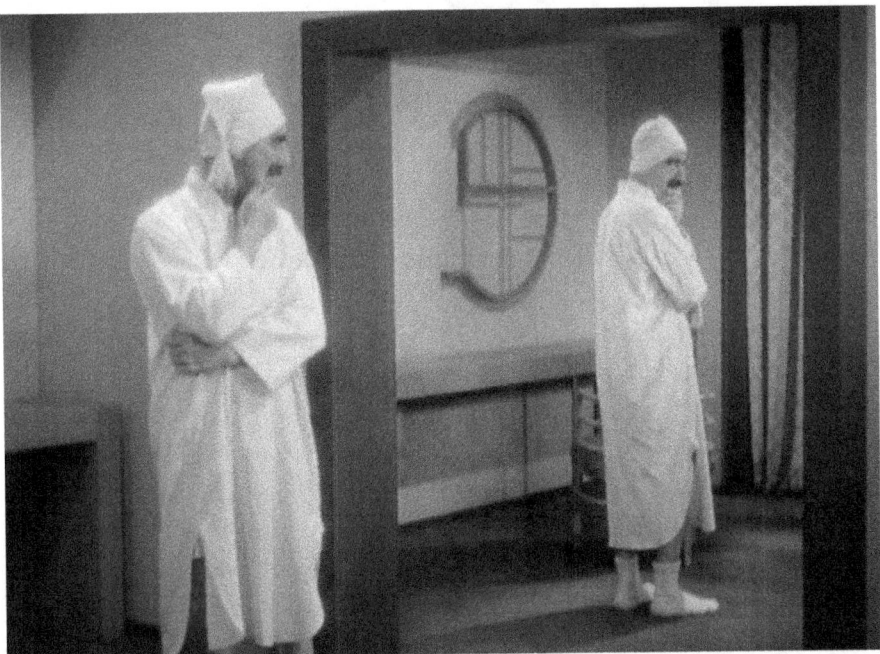

Figure 3.1 Groucho Marx sees his double in the "mirror" in the 1933 film *Duck Soup* (45:00)

the reflexive verb, a common construction in Dostoevsky.[30] In one representative sentence from *The Double*, Golyadkin "tore himself [*сорвался*] from where he was standing and charged [*бросился*] straight into the Director's office."[31] Grammatically, Golyadkin is both the subject and object of this violent movement.

While presenting Golyadkin as a self-harming clown in his own right, Dostoevsky also materializes the slapstick clown's "split" personality through the figure of the doppelgänger. Golyadkin Junior is a literal manifestation of Golyadkin Senior's fractured selfhood. The "double" is not just an uncanny trope, but also comic one; in fact, Dostoevsky originally conceived this novella as a picaresque with a "semicomic atmosphere."[32] Perhaps the most well-known doubling gag in Hollywood film is the mirror scene in the 1933 Marx Brothers film, *Duck Soup*, in which Groucho attempts to determine whether Harpo is his reflection or another being (Figure 3.1). As he "loses control" of his own

---

[30] Vinogradov notes the prevalence of these and other reflexive verbs, which indicate both the hero's movement and his emotional state (Vinogradov, "Stil' peterburgskoi poemy 'Dvoinik,'" 219). These verbs, which appear with similar frequency in Gogol's *Petersburg Tales*, indicate the ignobility and comic status of the characters whose movements they describe; for both Dostoevsky and his predecessor, they are associated with the ridiculous urban hero.

[31] *PSS*, 1: 165.

[32] Joseph Frank, *Lectures on Dostoevsky* (Princeton, NJ: Princeton University Press, 2019), 30.

"reflection," Groucho begins to question his own subjecthood. Crucial to the scene's comedy is the actors' family resemblance: they function as believable doubles. Just as Groucho is perturbed by Harpo, Golyadkin experiences his double as a threat to his subject status, complaining when his superiors view him as interchangeable with his double. Nussbaum confirms the objectifying power of the double, arguing that fungibility is another form of objectification.[33] The subjecthood of Golyadkin Junior negates that of Golyadkin Senior, leaving him feeling like a rag.

Yet, the appearance of Golyadkin Junior does not produce the Golyadkin Senior's clownish embodiment; it only exacerbates it. On several occasions, Dostoevsky directly states that a force is controlling Golyadkin. Sometimes this force is mechanical: "Mr. Golyadkin whizzed [*подался*] forward as if someone had touched off a spring [*пружина*] inside him."[34] In fact, Dostoevsky uses the adverb "mechanically" (*машинально*) six times in the novella to describe Golyadkin's movements. In other moments, the force is more nebulous: "He felt [...] that he was being borne along by some completely strange, alien force, that he himself wasn't walking at all—on the contrary: his legs were giving way and refused to obey him."[35] Unlike Dostoevsky's later heroes, who are commonly said to be physically taken over by ideas, the unintellectual Golyadkin is moved by some other power.[36] Dostoevsky's insistence on the mechanical quality of this movement—a detail that recurs in *Crime and Punishment*—points to the significance of modernity in these characters' embodiment. The socioeconomic pressures of Nikolaevan bureaucracy, and, in *Crime and Punishment*, nascent capitalism and its attendant ideologies, alter the physicality of Dostoevsky's characters, prompting their machine-like movements.

Working Hard and Hardly Working: Slapstick and Labor

In the early modern *commedia dell'arte* tradition, the socially "lowest" character type was the *zanni*, an uneducated migrant worker hired by prosperous

---

[33] Nussbaum, "Objectification," 257.
[34] Dostoevsky, "The Double," *PSS*, 1: 132–3.
[35] *PSS*, 1: 200.
[36] D. S. Mirsky, *A History of Russian Literature* (New York: Alfred A. Knopf, 1966), 271; William Mills Todd III, "The Ruse of the Russian Novel," in *The Novel. Volume I: History, Geography, and Culture.* Edited by Franco Moretti (Princeton: Princeton University Press, 2006), 422.

Figure 3.2 Tramp gets stuck in the factory gears in *Modern Times* (15:07)

characters to perform odd jobs. Many of his gags consisted in performing these tasks zealously but unsuccessfully. At its height between the sixteenth and eighteenth centuries, *commedia dell'arte* coincided with the rise of capitalism in Europe. The *zanni*, historically defined, was an agricultural worker pushed out by land enclosure movements in search of wage labor. The *zanni* thus inaugurated the clown's enduring status as a representative of the worker's precarity under capitalism. The classic example is Tramp in Charlie Chaplin's *Modern Times* (1936), who proves unable to conform to the demands of factory work, even as the factory machines deform him (Figure 3.2).

In Sianne Ngai's analysis, which ranges from *commedia dell'arte* to contemporary performance, the aesthetic of zaniness (from the word *zanni*) reflects "a precariousness created specifically by the capitalist organization of work."[37] The zany worker is desperate, stressed, and visibly strained.[38] Within the fictive narrative, they are observed and chastised by some sort of "boss," a figure

---

[37] Sianne Ngai, *Our Aesthetic Categories: Zany, Cute, Interesting* (Cambridge, MA: Harvard University Press, 2012), 188.
[38] Ibid., 185.

who expects productivity.[39] While the clown is innocently trying to do a good job, the slapstick viewer may feel anxiety on their behalf or, alternatively, pleasure at their anarchic refusal of efficiency. Though slapstick often involves violence against the clown, as a genre it is a slap in the face of "bourgeois legibility and rationality."[40]

While the socioeconomic dimension of Dostoevsky's characterizations has largely been dismissed—George Steiner comments that these characters "always have leisure for chaos" and are "available day and night"—Vadim Shneyder has recently brought this issue to light, noting that most characters in *Crime and Punishment* "spend their time performing odd jobs in the gig economy of postreform Russia."[41] Ngai's formulation of zaniness, as I hope to demonstrate, clarifies the physical dimension of Dostoevsky's socioeconomic characterization. The heroes' slapstick gesture is motored by their socioeconomic precarity, or, in the case of Golyadkin, by "ambition," what in this period was, according to Dostoevsky scholar V.S. Nechaeva, "emotional turmoil resulting from the discrepancy between the assessment of a person's genuine merits and accomplishments related to his moral, social, official or age status, and their denial or belittling."[42] As Nechaeva demonstrates, ambition was promoted by a bureaucratic system that fed antagonism between workers and, ultimately, in Golyadkin, "generat[es] a feeling of uncertainty about the future, fear and distrust of his entire surroundings leading to a recognition of his loneliness."[43] What "zany" is to capitalism, "ambition" is to the Nikolaevan bureaucracy: both terms suggest the worker's overactive response to conflict with management, a constant state of "losing" despite always trying to "play by the rules of the game." Like zaniness, ambition boasts great comic potential.

Already in Gogol's *Petersburg Tales*, the workplace is presented as a comic setting. Shneyder identifies Gogol's bureaucratic office as the literary antecedent to the factory, a space with movement so dizzying as to defy the worker's comprehension.[44] Like Gogol's characters, Dostoevsky's Golyadkin

---

[39] Ibid., 11.

[40] Donald Crafton, "Pie and Chase: Gag, Spectacle and Narrative in Slapstick Comedy," in *Classical Hollywood Comedy*. Edited by Kristine Brunovska Karnick and Henry Jenkins (New York: Routledge, 1995), 116.

[41] Steiner, *Tolstoy or Dostoevsky*, 154; Vadim Shneyder, *Russia's Capitalist Realism: Tolstoy, Dostoevsky, and Chekhov* (Evanston, IL: Northwestern University Press, 2019), 2.

[42] V. S. Nechaeva, *Rannii Dostoevskii, 1821–1849* (Moskva: Nauka, 1979), 155.

[43] Ibid.

[44] Shneyder, *Russia's Capitalist Realism*, 43.

struggles in the claustrophobia-inducing hierarchy of the Table of Ranks. In this system, characters of lower status experience greater professional pressure, which prompts their ambition and resulting physical zaniness, which ironically undermines their quest for respect and social acceptance. This impossible system transforms these characters into zany clowns, whose "incessant activity" in fact stems from their impotence.[45] When Dostoevsky refers to a "spring" (*пружина*) motivating Golyadkin's movement, we might understand the "spring" as a metaphor for ambition, an emotion that drives the hero forward at breakneck speed, both through the plot and through space.

Many slapstick gags rely on speed, from chase scenes in traditional pantomime to those achieved in early cinema with special effects.[46] Accordingly, as Vinogradov notes, Golyadkin "almost does not walk, but instead 'flies,' 'jumps,' 'leaps,' and so forth."[47] In what is both a personal and professional frenzy—an attempt to enter the good graces of his boss, then later to escape or catch his double—Golyadkin rushes around Petersburg, climbing onto a moving carriage, pacing rapidly and abruptly changing direction, and losing his galosh while walking.[48] In his first appearance at his boss's house, Golyadkin leaves no guest unscathed:

> [...] propelled by that same spring [*пружина*] that had sent him whizzing uninvited into someone else's ball, he pressed on further and further. On his way he stumbled [*наткнулся*] into some counsellor, treading on his foot, at the same time he stepped on the dress of a respectable old lady and tore it slightly, bumped into a man with a tray, elbowed someone else and [...] forged [*пробираясь*] ahead, until suddenly he found himself [*очутился*] right in front of Klara Olsufyevna herself.[49]

While Golyadkin's various faux pas at this party appear only as social mistakes, in the world of nineteenth-century Russian bureaucracy, a private party is professional, and a faux pas is a type of zaniness.

Like most fantastical apparitions, Golyadkin's double does not experience socioeconomic stress; for this reason, while the double looks like Golyadkin, he

---

[45] Ngai, *Our Aesthetic Categories*, 187.
[46] Bowser, "Subverting the Conventions," 13.
[47] Vinogradov, "Stil' peterburgskoi poemy 'Dvoinik,'" 221.
[48] Dostoevsky, "The Double," *PSS*, 1: 205; 1: 128; 1: 139.
[49] *PSS*, 1: 133.

does not move like him. Golyadkin Junior is also speedy but, unlike Golyadkin Senior, he is nimble. And, just as Golyadkin's erratic movements mirror his incoherent speech, the agile double is also a smooth talker. Unlike Golyadkin, whose muteness and inarticulateness only contribute to his incompetence as a worker, this socially successful character is fluent in bureaucratese. The double doesn't experience ambition because his superiors, in fact, overvalue and overreward his contributions. The following description of the double's graceful movements reprises the earlier passage in which Golyadkin Senior stumbles over everyone he encounters:

> He grinned, gambolled, pranced and twisted around [осклабившись, вертясь, семеня] with a smile that seemed to say "Good evening" to everyone. He wormed [втерся] his way into the small crowd of clerks, shaking hands with one, patting another on the shoulder, hugging another, explaining to a fourth exactly the kind of mission His Excellency had employed him for, where he had gone, what he had done, what he had brought back with him. To a fifth—probably his best friend—he gave a smacking kiss, right on the lips.[50]

Golyadkin Junior's physical agility and verbal fluency—a parody of social nimbleness that is comic in its own way—mark him as successful. Conversely, the protagonist's verbal incompetence both indicates and exacerbates his socioeconomic precarity.

Twenty years later, in *Crime and Punishment*, precarity has come to bear ever more relentlessly on Dostoevsky's newest protagonist: Raskolnikov. At first glance, this hero is much more serious than Golyadkin—much more intellectual, at the very least. But the two heroes' embodiments are strikingly similar. Using the same phrase as in *The Double*, Dostoevsky narrates how, in a moment of frenzy, Raskolnikov "ripped himself [сорвался] from where he was standing and ran off."[51] Like Golyadkin, Raskolnikov seems to be moved by a mysterious force. After the murder, he suddenly finds himself at his friend Razumikhin's apartment, though he did not intend to go there. When Razumikhin offers Raskolnikov a freelance translation job, the protagonist enters another physical frenzy:

> Without saying a word, Raskolnikov took the pages of the German article, picked up the three rubles, and walked out in silence. Razumikhin followed him with his eyes in bewilderment. But, after having reached the First Line, Raskolnikov

[50] *PSS*, 1: 194–5.
[51] Dostoevsky, *Crime and Punishment*, *PSS*, 6: 341.

suddenly turned around, climbed the stairs back up to Razumikhin's, and, placing both the German pages and the three rubles down on the table, left again, without saying a word.[52]

In addition to illustrating Raskolnikov's physical erraticism, this passage points to Raskolnikov's particular form of socioeconomic precarity. Though he does not have a steady job (or, perhaps, because of this), Raskolnikov often moves like a *zanni*. Unlike Oblomov, who can permanently retire to his couch, Raskolnikov experiences the economic pressure that motivates zaniness.[53] In fact, when Raskolnikov visits the police station for the first time, he introduces himself as a "poor, sick student, oppressed [...] by poverty."[54]

Raskolnikov cannot be said to have Golyadkin's brand of ambition (*ambitsiia*); Dostoevsky never uses the term in relation to this hero. While Golyadkin doggedly tries to succeed within his workplace, Raskolnikov attempts in vain to escape the system altogether. Unemployed and no longer enrolled in university, Raskolnikov resembles Chaplin's Tramp, out of step with the speed of urban life, "stroll[ing] at a pace that only a millionaire or a tramp could afford."[55] After a glass of vodka and a pie, he sleeps in the bushes on Vasilievskii Island; a funny episode, insofar as outdoor napping is not an accepted public behavior. Later, when Raskolnikov wanders into the street, a cabman whips him, passers-by laugh at him, and an old woman offers him money.[56] Raskolnikov's appearance also marks him as a down-and-out character: "Judging by his clothes and appearance, they could easily have mistaken him for a beggar, someone out asking for half-kopeck pieces in the streets."[57] Even in the novel's opening passage he worries over his "funny-looking" (*смешная*) hat: "With my tattered clothes I really need a peaked cap, even an old one, flat as a pancake, not this monstrosity [*урод*]."[58] Urban socioeconomic precarity has turned Raskolnikov into a clown: one who performs private behaviors in public, wears ridiculous clothing, and moves either in circles or in sudden jolts. The hero's own

---

[52] *PSS*, 6: 89.

[53] Anne Lounsbery takes up this issue in her study of Goncharov's *Oblomov*, in which she contrasts the physicalities of the prone protagonist and the vertical, industrious Stolz: Anne Lounsbery, "The World on the Back of a Fish: Mobility, Immobility, and Economics in *Oblomov*," *Russian Review*, vol. 70, no. 1 (2011): 43–64.

[54] *PSS*, 6: 80.

[55] Clayton, *The Body in Hollywood Slapstick*, 67.

[56] *PSS*, 6: 89.

[57] Ibid.

[58] *PSS*, 6: 7.

frustration with his economic position is, of course, a self-professed motive for the murder. Rather than submitting to the demands of the economic system—as Golyadkin does, until his psychotic break—Raskolnikov attempts to "game the system." Simultaneously, he strives to assert his subject status, one that has been thoroughly undermined by the reifying powers of capital. In Raskolnikov's mind, murder and theft are acts of economic critique and self-realization, logical alternatives to years of ill-rewarded wage labor; a "leap" rather than a long-term progression toward economic stability.[59] Of course, this "leap" is completely individualistic; Raskolnikov is ensconced in the zero-sum vision of capitalist success. Considering the position of socialists, he says to himself: "No, life's been given to me once and it'll never come again; I don't want to wait for the 'common good.' I want to live myself, or else it's better not to live at all."[60] This perspective may be expected from a clown; Tramp, too, aspires only to provide his girlfriend, Ellen, with a home. When he is mistaken for a revolutionary leading a march, we are meant to laugh. The clown's critique of capitalism occurs, however paradoxically, at the individual level.

Bakhtin writes that "the major emotional thrust of all Dostoevsky's work [...] is the struggle against a *reification* of man, of human relations, of all human values under the condition of capitalism."[61] If we accept this observation—not claiming Dostoevsky's intentionality, but observing his sensitivity to a changing society, as Shneyder convincingly argues—then this anti-capitalist project is successful in large part thanks to Dostoevsky's use of the slapstick mode, a genre with an inborn critique of capitalism. Slapstick comedy often lampoons socioeconomic injustice, whether extradiagetically, as the viewer recognizes the absurdity of capitalist labor, or diagetically, as the clown attempts to cheat the system. The murder plot in *Crime and Punishment* is a grotesque exaggeration of this clownish tradition. In fact, the gestures with which Raskolnikov implements his plan are incredibly zany: he fumbles with the axe, runs around the pawnbroker's apartment, and gets blood everywhere. Insofar as Raskolnikov's economic positioning has produced in him a zany, slapstick physicality, it is possible that, even if Raskolnikov didn't really do it for the money, "money" made him do it. And what is intended as an efficient shortcut toward socioeconomic prosperity,

---

[59] Ilya Kliger, *The Narrative Shape of Truth: Veridiction in Modern European Literature* (University Park, PA: Pennsylvania State University Press, 2011), 125.
[60] *PSS*, 6: 211.
[61] Bakhtin, *Problems of Dostoevsky's Poetics*, 62.

and a symbolic critique of capitalism, ultimately proves to be a tumultuous detour on the hero's path to salvation.

By Hook or By Crook: Slapstick Detouring in the Murder Scene

On his way to Alyona Ivanovna's apartment, Raskolnikov "needed to hurry and, at the same time, to make a detour [*сделать крюк*]: he wanted to approach the building in a roundabout way [*в обход*], from the other side."[62] An aerial map of Raskolnikov's path during the murder would resemble a map of his Petersburg wanderings: circles and zig-zagging lines that suggest inefficient, excessive movement. Throughout the murder scene, Raskolnikov is incapable of moving directly from point A to point B, both in the literal and figurative senses. The word "*крюк*," here meaning "detour," signifies in another way: its suggestion of ineptitude will prove prophetic when Raskolnikov fumbles the murder as though he has "hooks for hands" (*руки-крюки*).

If a gag is a "detouring, if not derailing, of a rational system of discourse or action," then the murder scene certainly qualifies as an extended gag, in which the desired "action"—murdering Alyona Ivanovna, stealing the pledges, and leaving no trace—is completed inefficiently and incorrectly. Whether or not the scene elicits bemusement from its reader, it bears a strange formal tension, in which "tragic" action—murder—is performed with comic gesture. Like a zany clown, Raskolnikov lacks the physical and mental acuity to carry out "orders." In his case, the orders come from within, making the murder scene a moment of ridiculous self-sabotage. Raskolnikov is the quintessential slapstick clown: the objectified subject who, as we will see, has very little control over his body.

The murder scene itself is framed by a set of large-scale gags. While the zany worker sometimes misunderstands a directive and performs a task incorrectly, in other cases he understands a directive and carries it out *too* well, over-adapting to the norm. Raskolnikov kills two people instead of the one he intended. Moreover, in killing a pawnbroker at all, Raskolnikov is over-performing the role of the radical student. He takes theory too literally, unlike most students, who—like the young man whom Raskolnikov overhears at the tavern—are content to

---

[62] *PSS*, 6: 60.

talk about murder without committing it.⁶³ Another large-scale gag is the comic gap between Raskolnikov's conception of the murder and its implementation. With all his talk, Raskolnikov has primed the reader for a monumental event performed by a great man; instead, the reader witnesses grotesque and brutal buffoonery. After the murder, in burying the pledges instead of raising the money he needs, Raskolnikov underperforms his set task and fails to enact the crime's potential utilitarian payoff.

The murder scene is composed of a series of smaller gags, or detours. In the slapstick tradition of using exaggerated versions of everyday tools, Raskolnikov chooses an axe as his murder weapon. Apparently, "he couldn't rely on a knife or, particularly, on his own strength; therefore he had settled definitively on an axe."⁶⁴ The axe is a less efficient choice, a detour that will require additional preparations. Clowns prepare gags in a similar way, choosing props that, as Paul Bouissac writes, "can be made to behave in an odd or uncooperative manner" and thereby "reflect the odd, anarchical nature of [the clown's] mind."⁶⁵ Crucially, the axe undermines Raskolnikov's already fraught subject status. Though the murder is his attempt to assert his subjecthood and autonomy, the hero consciously chooses an object more powerful than he is, an instrument that will instrumentalize him.

Raskolnikov's other preparations function similarly, as both gags of unnecessary action and jabs at his subject-status. He sews a special loop inside his coat to hold the axe, thus adding an unnecessary step that might have been avoided if he had chosen a more practical weapon. Strangely, Raskolnikov seems to enjoy the preparation process. In his attempts to be crafty, he has become quite *crafty*, not only altering his coat but also fashioning a fake pledge out of found materials: a wooden block, metal strip, string, paper, and ribbon.⁶⁶ In preparing for an act that will ostensibly fortify his tenuous subject-status—along with his masculinity—Raskolnikov becomes a feminized craft hobbyist. Dostoevsky constructs a canonical sexist gag, in which the male-identifying clown takes on feminine occupations and performs them so well that he undermines his own masculinity. More specifically, Dostoevsky is disrupting the expected hypermasculinity of the criminal, a gag he frequently

---

⁶³ *PSS*, 6: 55.
⁶⁴ *PSS*, 6: 57.
⁶⁵ Paul Bouissac, *The Semiotics of Clowns and Clowning* (London: Bloomsbury, 2015), 61–2.
⁶⁶ *PSS*, 6: 57.

Figure 3.3 Tramp's cellmate, the hardened criminal, doing embroidery in *Modern Times* (23:56)

employs in *Notes from the House of the Dead* and one that Chaplin includes in *Modern Times*, when Tramp's burly jail cellmate takes out his embroidery hoop (Figure 3.3).

Raskolnikov's physicality, too, is a constant source of slapstick comedy in this scene. As he walks to Alyona Ivanovna's apartment, the hero exhibits an intensely zany, mechanical embodiment, later canonized by Chaplin's Tramp stuck in the gears in *Modern Times* (Figure 3.2):

> This last day, which had dawned so unexpectedly and resolved everything all at once, acted on him almost completely mechanically [*подействовал на него почти совсем механически*]: it was as if someone took him by the hand and pulled him along behind, irresistibly, blindly, with unnatural strength, without resistance. It was exactly as if a corner of his clothes had become enmeshed in the cogwheel of a machine and it had begun to pull him in.[67]

---

[67] *PSS*, 6: 58.

Here, Raskolnikov appears not as a self-powered motor, but rather as a "cogwheel of a machine." In contrast to Golyadkin, who is internally powered by the spring of ambition, Raskolnikov seems to be momentarily moved by the workings of a larger machine. Conscious of his loss of self-control, he considers how "the criminal himself, almost every one of them, at the very moment of the crime, is subject to some failure of willpower and reason, which are replaced, instead, by phenomenal childish thoughtlessness, precisely at the moment when reason and caution are most needed."[68] However, continues the narrator, "after arriving at these conclusions, he decided that in his own case, in this affair, there could be no such morbid reversals, that he would retain his reason and his willpower, essentially, all during the implementation of his plan."[69] Raskolnikov is conscious enough to consider the threat of irrationality but lacks the self-awareness to implicate himself. In the moments before the murder, he attempts to control his erratic physicality, walking "quietly and *steadily*, without hurrying, so as not to arouse any suspicions" and ringing the pawnbroker's doorbell "softly, firmly, without any impatience."[70] He is attempting to mediate the genre of his crime, aiming for deliberate, tragic heroism rather than chaotic, slapstick clownishness.

Once in the building, however, Raskolnikov is almost completely overcome by zaniness as he attempts to "finish the job." Struggling against the suspicious Alyona Ivanovna in the doorway, he grabs the door handle with such force that he "almost yanked her out onto the landing along with the door."[71] Inside the apartment, Raskolnikov attempts to speak "as casually as possible" but instead stutters, much like the inarticulate Golyadkin.[72] In this moment, Raskolnikov's words are not his own: "He hadn't planned to say this, but it was uttered just so, all by itself [*само вдруг выговорилось*]."[73] As the hero prepares to strike the unwitting Alyona, he loses even more bodily control: "His hands were terribly weak; he felt how with each moment they grew number and more wooden [*немели и деревенели*]."[74] In Russian, the verb "to go numb" is the same as "to go mute." The verb signifies doubly in this scene, emphasizing Raskolnikov's earlier muteness and increasing woodenness—in short, his puppetness.

---

[68] Ibid.
[69] *PSS*, 6: 59.
[70] *PSS*, 6: 60–1, emphasis in original.
[71] *PSS*, 6: 62.
[72] Ibid.
[73] Ibid.
[74] *PSS*, 6: 63.

During the first axe swing, Raskolnikov is completely disengaged from his body: "hardly aware of himself [*едва себя чувствуя*], and almost with no effort, almost mechanically [*машинально*], [he] brought the butt end down onto her head. It was as if he had no strength. But as soon as he lowered the axe [*опустил*] once, he felt a new strength in himself [*родилась в нем сила*]."[75] Raskolnikov feels empowered only when he lowers the axe (*опустил*), when the axe, driven by momentum, begins to function independently of him. Then, as if a spring had been released in him, Raskolnikov cannot stop attacking. He strikes Alyona Ivanovna twice more, expending extra energy when, for all he knows, the first strike was sufficient to kill the woman. The great irony of this scene is that Raskolnikov conceives of the murder as an escape route from the capitalist labor system, yet the murder itself is an enormously laborious task. The hero wants to free himself from capitalist objectification and mechanical embodiment, but, of all the novel's scenes, he is most zany and object-like during this one.

A short detour of my own: later in the novel, Raskolnikov dreams that he is chasing a stranger back to the old pawnbroker's apartment, where he sees her, bent over (*скрючившись*). He hits her with the axe, "But it was strange: she didn't even stir under the blows, as if she were made of wood [*деревянная*]."[76] The dream scenario reverses the puppet identities within the real murder scene: in reality, Raskolnikov resembled a puppet, his hands growing wooden [*деревенели*], but in the dream this role is played by the old woman, bent over like an off-duty marionette. However, she is no ordinary puppet. Raskolnikov bends down lower and lower, trying to glimpse her face, and finally sees that she's laughing. Only then he realizes that a surrounding crowd is laughing and whispering:

> Rage overcame him: he began striking the old woman on the head with all his strength, but with each blow of the axe the laughter and whispering from the bedroom sounded stronger and louder, and the old woman shook with mirth. He tried to flee, but the entire entryway was filled with people, the door to the staircase was open, and on the landing, the staircase, and below—stood a crowd of people, side by side, everyone looking, but everyone quiet, all waiting, all silent.[77]

---

[75] Ibid.
[76] *PSS*, 6: 213.
[77] Ibid.

Raskolnikov's dream recalls *balagan* puppet theater, as the hero comes to resemble a puppet master humiliated before a crowd by his suddenly animated puppet, no longer under his control. Indeed, Bakhtin compares Raskolnikov in this scene to a decrowned carnival king-pretender.[78] Raskolnikov's dream only recapitulates the performance motifs presented earlier in the murder scene; the puppet and puppetmaster serve as metaphors for agency and control.

Back to the murder scene itself: having killed Alyona Ivanovna, Raskolnikov only becomes more inept as he begins searching for the hidden pledges. He takes the pawnbroker's keys, runs to her bedroom, and then stops: "another distressing idea suddenly hit him on the head [*ударила ему в голову*]. All of a sudden it seemed to him that the old woman might still be alive and might revive."[79] This idea "hits" (*ударила*) Raskolnikov in the head; here Dostoevsky portrays Raskolnikov as a victim, hit by an idea, just as a clown is bonked on the head by a large rubber mallet—or, indeed, just as Alyona Ivanovna was struck by the hero moments before. Raskolnikov tosses the keys aside and rushes back to the main room, abandoning his search for the pledges, in order to verify that the pawnbroker is dead. He grabs hold of the axe again and raises it above the woman. In this ridiculous position, he realizes that she is dead. The gag resides in Raskolnikov's cognitive inability to recognize death and, again, his overwork in raising the axe for a fourth time. Immediately after this, Raskolnikov notices a cord on the body and struggles to pull it off. This struggle continues for a while; he is too weak to overpower even an inanimate cord. Exasperated, Raskolnikov considers taking the axe to the cord: another nod to the axe's ridiculous oversizedness, and the hero's inability to select the correct tool for a given task.

Back in Alyona Ivanovna's bedroom, Raskolnikov struggles to find the correct key. He is completely illogical: "he would see, for example, that a key wasn't the right one, it didn't work, but he kept on trying it."[80] When he finally has a new idea, he crawls under the bed—a location, as Erman has demonstrated, heavily associated with crisis in comic cuckold plays and Dostoevsky's works alike.[81] Raskolnikov is aware of this comic trope; later, remembering the murder, he recognizes the "low," "horizontal" nature of his crime by recalling this physical

---

[78] Bakhtin, *Problems of Dostoevsky's Poetics*, 168.
[79] Dostoevsky, *Crime and Punishment*, *PSS*, 6: 63.
[80] *PSS*, 6: 64.
[81] Erman, "'Husband under the Bed,'" 312.

position: "Would a Napoleon stoop to crawl under an 'old woman's' bed? Hey, what nonsense!"[82] As if all this weren't ridiculous enough, Raskolnikov also fails to leave no trace, as he wipes his bloody hands all over the pawnbroker's red brocade. "Red blood will be less noticeable on red silk," he reasons.[83]

To read the murder as slapstick is perhaps uncomfortable; however, it's important to recognize when the slapstick mode begins in order to identify when it ends. As soon as Lizaveta Ivanovna enters the apartment, the genre shifts from slapstick to melodrama. In slapstick, quick pacing "leaves no room for emotion or empathetic response" for victims of violence.[84] In contrast, during this second encounter, Dostoevsky slows the narrative pace and describes Lizaveta's face in great detail. The author also alters Raskolnikov's gesture, from a clown to an expert killer. When Raskolnikov finally strikes her, "The blow struck her right on the skull, with the blade of the axe [...] She collapsed onto the floor at once."[85] No longer fumbling, Raskolnikov murders Lizaveta in one strike.

The generic mode of the first murder elicits the reader's empathy for Raskolnikov. Laughter at clowns sometimes results not from sadistic amusement at their failings, but rather from identification and empathetic concern. Slapstick spectators are anxious to see the clown succeed, experiencing pity or frustration when he fails—laughter, in this case, is the release of anxious tension. In writing the murder scene largely in a slapstick mode, Dostoevsky primes his reader to relate to Raskolnikov as one would relate to a clown: with empathetic and perhaps condescending pity. What is perhaps most twisted is that, in eliciting this identification, Dostoevsky manipulates the reader into wanting Raskolnikov to succeed in murder.

When Raskolnikov kills Lizaveta Ivanovna, however, he transforms from a slapstick clown into a melodramatic villain. These two Raskolnikovs—the clown and the villain—are but another manifestation of the hero's essential "split" personality. Yet, Dostoevsky tempers this melodramatic characterization by indicating Raskolnikov's helplessness; something of the objectified clown remains. Because the subject of the sentence in which Lizaveta is killed is "the blow" (*удар*), Raskolnikov paradoxically—grammatically—never strikes. This is the melodramatic "metaphoricity of gesture" taken to an extreme: gesture,

---

[82] *PSS*, 6: 211.
[83] *PSS*, 6: 64.
[84] Andrin, "Back to the 'Slap,'" 229.
[85] *PSS*, 6: 65.

Figure 3.4 Ellen and Tramp walking toward the horizon at the end of *Modern Times* (1:26:24)

rather than the human agent, commits a moral offense. In this pivotal scene, Dostoevsky juxtaposes and then intermingles the aesthetics of slapstick and melodrama, evoking both the pitiful humanity of Raskolnikov and the horror of the murders. The delicate aesthetic balance in the murder scene legitimizes the novel's conclusion: Raskolnikov's spiritual salvation.

Escape from the Machine

When Sonia learns of Raskolnikov's crime, she reacts with an almost maternal pity: "What have you done, what have you done to yourself?"[86] Raskolnikov's detour into criminality is often framed as naïve self-sabotage, an instance of "crooked," childlike logic gone wrong. The criminal, like the clown, is pitifully incapable of following the rules. By laughing at them, in Henri Bergson's view,

---

[86] *PSS*, 6: 316.

we "correct" for their socially flawed attitudes.[87] Slapstick comedy, in this sense, shares with Dostoevsky's Orthodoxy the tendency to pity the criminal instead of punishing him. Murder is simply a detour on the path to salvation.

If, as Caryl Emerson argues, Dostoevsky's "grisly detail serves the potential for transcendence," then I would add that it does so through the intermediary step of comedy.[88] The detailed description of the murder scene—not only the blood and bones, but Raskolnikov's ridiculous gestures—topples the hero's pretensions and emphasizes the banal ugliness of his act. And, rather than distancing the reader from the hero, this bathos cues us to react like slapstick viewers—indeed, like Orthodox believers: to pity the hero and desire his escape from an eternity of zany detours.

Escape, for Raskolnikov, is not the revolutionary overthrow of capitalism in Petersburg, or a jailbreak from the penal colony, but spiritual transcendence. In Siberia, he will continue to endure material precarity, but his physicality will no longer reflect this. Still, *Crime and Punishment* does not thwart slapstick's potential for economic critique. The novel expresses both the claustrophobic predicament of the worker under capitalism and Dostoevsky's own dearly held theological tenets. His heroes' object-adjacency and zaniness signal both the degrading effects of capitalism and the indignity of earthly existence. The endings of both *Modern Times* and *Crime and Punishment* epitomize these simultaneous meanings. Tramp and Ellen, walking cheerfully into the dustbowl-era American heartland, resemble the spiritually renewed Raskolnikov and Sonia gazing out onto the Siberian expanse in Dostoevsky's epilogue (Figure 3.4). These *zanni* have transcended capitalism, moving beyond the industrialized urban environment into a wide-open space where the only overbearing boss is God himself. For the reader with a more collectivist vision of utopia, this ending is, perhaps, the novel's final joke—the one joke Dostoevsky isn't in on. But, of course, Dostoevsky never promised utopia. He offers transcendence. And I, for one, will not begrudge these clowns their happy endings.

---

[87] Henri Bergson, *Laughter: An Essay on the Meaning of the Comic*. Translated by Cloudesley Brereton and Fred Rothwell (Los Angeles: Green Integer Books, 1991), 24.
[88] Caryl Emerson, *All the Same The Words Don't Go Away: Essays on Authors, Heroes, Aesthetics, and Stage Adaptations from the Russian Tradition* (Brighton, MA: Academic Studies Press, 2011), 217.

Bibliography

Andrin, Muriel. "Back to the 'Slap': Slapstick's Hyperbolic Gesture and the Rhetoric of Violence," in *Slapstick Comedy*. Edited by Tom Paulus and Rob King, 226–35. New York: Routledge, 2010.

Bagby, Lewis. *First Words: On Dostoevsky's Introductions*. Brighton, MA: Academic Studies Press, 2016.

Bakhtin, Mikhail. *Problems of Dostoevsky's Poetics*. Translated by Caryl Emerson. Minneapolis: University of Minnesota Press, 1999.

Bergson, Henri. *Laughter: An Essay on the Meaning of the Comic*. Translated by Cloudesley Brereton and Fred Rothwell. Los Angeles: Green Integer Books, 1991.

Bouissac, Paul. *The Semiotics of Clowns and Clowning*. London: Bloomsbury, 2015.

Bowser, Eileen. "Subverting the Conventions: Slapstick as Genre," in *The Slapstick Symposium*. Edited by Eileen Bowser, 13–17. Brussels: FIAF, 1988.

Brooks, Peter. *The Melodramatic Imagination: Balzac, Henry James, Melodrama, and the Mode of Excess*. New Haven: Yale University Press, 1976.

Clayton, Alex. *The Body in Hollywood Slapstick*. Jefferson, NC: McFarland & Company, 2007.

Crafton, Donald. "Pie and Chase: Gag, Spectacle and Narrative in Slapstick Comedy," in *Classical Hollywood Comedy*. Edited by Kristine Brunovska Karnick and Henry Jenkins, 106–20. New York: Routledge, 1995.

Dale, Alan. *Comedy Is a Man in Trouble: Slapstick in American Movies*. Minneapolis: University of Minnesota Press, 2000.

Dostoevsky, Fyodor. *Crime and Punishment*. Translated by Michael Katz. New York: W. W. Norton & Company, 2019.

Dostoevsky, Fyodor. *Notes from the Underground and the Double*. Translated by Ronald Wilks. New York: Penguin, 2009.

Dostoevsky, Fyodor. *Polnoe sobranie sochinenii v tridtsati tomakh*. Leningrad: Nauka, 1972–90.

Emerson, Caryl. *All the Same the Words Don't Go Away: Essays on Authors, Heroes, Aesthetics, and Stage Adaptations from the Russian Tradition*. Brighton, MA: Academic Studies Press, 2011.

Erman, Irina. "'Husband under the Bed': Specular Enclosures, Cuckoldry, and Logorrhea in Dostoevsky's Early Works," *The Russian Review*, vol. 76, no. 3 (2017): 311–30.

Frank, Joseph. *Lectures on Dostoevsky*. Princeton, NJ: Princeton University Press, 2019.

Fusso, Susanne. "Husbands and Lovers: Vaudeville Conventions in 'Another Man's Wife,' 'The Jealous Husband,' and *The Eternal Husband*," in *Before They Were Titans: Essays on the Early Works of Dostoevsky and Tolstoy*. Edited by Elizabeth Cheresh Allen, 61–92. Brighton, MA: Academic Studies Press, 2015.

Gunning, Tom. "Mechanisms of Laughter: The Devices of Slapstick," in *Slapstick Comedy*. Edited by Tom Paulus and Rob King, 137–51. New York: Routledge, 2010.

Iakubova, Rima. "Dostoevsky's Novel *Demons* and Russian *Balagan*," in *The New Russian Dostoevsky: Readings for the Twenty-First Century*. Edited by Carol Apollonio, 217–28. Bloomington, IN: Slavica, 2010.

Ivanov, Viacheslav. *Sobranie sochinenii v chetyrekh tomakh*, vol. 4. Briussel: Foyer Oriental Chrétien, 1987.

Karlinsky, Simon. *Russian Drama from Its Beginnings to the Age of Pushkin*. Berkeley, CA: University of California Press, 1985.

Katz, Monika. *F. A. Koni und das russische Vaudeville: Zur Geschichte des Unterhaltungstheaters in St. Petersburg 1830–1855*. Berlin: Frank & Timme, 2017.

Keaton, Buster. *My Wonderful World of Slapstick*. Garden City, NY: Doubleday & Company, 1960.

Kliger, Ilya. *The Narrative Shape of Truth: Veridiction in Modern European Literature*. University Park, PA: Pennsylvania State University Press, 2011.

Lotman, Iurii. "Theater and Theatricality in the Order of Early Nineteenth Century Culture," in *Semiotics and Structuralism: Readings from the Soviet Union*. Edited by Henryk Baran, 33–63. White Plains, NY: International Arts and Sciences Press, 1976.

Martinsen, Deborah. *Surprised by Shame: Dostoevsky's Liars and Narrative Explorers*. Columbus: The Ohio State University Press, 2003.

Meade, Marion. *Buster Keaton: Cut to the Chase*. New York: Harper Collins Publishers, 1995.

Mirsky, D. S. *A History of Russian Literature*. New York: Alfred A. Knopf, 1966.

Nechaeva, V. S. *Rannii Dostoevskii, 1821–1849*. Moskva: Nauka, 1979.

Ngai, Sianne. *Our Aesthetic Categories: Zany, Cute, Interesting*. Cambridge, MA: Harvard University Press, 2012.

Nussbaum, Martha. "Objectification," *Philosophy and Public Affairs*, vol. 24, no. 4 (1995): 249–91.

Shneyder, Vadim. *Russia's Capitalist Realism: Tolstoy, Dostoevsky, and Chekhov*. Evanston, IL: Northwestern University Press, 2019.

Steiner, George. *Tolstoy or Dostoevsky: An Essay in Contrast*. London: Faber and Faber, 1980.

Todd, William Mills III. "The Ruse of the Russian Novel," in *The Novel. Volume I: History, Geography, and Culture*. Edited by Franco Moretti, 401–23. Princeton: Princeton University Press, 2006.

Vinogradov, V. V. "Stil' peterburgskoi poemy 'Dvoinik,'" in *Stat'i i materialy*. Edited by A. S. Dolinin, 209–54. Peterburg: Mysl, 1922.

4

Sensations of Laughter: Mind and Matter in *The Brothers Karamazov*

Melissa Frazier

Theories of comedy, like theories of science, often revolve around the vexed question of the relationship between mind and material world. While many emphasize the primacy of mind over body or the other way around, most also trace the effects of humor to a gap, or "hiatus" between the two; as Simon Critchley puts it, "[h]umour functions by exploiting the gap between being a body and having a body, between—let us say—the *physical* and *metaphysical* aspects of being human."[1] Dostoevsky puts this mismatch to often wildly comical effect, for example in *Demons* (1872) when the same "progressive" picnic that in Nikolai Chernyshevsky's *What Is To Be Done?* (1863) is all merriment and laughter devolves into an unseemly and drunken cancan, or when the body of the aptly named Virginsky rebels against his attempt to realize his own Chernyshevskiian ideals. Virginsky, as the narrator says, "got everything out of books," including the offer to give way in favor of his wife's lover in imitation of Chernyshevsky's hero Lopukhov.[2] Unfortunately, as it turns out, books can get even an ardent believer only so far. "It was asserted," the narrator explains, "that when his wife announced his retirement, Virginsky said to her: 'My friend, up to now I have only loved you, but now I respect you.'" "But," the narrator then adds, "it is hardly possible that such an ancient Roman utterance was actually spoken; on the contrary, they say he wept and sobbed."[3] For all its often slapstick hilarity, however, comedy in Dostoevsky also goes beyond the easy effects of mismatch. As Alenka Zupančič writes in *The Odd One In: On Comedy*, "[W]

---

[1] Simon Critchley, *On Humour* (London: Routledge, 2002), 43.
[2] Fyodor Dostoevsky, *Demons*. Translated by Richard Pevear and Larissa Volokhonsky (New York, Vintage, 1994), 31; Fyodor Dostoevsky, *PSS* (Leningrad: Nauka, 1974), 10: 28.
[3] Dostoevsky, *Demons*, 32; *PSS*, 10: 29.

hat is comic (and productive) is not simply the discrepancy between the spirit and the letter, their divergence, but also and above all their mutual implication."[4] Underpinning this two-step approach to comedy is a more complicated science of mind and body, one that casts the two not in terms of a simple opposition, but as two aspects of a single whole.

The science that students of Russian literature know best assumes an opposition instead, as in the would-be material monism that Chernyshevsky himself made famous. Chernyshevsky's insistence in *What Is To Be Done?* on the determining role of the physical environment marks him as a supporter of the combined philosophical and scientific stance that we loosely term Russian Nihilism. It also reflects his reading of the so-called "vulgar" materialists, Karl Vogt (1817–95), Jakob Moleschott (1822–93), and Ludwig Büchner (1824–99).[5] While Victoria Frede summarizes the argument of all three in their famous slogan, "Keine Kraft ohne Stoff," "no force without matter," readers might also recall philosopher Ludwig Feuerbach's précis of Moleschott's claims in particular.[6] As Feuerbach writes in his review of Moleschott's *Die Lehre der Nahrungsmittel: Für das Volk* (1850; translated into English in 1856 as *The chemistry of food and diet, with a chapter on food adulterations*), "Der Mensch ist was er ißt," "Man is what he eats."[7] In *What Is To Be Done?* the "vulgar" commitment to a world of matter alone is apparent in the scientist-heroes' tendency to pepper their conversations with references to the "optical nerve" and "artificial albumin," as in the narrator's repeated emphasis on the material underpinnings of what we might take to be mental or spiritual states. Marya Aleksevna's selfish and grasping ways are presented as the direct effect of her environment, for example, while the two morphine pills that a troubled Lopukhov takes to help him sleep tell the narrator that his "spiritual travail was roughly equivalent in strength (according to Lopukhov's materialist viewpoint) to four cups of strong coffee."[8]

---

[4] Alenka Zupančič, *The Odd One In: On Comedy* (Cambridge, MA: MIT Press, 2008), 120–1.

[5] The label comes from Friedrich Engels who famously described the scientific stance of all three, Vogt, Moleschott, and Büchner, as "vulgar itinerant preacher materialism." Friedrich Engels, "Old Preface to *Anti-Dühring*. On Dialectics," in Karl Marx and Friedrich Engels, *Collected Works*, vol. 25 (New York: International Publishers, 1975), 340.

[6] Victoria Frede, "Materialism and the Radical Intelligentsia: The 1860s," in *A History of Russian Philosophy 1830–1930*. Edited by Gary M. Hamburg and Randall A. Poole (Cambridge: Cambridge University Press, 2012), 10.

[7] Melvin Cherno, "Feuerbach's 'Man Is What He Eats': A Rectification," *Journal of the History of Ideas*, vol. 24, no. 3 (1963): 399.

[8] Nikolai Chernyshevsky, *What Is to Be Done?*. Translated by Michael R. Katz (Ithaca: Cornell University Press, 1989), 252.

Dostoevsky's most obvious response to Chernyshevsky's "vulgarity" is his insistence on a higher, spiritual reality expressed most memorably in *The Brothers Karamazov* (1880) in a devil who pointedly may or may not appear to Ivan in tangible form. His answer is also the advocacy of a different strain of nineteenth-century science, one that posits a living and always changing material world that is no less real for its spiritual and/or psychological underpinnings and effects. As I have argued elsewhere, Dostoevsky's commitment to this more complicated materiality is evident in his recourse to the literary devices of "sensation," or a kind of writing that takes aim at readers' bodies together with their minds.[9] The novel of sensation has often been read in starkly materially determinist terms, as an attempt to address readers' bodies alone. It is also not usually associated with laughter. Set in the context of a nineteenth-century science of mind and body, however, "sensation" gains not just in more pleasurable effects, but in psycho-physiological complexity.

Just as Bruno Latour in our own day insists that we understand mind itself as "a wriggling and squiggling part of nature," so the most significant of nineteenth-century scientists, including physiologists George Henry Lewes and Hermann von Helmholtz, physicist James Clerk Maxwell, and evolutionary biologist Charles Darwin, started with a premise of what Richard Menke calls "dual-aspect monism."[10] Rather than subsuming mind into matter or the other way around, this more sophisticated science posits both sides, mind and matter, as operating always in tandem, as simultaneously both cause and effect. While Dostoevsky's reliance on the more lurid effects of "sensation" is already an expression of this scientific worldview, when he asks that we laugh at a Nihilist confusion of levels and kinds of materiality, he evokes the truths of what he calls "living life" with a degree of over-determination that is itself very funny.[11] My claim here is that Dostoevsky's many comic riffs on (im)materiality, above all in *The Brothers Karamazov*, make the case for the mutual implication of mind and matter on two mutually reinforcing levels. As his jokes tell the very story that his recourse to "sensation" also enacts, Dostoevsky's "dual-aspect monism" finally

---

[9] See Melissa Frazier, "The Science of Sensation: Dostoevsky, Wilkie Collins and the Detective Novel," *Dostoevsky Studies*, vol. 19 (2015): 7–28.

[10] Bruno Latour, *Pandora's Hope* (Cambridge, MA: Harvard University Press, 1999), 10; Richard Menke, "Fiction as Vivisection: G. H. Lewes and George Eliot," *ELH*, vol. 67, no. 2 (Summer, 2000): 623.

[11] Fyodor Dostoevsky, *Notes from Underground*. Translated by Richard Pevear and Larissa Volokhonsky (New York: Vintage, 1993), 129; *PSS*, 5: 178.

makes explicit the operation of comedy exactly as Zupančič describes it: what is funny is not a gap, but the (dis)juncture of mind and material world as two halves that make up a single whole.

Dead Matter

Much of the humor in *The Brothers Karamazov* derives from the characters' efforts to sort through the implications of material monism, for example, when Fyodor Pavlovich attempts to discuss theology with his son Alyosha. Fyodor Pavlovich with his crude sexuality, his spitting, and the bobbing of his Adam's apple is mired in a particularly dead sort of materialism evident also in his inability to imagine hell other than in the physical terms of life as we know it here on Earth. If devils are to drag him down with hooks, Fyodor Pavlovich asks, "Where do they get them? What are they made of? Iron? Where do they forge them? Have they got some kind of factory down there?"[12] In comedic terms, what is funny is the incongruity that persists despite Fyodor Pavlovich's efforts to explain the "other" world in terms of what he takes to be the reality of this one. The same incongruity then repeats to more disconcerting effect in the case of Father Ferapont's holy foolishness.

For Ferapont as Father Zosima's great rival at the monastery, holiness is measured in the corporeal terms of the proper observance of fasts, and devils again enjoy a pointedly material reality. As Ferapont explains to an eager interlocutor:

> As I was leaving the Superior's, I looked—there was one hiding from me behind the door, a real beefy one, a yard and a half tall or more, with a thick tail, brown, long, and he happened to stick the top of it into the doorjamb, and me being no fool, I suddenly slammed the door shut and pinched his tail. He started squealing, struggling, and I crossed him to death with the sign of the Cross, the triple one. He dropped dead on the spot, like a squashed spider.[13]

Like Fyodor Pavlovich with his hooks, what is funny is Ferapont's juxtaposition of what would seem a purely symbolic gesture, however emphatic—the triple one!—with such crudely physical effects. In both instances, and as so often in *The*

---

[12] Fyodor Dostoevsky, *The Brothers Karamazov*. Translated by Richard Pevear and Larissa Volokhonsky (New York: Farrar, Straus and Giroux, 1990), 24; *PSS*, 14: 23.

[13] Dostoevsky, *The Brothers Karamazov*, 169; *PSS*, 14: 153–4.

Brothers Karamazov, the joke on the "father" is also a comment on one "son" in particular: Ivan. Ivan as a would-be Nihilist tries to understand both this world and the next in the same tangible terms, so that a "loathsome" action can only be what you do, not what you don't, and the devil again real only if he enjoys a fleshly existence.[14] While the mistake of all three is a refusal even to entertain the possibility of a higher, more transcendent reality, Ivan is also explicitly limited by his commitment to a certain kind of science.

Ivan with his training in the natural sciences starts the novel a confirmed Nihilist, his "half-science" amplified not just by Smerdyakov, but by Rakitin and by the young Kolya Krasotkin.[15] As the thirteen-year-old Kolya explains, "I only respect mathematics and natural science." Rakitin is an older and seedier version of the same set of ideas, for example, when he insists that Alyosha in his innate sensuality is a "full-fledged Karamazov" after all, and "so race and selection do mean something."[16] Darwin in Rakitin's reading provides a natural law, a given cause that produces a necessary effect, as does his Claude Bernard. When Alyosha visits Dmitri in prison, he is surprised at Dmitri's sudden question, "Who is this Carl Bernard?" "No, not Carl, wait," he then adds, "I've got it wrong: Claude Bernard. What is it? Chemistry or something?"[17] It's physiology, not chemistry, but Dmitri has evidently grasped the basic idea. In Michael Katz's summary, Bernard "believed in the absolute determinism of natural science; in his words: 'the conditions of a phenomenon once known and fulfilled, the phenomenon must occur,'" and Rakitin seems to have explained as much.[18] According to Dmitri, Rakitin plans to write an article "with a tendency: 'It was impossible for him [Dmitri] not to kill, he was a victim of his environment.'"[19] As Dmitri explains:

> Imagine: it's all there in the nerves, in the head, there are these nerves in the brain (devil take them!) ... there are little sorts of tails, these nerves have little tails, well, and when they start trembling there ... that is, you see, I look at something with my eyes, like this, and they start trembling, these little tails ... and when they tremble, an image appears, not at once, but in a moment, it takes a second,

---

[14] Ibid., 276; *PSS*, 14: 251.
[15] The term "half-science" is Shatov's in *Demons* (Dostoevsky, *Demons*, 251; *PSS*, 10: 199).
[16] Dostoevsky, *The Brothers Karamazov*, 551, 80; *PSS*, 14: 497, 74.
[17] Ibid., 588; *PSS*, 15: 27.
[18] Michael Katz, "Dostoevsky and Natural Science," *Dostoevsky Studies*, vol. 9 (1988): 72.
[19] Dostoevsky, *The Brothers Karamazov*, 588; *PSS*, 15: 28.

and then a certain moment appears, as it were, that is, not a moment—devil take the moment—but an image, that is, an object or an event, well, devil take it—and that's why I contemplate, and then think ... because of the little tails, and not at all because I have a soul or am sort of image and likeness ....[20]

While Rakitin associates this material determinism with two rather more famous figures in nineteenth-century science, his more immediate source is Chernyshevsky.

Like the "vulgar" materialists, Nikolai Chernyshevsky (1828–89) claims a world of matter alone, including not just the bodies that respond to similar chemical stimuli in the same way, but also the environmental conditions that dictate particular forms of behavior. *What Is To Be Done?* accordingly lays great emphasis not just on the physical dimensions of his heroes—Lopukhov's broad shoulders, or Vera Pavlovna's ample bosom—but also on the actual functioning of their bodies, including not just Lopukhov's recourse to sleeping pills, but the tendency of Vera Pavlovna and her second husband to interrupt their discussions of physiology with discreet references to actual sexual encounters. In a curious reversal that marks most attempts at material monism, however, even as Chernyshevsky relegates mind to an effect of matter, his project as a whole relies on a causality that works the other way. As his enlightened heroes model for eager readers the refashioning of their world along proper ideological lines, the determining factor turns out to be mind as separate from matter instead.

Despite his Nihilist claims to the primacy of matter, Chernyshevsky's "New People" regularly make use of ideological assumptions in reshaping their physical environment, in Rakhmetov's overcoming of his own aristocratic origins to revolutionary effect, for example, or Vera Pavlovna's increasing mastery over her "natural" emotions. Chernyshevsky also openly aspires to instill the same primacy of thought in his reader. Rakhmetov can protest as much as he likes that his weakness for cigars only serves to demonstrate that he, too, is "not an abstract idea, but a human being, one who longs to live life," but the narrator readily acknowledges that his "extraordinary" man is a "type," albeit "a specimen of a very rare breed," as are the only slightly less remarkable Lopukhov and Kirsanov. If his heroes already explicitly function not as characters in their own plot complete with their own (fictional) bodies, but as templates for readers' lives, Chernyshevsky is also careful to reiterate his point on yet another level. As

---

[20] Ibid., 589; *PSS*, 15: 28.

ultimately insubstantial as his plot and characterization may be, Chernyshevsky often casts both aside in favor of extra-diegetic explanation.

The narrator's repeated rejection of the plot that he lifted from Georges Sand in the first place is expressly an appeal to readers to do without the "embellishments" that literary fiction usually entails.[21] Although the novel begins with an apparent suicide and a love affair gone wrong, the narrator immediately disavows the enticements of plot that he has already set in motion. As he explains:

> Yes, the first pages of my story reveal that I have a very poor opinion of my public. I employed the conventional ruse of a novelist: I began my tale with some striking scenes taken from the middle or the end, and I shrouded them with mystery. You, the public, are kind, very kind indeed, and therefore undiscriminating and slow-witted [....] So I was obliged to bait my hook with striking scenes.[22]

As Chloë Kitzinger argues, it is largely because Chernyshevsky eschews literariness along with what she calls the "messiness and contingency" of actual human beings that *What Is To Be Done?* was so successful "at producing positive models of human behavior that 1860s Russian readers could actively use."[23] For all its gestures at transparency, however, Chernyshevsky's repeated and strenuous recourse to "types" only pretends to engage with actual living matter while really offering pseudo-scientific abstraction, an intellectual leap forward into a much-desired future that is also a retreat from the very life that his science purports to explain.

This retreat takes a still darker turn in Bernard's *Introduction to the Study of Experimental Medicine* (1865). While Claude Bernard was among the most serious and scientifically grounded advocates of material determinism, still his attempt to reduce all of life to the law-like effects of quantifiable material conditions produces a similarly lifeless result. Although physiology, as he writes in the *Introduction*, is "the science whose object is to study the phenomena of living beings and to *determine* the material conditions in which they appear," Bernard was controversial in his own day for his reliance on the practice of vivisection.[24] "If a comparison were required to express my idea of the science

---

[21] Chernyshevsky, *What Is to Be Done?*, 48.
[22] Ibid., 47.
[23] Chloë Kitzinger, *Mimetic Lives: Tolstoy, Dostoevsky, and Character in the Novel* (Evanston, IL: Northwestern University Press, 2021), 158.
[24] Claude Bernard, *An Introduction to the Study of Experimental Medicine* (New York: Dover, 1957), 66.

of life," he explains, "I should say that it is a superb and dazzlingly lighted hall which may be reached only by passing through a long and ghastly kitchen."[25] In *Dying to Know* (2002), George Levine's exploration of the conjoined workings of nineteenth-century literature and science, he justifies Bernard's recourse to actual dismemberment when he posits a "desire for death" as "a central aspect of modern epistemology." "Or perhaps it might be said," he adds, "that modern scientific epistemology is a perfect medium through which the desire for death might get expressed."[26] If Bernard's material determinism leads once more to a literal dead end, "modern scientific epistemology" doesn't have to go that way.

In Rakitin's interpretation, Charles Darwin, like Bernard, traces a relentless passage from cause to effect. "So race and selection do mean something," Rakitin says, and the result is again death: "It was impossible for him not to kill." In Gillian Beer's reading in *Darwin's Plots*, however, Darwin's science seeks instead to accommodate the particularity and contingency that mark the functioning of living bodies in the world. "Darwinian theory," Beer writes, "will not resolve to a single significance nor yield a single pattern. It is essentially multivalent. It renounces a Descartian clarity, or univocality."[27] While Beer confines her argument to Darwin, the commitment to contingency and the specificity of individual experience that she describes was shared by many of the most significant figures in nineteenth-century science. It also lent itself to a different kind of literature.

Both physicist James Clerk Maxwell and pioneering psychological physiologist George Henry Lewes, for example, are explicit in their understanding of science as an area of inquiry as defined by what Rick Rylance calls its "provisionality, openness, revisability, and collective endeavor."[28] As practicing scientists, they also relied on empirical evidence that remains always subject to re-interpretation and review. Maxwell is equally famous for his extraordinary discovery of the equations that describe the phenomena of electromagnetism, including light, as for his claim to ultimate uncertainty in the thought experiment that we know as "Maxwell's Demon." As Louis Menand summarizes his stance in the

---

[25] Ibid., 15.

[26] George Levine, *Dying to Know* (Chicago: University of Chicago Press, 2002), 2.

[27] Gillian Beer, *Darwin's Plots: Evolutionary Narrative in Darwin, George Eliot and Nineteenth-Century Fiction* (New York: Cambridge University Press, 2009), 6.

[28] Rick Rylance, *Victorian Psychology and British Culture, 1850–1880* (New York: Oxford University Press, 2000), 301.

latter, "Scientific laws rely on the assumption that like causes always produce like effects, but as Maxwell himself once put it, this assumption is a 'metaphysical doctrine,' one of 'not much use in a world like this, in which the same antecedents never again concur, and nothing ever happens twice.'"[29] Maxwell also shared Lewes's fully scientific belief in the mutual implication of mind and material world.

As Lewes explains in his partly posthumously published *Problems of Life and Mind* (1873), "[E]very mental phenomenon has its corresponding neural phenomenon (the two being as the convex and concave surfaces of the same sphere, distinguishable yet identical), and ... *every neural phenomenon involves the whole Organism.*"[30] This "dual-aspect monism" not only complicates our understanding of cause and effect, but also guarantees the impossibility of a single objective reality "out there." For Maxwell, "[T]he only laws of matter are those which our minds must fabricate, and the only laws of mind are fabricated for it by matter"; for Lewes, "[O]bjective existence *is* to each what it is felt to be."[31] Dostoevsky asserts a similarly complicated materiality when his hero Razumikhin in *Crime and Punishment* makes vehement claim to "the *living* process of life," or when the unnamed narrator in *Notes from Underground* insists on our attention to "living life."[32] He also embodies its truths in a literary style marked by a "bait[ing of the] hook" of exactly the sort that Chernyshevsky claims to deplore. In Great Britain at the same time, this kind of writing was known as "sensation."

---

[29] Louis Menand, *The Metaphysical Club*, 1st ed. (New York: Farrar, Straus, and Giroux, 2001), 222. While we know that Dostoevsky was familiar with many of the most significant proponents of a more contingent and specific sort of science, including not just Lewes (see below) as well as Darwin, but also physiologist and physicist Hermann von Helmholtz, as far as I know there is no evidence that he knew Maxwell. It nonetheless speaks to the widespread discomfort at a science predicated on what Darwin's critics famously called "the law of higgledy-piggledy" that Maxwell, like Dostoevsky, cast its unsettling effects in terms of demons.

[30] George Henry Lewes, *Problems of Life and Mind: First Series, the Foundations of a Creed*, vol. 1 (Boston: Houghton, Osgood, 1875–80), 103–4.

[31] Ivan Tolstoy, *James Clerk Maxwell: A Biography* (Chicago: University of Chicago Press, 1981), 77; Lewes, *Problems of Life and Mind*, 175–6.

[32] Fyodor Dostoevsky, *Crime and Punishment*. Translated by Richard Pevear and Larissa Volokhonsky (New York: Vintage, 1993), 256; *PSS*, 6: 197; Dostoevsky, *Notes from Underground*, 129; *PSS*, 5: 178. Note that Dostoevsky was well aware of Lewes's example. Although Lewes's enormously influential *Problems of Life and Mind* (1873) appeared in Russian translation only in 1876, his *Physiology of Everyday Life* (1859) not only makes a cameo appearance in *Crime and Punishment*, but was the subject of a favorable review in the Dostoevsky brothers' journal *Time* in 1861; Dostoevsky is also likely to have known Lewes's science of mind and body from his novel *Ranthorpe* (1847), published in Russia in 1859 as *A Poet's Life*.

"Sensation"

Despite Chernyshevsky's disdain for its effects, the novel of sensation is most often cast in terms of the same commitment to material determinism that Chernyshevsky himself so unevenly expresses. As Nicholas Daly writes, the genre as it appeared in the wake of Wilkie Collins's *The Woman in White* (1859) is an attempt to "conjure up a corporeal rather than a cerebral response in the reader"; in the words of D. A. Miller, "sensation" offered "one of the first instances of modern literature to address itself primarily to the sympathetic nervous system, where it grounds its characteristic adrenalin effects: accelerated heart rate and respiration, increased blood pressure, the pallor resulting from vasoconstriction, and so on."[33] This response is usually attributed to an extreme reliance on lurid elements of plot, including, as Richard Fantina writes, "the themes of inheritance, bigamy, poisoning, drug abuse, and adultery, and … frequent employment of the *deus ex machina* and other startlingly improbable coincidences …."[34] These "sensational" twists and turns were widely held to achieve their effect on readers' bodies both on their own and by eliciting a sympathetic identification with the characters' often fraught physical states.

In her 1862 review, for example, novelist Margaret Oliphant marvels at the effect produced when the "Woman in White" reaches out to touch Walter's shoulder: "Few readers will be able to resist the mysterious thrill of this sudden touch. The sensation is distinct and indisputable. The silent woman lays her hand upon our shoulder as well as upon that of Mr Walter Hartright." Noting that the effect is then repeated when Walter makes the connection between his chance companion and Laura, Oliphant concludes: "These two startling points of this story do not take their power from character, or from passion, or any intellectual or emotional influence. The effect is pure sensation, neither more nor less."[35] Only a year later, the Rev. Henry Mansel argues, sensation had become the marker of all current British writing:

> A great philosopher has enumerated in a list of sensations 'the feelings from heat, electricity, galvanism, &c.,' together with 'titillation, sneezing, horripilation,

---

[33] Nicholas Daly, *Literature, Technology, and Modernity, 1860–2000* (Cambridge: Cambridge University Press, 2004), 40; D. A. Miller, *The Novel and the Police* (Berkeley: University of California Press, 1988), 146.

[34] Richard Fantina, *Victorian Sensational Fiction: The Daring Work of Charles Reade* (New York: Palgrave Macmillan, 2010), 23.

[35] Norman Page, ed., *Wilkie Collins: The Critical Heritage* (London: Routledge, 1974), 119.

shuddering, the feeling of setting the teeth on edge, &c.'; and our novels might be classified in like manner, according to the kind of sensation they are calculated to produce. There are novels of the warming-pan, and others of the galvanic-battery type—some which gently stimulate a particular feeling, and others which carry the whole nervous system by steam. There are some which tickle the vanity of the reader, and some which aspire to set his hair on end or his teeth on edge; while others, with or without the intention of the writer, are strongly provocative of that sensation in the palate and throat which is a premonitory symptom of nausea.[36]

Mansel's criticism, like Oliphant's, reflects a conservative British literary establishment highly uncomfortable at what an anonymous review in the *Christian Remembrancer* in 1864 described as an appeal to "the animal part of our nature."[37] In Russia, the same concern was expressed by the radical left.

Like his fellow Nihilist Chernyshevsky, Pyotr Tkachev (1844–86) combined a commitment to material determinism with a paradoxical insistence on maintaining and even extending intellectual control, and in his 1873 review of *Demons*, "Sick People" ("Больные люди"), he faults Dostoevsky on the latter score. For Tkachev, the "sick people" of his title are first Dostoevsky and then his characters, all of whom he sees as suffering from a sort of schizophrenia. His real concern, however, is for a reading public that apparently suffers in Russia as in Great Britain from a new literature of "sensation." Dostoevsky's writing, Tkachev argues, reflects an impoverished literary environment so desperate for "nervous irritation [*нервного раздражения*]: scandals, horrors, piquancy" that it makes recourse to "police agents, examining magistrates, and even just district court stenographers." He is appalled at what he describes as Dostoevsky's method in *Demons*: "Give us more and more gossip, scandal, irritate all the more strongly the reader's spinal cord [*спинной мозг*], make his hair stand on end, entertain him, amuse [*потешайте*] or frighten him, but just don't make him think or look up from the page."[38]

In his influential article "A Cruel Talent" ("Жестокий талант," 1882), Nikolai Mikhailovsky (1842–1904) makes the same point with regard to Dostoevsky's oeuvre as a whole. While Mikhailovsky grants Dostoevsky a formal ability, he

---

[36] Henry L. Mansel, "Sensation Novels," *Quarterly Review*, vol. 113, no. 226 (1863 April): 487.
[37] Anon. "Our Female Sensation Novelists," in *Varieties of Women's Sensation Fiction, 1855–1890*. Edited by Andrew Maunder, vol. 1 (London: Pickering and Chatto, 2004), 108.
[38] P. N. Tkachev, "Bol'nye liudi: 'Besy,' roman Fedora Dostoevskogo, v trekh chastiakh," in *Kritika 70-kh godov XIX veka*. Edited by S. F. Dmitrenko (Moscow: Olimp, 2002), 75–6.

again decries what he sees a deliberate and sustained attempt to inflict suffering on the reader through the use of "excessive and entirely inartistic longeurs, introductory scenes ... [and] ... digressions."[39] This "cruel talent," Mikhailovsky continues:

> will cloud your mind with its images and pictures and make your heart beat faster, and only in those *lucida intervalae* when in the course of reading sobriety returns to us, will you ask yourself: Why is he so tormenting that Sidorov or Petrov? Why is he is titillating [щекочет] me, too, in such tormenting fashion?

In fact, Mikhailovsky explains, there is no purpose to this suffering other than to create "sensations [ощущений] that become a need," as he argues that Dostoevsky's writing serves Russian society as nothing more than a kind of "narcotic" [наркотического свойства].[40] While readers in our own day are hardly likely to read Dostoevsky of all writers as so lacking in philosophical intent, the real flaw in Mikhailovsky's argument is his limited understanding of what "sensation" entails. From the point of view of "dual-aspect monism," the intent of "sensation" is not to by-pass cognition—as if any act of reading could!—but rather to engage readers' minds as implicated in and through their bodies. In Beer's terms, both approach and effect reflect what she calls a Darwinian "emphasis on substantiation."[41]

In the emerging novel of sensation, as in Darwin and in Charles Dickens as Darwin read him, Beer identifies an "identical drive towards confirming experience by appeal to the physical and the material, changing language into physical process."[42] In the novel of sensation, this "confirmation" is readily apparent in the combined physical and spiritual sickness that, as Tkachev notes, so often afflicts Dostoevsky's heroes. It is also at stake in the climactic moment of Collins's *The Moonstone* (1868) when Ezra Jennings, author of a never-to-be-published work "on the intricate and delicate subject of the brain and the nervous system," proves that the diamond was stolen under the influence of

---

[39] N. K. Mikhailovsky, "Zhestokii talant," in *F. M. Dostoevskii v russkoi kritike*. Edited by A. A. Belkin (Moscow: Khudozhestvennaia literatura, 1956), 332.

[40] Mikhailovsky, 333–4. Note that Mikhailovsky's "*щекочет*" can also refer to a "tickling" of a more innocent and less "titillating" kind.

[41] Beer, *Darwin's Plots*, 41.

[42] Ibid., 41. Marina Kostalevsky argues exactly for Dostoevsky's transformation of "language into physical process," although with reference not to "sensation," but to Russian Orthodoxy, see her "Sensual Mind: The Pain and Pleasure of Thinking," in *A New Word on "The Brothers Karamazov."* Edited by Robert Jackson (Evanston, IL: Northwestern University Press, 2004), 200–209.

a dose of opium that the culprit didn't know that he had taken.[43] The effects of this "appeal" are finally most importantly felt in a reader who is cast in real rather than imagined terms. As Beer writes, "[W]e are to laugh and weep as we read: rictus and wetness. We are to be physically disarranged by the reading experience."[44] While Dostoevsky's radical critics evidently experienced the "physical disarrangement" that "sensation" intends, the nuance of an appeal not to bodies, but to embodied minds, seems to have entirely escaped them. Despite Tkachev's passing reference to "amusement" [потешать], and Mikhailovsky's, like Mansel's, to an apparently uncomfortable sort of "tickling," they also strikingly fail to find Dostoevsky funny.

That reading is still with us, as a 2001 survey of readers in Cheliabinsk would suggest. The survey lists among the "associations" that readers make with Dostoevsky not just physical items (axes) and topoi (St. Petersburg), but also "sensations" [ощущения] and "states" [состояния] including "pain," "sickness," "nerves," and "hysteria."[45] For these respondents, as for Tkachev and Mikhailovsky, the overwhelming effect of Dostoevsky's writing is one of "horripilation," or what the survey calls "discomfort" [дискомфорт]. It is certainly true that Dostoevsky's investment in what Vadim Shneyder calls a "stubborn [прочная]" materiality is often and perhaps most memorably reflected in his sustained attention to ill and otherwise abnormal bodies, including not just Ivan Karamazov's brain fever, but Myshkin with his epileptic fits in *The Idiot*, or Raskolnikov with the feverish dreams that derive, as the narrator explains, from the "morbid condition" that tends to give dreams a "remarkably graphic, vivid, and extremely lifelike quality."[46] Even as "sensation" as a whole is notable for its reliance on more uncomfortable effects, as Beer writes, "The need to *please* his

---

[43] Wilkie Collins, *The Moonstone* (New York: Modern Library, 2001), 382.

[44] Beer, *Darwin's Plots*, 41.

[45] M. V. Zagidullina, "Dostoevskii glazami sootechestvennikov," *Roman F. M. Dostoevskogo "Idiot": Sovremennoe sostoianie izucheniia*. Edited by T. A. Kasatkina (Moscow: Nasledie, 2001), 527.

[46] Vadim Shneyder "Kapitalizm kak povestvovatel'naia problema, ili Pochemu den'gi ne goriat v romane F. M. Dostoevskogo 'Idiot,'" *Russkii realism XIX veka*. Edited by M. Vaisman, A. Vdovin, I. Kliger and K. Ospovat (Moscow: Novoe literaturnoe obozrenie, 2020), 77; Dostoevsky, *Crime and Punishment*, 54; *PSS*, 6: 45. As Audrey C. Peterson explains, for all its symbolic value in literary texts ranging from *Wuthering Heights* to *Madame Bovary*, brain fever in the nineteenth century was also a legitimate medical condition, the physiological symptoms of which corresponded to some extent to what we now understand as meningitis or encephalitis. In the original Russian, the narrator diagnoses Ivan as suffering from "*белая горячка*" (Dostoevsky, *PSS*, 15: 70), "*delirium tremens*" or "delirium" more generally; he also quotes a doctor's diagnosis of "*расстройства в мозгу*," "disturbances in the brain." See Peterson, "Brain Fever in Nineteenth Century Literature: Fact and Fiction," *Victorian Studies*, vol. 19, no. 4 (1976 June): 445–64.

readers as well as to unsettle and disturb them is as vital to Darwin as it was to Dickens."⁴⁷ The same is also true for Dostoevsky.

Dostoevsky's sense of the human mind and body as aspects of a natural world that enjoy their own agency finds especially beautiful expression in Ivan Karamazov's love for the "sticky little leaves that come out in spring" as in Father Zosima's belief that animals, too, have souls.⁴⁸ "But can it be that they, too, have Christ?" a young companion asks. "How could it be otherwise," Zosima answers, "for the Word is for all, all creation and all creatures, every little leaf is striving towards the Word, sings glory to God, weeps to Christ, unbeknownst to itself, doing so through the mystery of its sinless life."⁴⁹ Just as Zosima's vision of a material world in possession of its own spirituality evokes a feeling of gladness, so dreams in Dostoevsky can be bright as well as dark. While Dmitri Karamazov's dream of the "wee one" derives from an equally fraught physical state, for example, its effect on Dmitri and by extension the reader is one instead of great peacefulness: "I had a good dream, gentlemen," Dmitri says, as the narrator adds, "somehow strangely, with a sort of new face, as if lit up with joy."⁵⁰ Even as his brother Alyosha grieves the death and the bodily corruption of his mentor Zosima, the effects of Alyosha's dream of the marriage of Cana are still happier.

Alyosha is "very worn out" when he dozes off to the sound of Father Paissy reading and dreams of the resurrected Zosima welcoming him to the very feast that Paissy's words describe.⁵¹ As Zosima in the dream invites Alyosha to look on the God, "Something burned in Alyosha's heart, something suddenly filled him almost painfully, tears of rapture nearly burst from his soul." The apparent pain wakes him from his sleep and Alyosha goes outside to find himself one not just with his own mind and body, but with the material world around him. As the narrator explains:

> Over him the heavenly dome, full of quiet, shining stars, hung boundlessly. From the zenith to the horizon the still-dim Milky Way stretched its double strand. Night, fresh and quiet, almost unstirring, enveloped the earth. The white towers and golden domes of the church gleamed in the sapphire sky.

---

[47] Beer, *Darwin's Plots*, 35.
[48] Dostoevsky, *Brothers Karamazov*, 230; *PSS*, 14: 210.
[49] Ibid., 295; *PSS*, 14: 268.
[50] Ibid., 508; *PSS*, 14: 457.
[51] Ibid., 360; *PSS*, 14: 326.

The luxuriant autumn flowers in the flowerbeds near the house had fallen asleep until morning. The silence of the earth seemed to merge with the silence of the heavens, the mystery of the earth touched the mystery of the stars ....

As Alyosha falls to embrace the earth, he "vow[s] ecstatically to love it, to love it unto ages of ages." "What was he weeping for?" the narrator asks and answers with reference to Zosima's earlier instruction: "Oh, in his rapture he wept even for the stars that shone on him from the abyss, and 'he was not ashamed of his ecstasy.' It was as if threads from all those innumerable worlds of God all came together in his soul, and it was trembling all over, 'touching other worlds.'"[52] As Dostoevsky here as elsewhere both represents and evokes bodies as well as minds, he finally elicits in his readers not just joy, but also laughter at the Nihilists' expense. Where Chernyshevsky claims to believe in material determinism only to tell his readers what to think, Dostoevsky engages readers' minds and bodies at the same time, only most pleasurably in his many jokes that explain the very problem of Nihilist disembodiment that our sensations of laughter would address.

Laughter and "Living Life"

Although "sensation" already operates in terms of a "dual-aspect monism" of mind and matter, laughter offers a special case. In *The Odd One In*, Alenka Zupančič lends herself to long-standing tradition when she describes comedy as an "encounter of two different (often directly opposed) levels or experiences."[53] Although, as Zupančič notes, "there is no lack of descriptive and occasional possible designations of these two levels," she also subscribes to the Bergsonian view that the pair "living-mechanical" is the "real core" or "matheme" of everything funny.[54] It is Henri Bergson's much-quoted claim in *Laughter: An Essay on the Meaning of the Comic* (1900) that what is funny is "[s]*omething mechanical encrusted on the living.*"[55] Where Bergson starts and stops at the fact of incongruity, however, Zupančič goes on to argue for the mutual implication of the two halves of the single comic whole.

---

[52] Ibid., 362; *PSS*, 14: 327–8.
[53] Zupančič, *The Odd One In*, 111.
[54] Ibid., 112.
[55] Henri Bergson, *Laughter: An Essay on the Meaning of the Comic* (Los Angeles: Green Integer, 1999), 37. Italics Bergson's.

Bergson's theory, Zupančič argues, is limited by the "aprioristic and rather abstract duality of his basic philosophical position, which perpetuates in more than one aspect the dualism of matter and spirit, body and soul."[56] Bergson, she writes, "remains caught in an abstract dualism of the concrete and the universal" that only distances him from the "living life" that is his aim as it is Dostoevsky's.[57] What Zupančič calls "true" comedy instead unfolds as a combination of two and one that she depicts not in the Lewesian terms of the "convex and concave surfaces of the same sphere, distinguishable yet identical," but as a Möbius strip with "two sides" but "*only one surface.*"[58] "Comedy is materialistic," she writes, "because it sees the turning of materiality into pure spirit and of pure spirit into something material as *one and the same movement*, driven by a difficulty inherent to materiality itself."[59] Zupančič's readers may well question her assumption that theories of comedy can or should distinguish "true" comedy from "false"; as Critchley writes, "When it comes to what amuses us, we are all authorities, experts in the field. We *know* what we find funny."[60] Her so-called "true" comedy in content as well as form is nonetheless exactly the kind that Dostoevsky practices, above all in Ivan Karamazov's encounter with his devil.

While there is an explicitly Faustian element to Dostoevsky's repeated association of laughter with the demonic, his demons also always make the same joke.[61] Like the demons in *Demons*, Ivan's devil complicates our understanding of what material reality might entail, starting with the narrator's attempt to frame the devil's appearance as a figment of Ivan's apparently objectively disordered body and so mind, not that we know for sure, as the narrator with his characteristic combination of apparent certainty and equally evident doubt

---

[56] Zupančič, *The Odd One In*, 114.

[57] Ibid., 31. In Zupančič's argument, the similarity is not coincidental. In accounting for the contradictions that mark Bergson's theory, Zupančič describes a tension between two different "modalities," the first a "concept of 'life' which comes from the wider background of his own philosophical edifice (*élan original, vital*)," and the second "something that, historically speaking, fully escalated precisely in Bergson's time, penetrating all segments of human life: mechanics, and an overwhelming advance in establishing firm laws on all possible levels of existence" (Ibid., 113).

[58] Ibid., 54.

[59] Ibid., 47.

[60] Critchley, *On Humour*, 2.

[61] While William J. Leatherbarrow associates the Russian preference for a "shabby, down-at-heel devil" with Goethe (pg. 17), note that his longer discussion of laughter and the demonic in *Demons* focuses on Russian folklore and the folk puppet theater instead. See his chapter 4, "A Devil's Vaudeville: The Devils," in *A Devil's Vaudeville: The Demonic in Dostoevsky's Major Fiction* (Evanston, IL: Northwestern University Press, 2005).

begins with a disclaimer only to immediately follow with a definite statement. "I am not a doctor," he says:

> but nevertheless I feel the moment has come when it is decidedly necessary for me to explain to the reader at least something of the nature of Ivan Fyodorovich's illness. Getting ahead of myself, I will say only one thing: he was, that evening, precisely just on the verge of brain fever, which finally took complete possession of his organism, long in disorder but stubbornly refusing to succumb.[62]

If the narrator's incongruous prose style, veering from "not a doctor" to "decidedly necessary" and "precisely just on the verge," is funny all on its own, the argument that he advances so unevenly is also absurd. To claim the effects of delirium, after all, is neither to deny material reality, nor to prove that apparently supernatural beings don't exist. As Svidrigailov puts it in *Crime and Punishment*, "I agree that ghosts come only to sick people; but that only proves that ghosts cannot appear to anyone but sick people, not that they themselves do not exist."[63] Like the narrator but only more so, Ivan craves certainty, and he wants desperately to believe in that paradoxical creation of the material monists, a fully rational world made up of matter alone. To our amusement, the devil then arrives (or not) to mock Ivan's Nihilist assumptions and expectations of materiality, as well as our own.

Where devils, as Father Ferapont would have them, come equipped with tail and horns, this one manifests as an unremarkable if down-at-heels gentleman "*qui frisait la cinqantaine.*"[64] The narrator then goes on to describe this apparently well-known type at length and by way of the most mundane of details, from his no longer fashionable brown jacket, his dirty linen and checked trousers, to his card-playing habits and usually estranged children. The joke now is that a supernatural being is not made either more or less real by his apparent lack of supernatural attributes; as the devil himself says: "The other world and material proofs, la-di-da!"[65] Having made his point by means of his appearance alone, the devil then revisits the possibility of Ivan's physical disorder as he shifts the question of (ir)reality to take in the "sensational" effects that Dostoevsky's writing was itself known for. "Listen," the devil says:

---

[62] Dostoevsky, *Brothers Karamazov*, 634–5; *PSS*, 15: 69–70.
[63] Dostoevsky, *Crime and Punishment*, 289; *PSS*, 6: 221.
[64] Dostoevsky, *Brothers Karamazov*, 635; *PSS*, 15: 70.
[65] Ibid., 636–7; *PSS*, 15: 71.

in dreams and especially in nightmares, well, let's say as a result of indigestion or whatever, a man sometimes sees such artistic dreams, such complex and real actuality, such events, or even a whole world of events, woven into such a plot, with such unexpected details, beginning from your highest manifestations down to the last shirt button, as I swear even Leo Tolstoy couldn't invent.[66]

His most sustained mockery, however, lays bare the problem of materiality from a scientific point of view.

Although the devil acknowledges matter as the only measure of reality in his desire "to become incarnate, but so that it's final, irrevocable, in some fat, two-hundred-and-fifty-pound merchant's wife," like many a Nihilist, he also makes recourse to mathematics.[67] "[L]ike you," he tells Ivan, "I suffer from the fantastic, and that is why I love your earthly realism. Here you have it all outlined, here you have the formula, here you have geometry and with us it's all indeterminate equations!"[68] Now the joke is that "earthly realism" in fact doesn't offer either "the formula" or "geometry," despite Ivan's earlier attempts to argue otherwise; unfortunately for the certainty that Ivan seeks, as Ivan himself is well aware, non-Euclidean geometry as it was already understood by the mid-nineteenth century was only the latest advance in a science that called into question the relationship of formal axiomatic systems with what we take to be empirical proof. As Maxwell argued in 1867 when he posited his own demon, an imaginary creature stationed at a door separating two halves of a gas-filled container who busily sorts fast gas molecules from slow ones and so contravenes the second law of thermodynamics, from a fully scientific point of view, material reality doesn't lend itself to certainty, only probability. There is also no evidence that Earth as we know it excludes other possibilities.

Ivan's devil has more to say, all of it funny, much of it amusingly decorated with French, about the atheist who walks a quadrillion kilometers to reach paradise, the struggle between belief and disbelief, the exigencies of a materially determining "nature," and even Ivan's own literary efforts, but the workings of comedy are often the same, as evident not least in Ivan's response. As Ivan laughs, cries out in anger, and finally throws a glass at the devil whose material reality he would deny, his living body demonstrates the claims of the more

---

[66] Ibid., 639; *PSS*, 15: 74.
[67] Ibid., 638–9; *PSS*, 15: 73–4.
[68] Ibid., 638; *PSS*, 15: 73.

complicated materiality that his Nihilist mind rejects. In Zupančič's terms, what is funny is that "One splits into two," on the level of form as well as content, even as "the duality produced in the comic split encounters the impossibility of the two terms ever becoming completely independent, separate from each other."[69] As Dostoevsky mocks a "vulgar" materialism that empties the material world of the very matter that it claims, the sensations of laughter that we feel make the case for "dual-aspect monism" in the embodied experience of our own reading. When we laugh at Ivan's predicament, even when we smile, we restore bodies to minds and the two together to "living life," as Dostoevsky would have it.

Bibliography

Anon. "Our Female Sensation Novelists," in *Varieties of Women's Sensation Fiction, 1855–1890*. Edited by Andrew Maunder, et al., vol. 1, 105–14. London: Pickering and Chatto, 2004.

Beer, Gillian. *Darwin's Plots: Evolutionary Narrative in Darwin, George Eliot and Nineteenth-Century Fiction*. New York: Cambridge University Press, 2009.

Bergson, Henri. *Laughter: An Essay on the Meaning of the Comic*. Los Angeles: Green Integer, 1999.

Bernard, Claude. *An Introduction to the Study of Experimental Medicine*. New York: Dover, 1957.

Cherno, Melvin. "Feuerbach's 'Man Is What He Eats': A Rectification," *Journal of the History of Ideas*, vol. 24, no. 3 (1963): 397–406, https://doi.org/10.2307/2708215.

Chernyshevsky, Nikolai. *What Is to Be Done?*. Translated by Michael R. Katz. Ithaca: Cornell University Press, 1989.

Collins, Wilkie. *The Moonstone*. New York: Modern Library, 2001.

Critchley, Simon. *On Humour*. London: Routledge, 2002.

Daly, Nicholas. *Literature, Technology, and Modernity, 1860–2000*. Cambridge: Cambridge University Press, 2004.

Dostoevsky, Fyodor. *Polnoe sobranie sochinenii v tridtsati tomakh*. Leningrad: Nauka, 1972–90.

Dostoevsky, Fyodor. *The Brothers Karamazov*. Translated by Richard Pevear and Larissa Volokhonsky. New York: Vintage, 1990.

Dostoevsky, Fyodor. *Crime and Punishment*. Translated by Richard Pevear and Larissa Volokhonsky. New York: Vintage, 1993.

---

[69] Zupančič, *The Odd One In*, 122.

Dostoevsky, Fyodor. *Demons*. Translated by Richard Pevear and Larissa Volokhonsky. New York: Vintage, 1994.

Dostoevsky, Fyodor. *Notes from Underground*. Translated by Richard Pevear and Larissa Volokhonsky. New York: Vintage, 1993.

Engels, Friedrich. "Old Preface to *Anti-Dühring*. On Dialectics," in *Collected Works*. Edited by Karl Marx and Friedrich Engels, vol. 25, 336–44. New York: International Publishers, 1975.

Fantina, Richard. *Victorian Sensational Fiction: The Daring Work of Charles Reade*. New York: Palgrave Macmillan, 2010.

Frazier, Melissa. "The Science of Sensation: Dostoevsky, Wilkie Collins and the Detective Novel," *Dostoevsky Studies*, vol. 19 (2015): 7–28.

Frede, Victoria. "Materialism and the Radical Intelligentsia: The 1860s," in *A History of Russian Philosophy 1830–1930*. Edited by Gary M. Hamburg and Randall A. Poole, 69–89. Cambridge: Cambridge University Press, 2012.

Katz, Michael. "Dostoevsky and Natural Science," *Dostoevsky Studies*, vol. 9 (1988): 63–77.

Kitzinger, Chloë. *Mimetic Lives: Tolstoy, Dostoevsky, and Character in the Novel*. Evanston, IL: Northwestern University Press, 2021.

Kostalevsky, Marina. "Sensual Mind: The Pain and Pleasure of Thinking," in *A New Word on "The Brothers Karamazov."* Edited by Robert Jackson, 200–9. Evanston, IL: Northwestern University Press, 2004.

Latour, Bruno. *Pandora's Hope*. Cambridge, MA: Harvard University Press, 1999.

Leatherbarrow, William J. *A Devil's Vaudeville: The Demonic in Dostoevsky's Major Fiction*. Evanston, IL: Northwestern University Press, 2005.

Levine, George. *Dying to Know*. Chicago: University of Chicago Press, 2002.

Lewes, George Henry. *Problems of Life and Mind: First Series, the Foundations of a Creed*, vol. 1. Boston: Houghton, Osgood, 1875–80.

Mansel, Henry L. "Sensation Novels," *Quarterly Review*, vol. 113, no. 226 (April 1863): 482–514.

Menand, Louis. *The Metaphysical Club*, 1st ed. New York: Farrar, Straus, and Giroux, 2001.

Menke, Richard. "Fiction as Vivisection: G. H. Lewes and George Eliot," *ELH*, vol. 67, no. 2 (Summer, 2000): 617–53.

Mikhailovsky, N. K. "Zhestokii talant," in *F. M. Dostoevskii v russkoi kritike*. Edited by A. A. Belkin, 306–85. Moscow: Khudozhestvennaia literatura, 1956.

Miller, D. A. *The Novel and the Police*. Berkeley: University of California Press, 1988.

Page, Norman (ed.). *Wilkie Collins: The Critical Heritage*. London: Routledge, 1974.

Peterson, Audrey C. "Brain Fever in Nineteenth Century Literature: Fact and Fiction." *Victorian Studies*, vol. 19, no. 4 (June 1976): 445–64.

Rylance, Rick. *Victorian Psychology and British Culture, 1850–1880*. New York: Oxford University Press, 2000.

Shneyder, Vadim. "Kapitalizm kak povestvovatel'naia problema, ili Pochemu den'gi ne goriat v romane F. M. Dostoevskogo 'Idiot,'" in *Russkii realism XIX veka*. Edited by M. Vaisman, A. Vdovin, I. Kliger and K. Ospovat, 272–95. Moscow: Novoe literaturnoe obozrenie, 2020.

Tkachev, P. I. "Bol'nye liudi: 'Besy,' roman Fedora Dostoevskogo, v trekh chastiakh," in *Kritika 70-kh godov XIX veka*. Edited by S. F. Dmitrenko, 67–122. Moscow: Olimp, 2002.

Tolstoy, Ivan. *James Clerk Maxwell: A Biography*. Chicago: University of Chicago Press, 1981.

Zagidullina, M. V. "Dostoevskii glazami sootechestvennikov," in *Roman F. M. Dostoevskogo "Idiot": Sovremennoe sostoianie izucheniia*. Edited by T. A. Kasatkina, 508–39. Moscow: Nasledie, 2001.

Zupančič, Alenka. *The Odd One in: On Comedy*. Cambridge, MA: MIT Press, 2008.

Having the Last Laugh: Ontological Jokes and Dostoevsky's Comedic Genius

Alina Wyman

For all the seriousness of Dostoevsky's notorious "accursed questions," his prose is saturated with comedy, often of the most outrageous and indecorous kind. Fyodor P. Karamazov routinely practices stand-up comedy that would likely impress the audiences of The Second City or The Annoyance Theater. Captain Lebyadkin spews out poems of such hilarious ludicrousness that they could be rivaled only by transrational experiments of Russian avant-garde poets more than half a century later. Kirillov, often puzzled by a comic turn of phrase, is unable to recognize, let alone understand, jokes, but wants to decorate his suicide note with a crudely caricatured face sticking out its tongue in a gesture of ultimate mockery. Understanding Stepan Trofimovich's peculiar, multilingual jokes, that flip coquettishly between languages and stylistic registers, requires knowing French and German as well as the Russian folk idiom whereas the Prince of the preliminary plans for *The Idiot* is said to "deflect laughter"[1] and Stavrogin is mortally afraid of public laughter and ridicule. Dostoevsky's hero may be funny or ridiculous or markedly devoid of a sense of humor, as it were, born without a funny bone, yet, no matter what it may be, the character's relationship with humor, his "comedy coefficient," so to speak, is always important and philosophically relevant in Dostoevsky's world.

Because philosophical ideas and metaphysical dilemmas are often magnified, theoretically or fantastically expanded to reach gargantuan proportions in Dostoevsky's world, the phenomenon of the global or "ontological joke" is an important, if peculiar, subcategory of Dostoevskian humor and an essential part of his comedic economy. The questions I propose to raise in the context of this

---

[1] "*Как он отклоняет смех.*" PSS, 9: 242.

volume's timely theme, Dostoevsky's under-acknowledged funniness, are: (1) can one have a (spiritually) productive response to the ontological joke in Dostoevsky's universe? and (2) if so, what does such a response entail from a philosophical-psychological perspective? What follows are some preliminary answers to these moderately funny questions. Addressing them will entail explicating the motif of the ontological joke in the context of what Friedrich Nietzsche and Max Scheler call a *ressentiment* conflict; a brief examination of the Underground Man's responses to this comically phrased *ressentiment* dilemma and, finally, a (moderately serious) discussion of Dostoevsky's strategic use of tragicomedy in depicting the presumed objects of ontological mockery in *The Idiot*.

As a distinct philosophical motif in Dostoevsky's writings, the phenomenon of ontological jest or derision ("*ontologicheskaia nasmeshka*") has been studied by Boris Tikhomirov in "Khristos i Istina v poeme Ivana Karamazova 'Velikii inkvizitor'" (2012) and "Kto zhe eto tak smeetsia nad chelovekom?" (2013), where it is analyzed as part of the integral ideology of metaphysical rebel characters, engaged in anti-Christian polemics.[2] Because I see ontological or existential jest as a broader motif, already distinctly present in *Notes from Underground* and integrally linked to the question of value in Dostoevsky's world, my definition of the phenomenon and analytical focus are different from Tikhomirov's. Largely focusing on the connection between ontological jest and Christological and Gnostic themes, Tikhomirov explicates the identity of "the agent of ontological mockery" in *The Brothers Karamazov*, *Demons*, *The Idiot*, and *Diary of a Writer* and his analysis largely bypasses the comical aspects of the problem. While also attentive to its philosophical underpinnings, my analysis aims to elucidate the significance of the consistently *comical* phrasing of the conflict in Dostoevsky and contains a preliminary discussion of humorous responses to ontological jokes.

Without tracing the literary and philosophical roots of the ontological joke motif in Dostoevsky's work,[3] let us briefly define the content of this important thematic variant, which gains considerable philosophical depth in Dostoevsky's post-Siberian works: (1) a hero typically faces a frustrating contradiction

---

[2] Boris Tikhomirov, "Kto zhe eto tak smeetsia nad chelovekom: Motif 'ontologicheskoi nasmeshki' v tvorchestve Dostoevskogo," *Dostoevsky Studies*, vol. 17 (2013): 74.

[3] Somewhat similar, if less philosophically elaborate, musings can be found in the works of Russian Romantics, for example, Lermontov and Baratynsky, and the kernel of the ontological jest motif can arguably be detected in E.T.A. Hoffmann's darker works. Boris Tikhomirov notes that the later formulations of the ontological jest narrative in Dostoevsky's novels contain Gnostic motifs, without directly linking the novelist with specific Gnostic sources. Tikhomirov, "Kto zhe eto tak smeetsia nad chelovekom," 74–7.

between irreconcilable (or seemingly irreconcilable) ideas, desires or whole systems of value, which exercises a considerable strain ("*nadryv*") on his mental and emotional life, and (2) proceeds to universalize this debilitating dilemma, conceptualizing it as a *global joke* at his or, more precisely, humanity's expense. "Who is laughing at us humans up there?," Dostoevskian heroes typically ask.[4] This basic question is variously expanded and elaborated in several novels and in prose miniatures of *A Writer's Diary*, as it is in the sketch "Judgment," whose suicidal narrator takes nature, the global comedian, to task for creating rational creatures endowed with an irrational desire for eternal life, tragically, or perhaps tragicomically, conscious of their own mortality: "[O]ne can't avoid an extremely amusing [...] thought: what if humans were unloosed upon the earth as part of some impudent experiment, only to see whether this kind of creature would survive on earth?"[5] In the words of Ippolit Terentiev in *The Idiot*, human beings are subjected to ontological mockery, placed in deliberately "insulting [насмешливые]" conditions by "nature" or "providence," equated to a terrifying tarantula-God in the boy's tubercular nightmares.[6]

Like the Underground Man's emphatically impersonal universe, the ontological joker is usually anonymous, represents the universe's higher power—often being a gruesome or absurd stand-in for the benevolent Divine Other—and uses his unquestionable surplus of power and knowledge to mock, jeer and laugh at humanity ("*nasmekhat'sia;*" "*kalambur*[*it'*]"; "*smeiat'sia*"). He comedically ambushes his human subject, who can't fully understand the joke but is becoming uncomfortably, if only dimly, aware of being the butt of someone else's comic routine. Humiliated by such anti-dialogical ridicule, Dostoevsky's hero fires back by attempting to disrupt the joke through analysis or to laugh back, ridiculing, scandalizing, but also inevitably *personalizing* the global joker in the process. I will argue that it is when the hero offers an emphatically comedic response to the ontological joke, beginning to laugh at the invisible comedian or even *with* him, however timidly or desperately, that he achieves some spiritual progress. Conversely, the serious, mainly or exclusively analytical responses come short of freeing the hero, instead plunging him deeper into existential despair fraught with *ressentiment*.

---

[4] The closest variant of this query is found in *The Brothers Karamazov*, formulated by Fyodor Pavlovich: "Кто же это так смеется над человеком?," to which Ivan Fyodorovich decorously answers "черт," the devil, but a less pious and more sinister answer is certainly implied. *PSS*, 14: 232.

[5] *PSS*, 23: 147.

[6] *PSS*, 8: 344, 323–4.

The Presumption of Ontological Mockery and Its *Ressentiment* Potential

Max Scheler and Friedrich Nietzsche, whose thought is arguably compatible with Dostoevsky's because they consistently connect the psychological sphere with the ethical and spiritual realms, point out that mentally or spiritually "straining" dilemmas, like the ones that usually result in the presumption of an ontological jest in Dostoevsky, may lead to a so-called *ressentiment* revolt. In *Beyond Good and Evil* and *Toward a Genealogy of Morals*, Nietzsche describes *ressentiment* as a possible psychological response to coercion, where the subjects of oppression, deprived of any means of voicing both their true desires and their protest directly, find roundabout, often peculiar ways of channeling and cunningly targeting their rage against the oppressor. When one's desire for action and power is repeatedly frustrated, the initial, outward-oriented impulse for revenge turns inward: hurt may be visited upon the self in order to eventually hurt the oppressor.[7]

Nietzsche sees the culmination of this highly sublimated form of revenge in the act of the revaluation of values, which he associates with the "slave revolt in morality." In a gesture of subversive protest, the oppressed embrace their own debasement and cunningly endorse their very powerlessness as their highest value, thereby devaluing the desired but unattainable values of power and happiness. All of this is done with a sideward glance at the oppressor, with a covert goal of affecting and ultimately sabotaging his own value barometer.[8] However, if the avenger relies on the passive-aggressive *ressentiment* solutions exclusively, without at least periodic recourse to affirmative, active behaviors, he runs the risk of forgetting about this temporary or provisional switch and no longer recognizing the initial values as such, eventually succumbing to a full-blown *ressentiment* delusion. Max Scheler calls this, usually irreversible, stage of *ressentiment*—when the true value is no longer transparent, as it were, shimmering behind the substituted and objectively false value—"organic *ressentiment*" or "organic mendacity."[9]

---

[7] Friedrich Nietzsche, *The Complete Works of Friedrich Nietzsche*. Edited by Oscar Levy. Translated by Horace B. Samuel, 18 vols. (Edinburgh and London: T.N. Fouli, 1909–13), 13: 34.

[8] Nietzsche, *The Complete Works*, 13: 30, 32.

[9] Max Scheler, *Ressentiment*. Edited by Lewis A. Coser. Translated by William W. Holdheim (New York: Free Press of Glencoe, 1961), 77–8.

It is likely that Nietzsche's concept of *ressentiment* and the image of its "practitioner," "the man of *ressentiment*," were themselves inspired by Dostoevsky, as suggested by Paolo Stellino and Charles Miller.[10] Stellino links Nietzsche's definitions and descriptions of the phenomena in *Toward a Genealogy of Morals* to specific passages in *Notes from Underground*; however, Miller's detailed analysis of the extremely distorted French translation of Dostoevsky's novella read by Nietzsche, in which a haphazardly condensed version of *Notes* was combined with *The Landlady* and presented as a single work, makes it impossible to speak of Dostoevsky's direct or straightforward influence.[11]

Scheler, who has revised, expanded, and nuanced Nietzsche's theory of *ressentiment*, also points out that the externally oriented revenge-drive is likely to be transformed into the passive-aggressive, often inward-directed energy of *ressentiment* in "lasting situations which are felt to be injurious but beyond one's control—in other words, *the more the injury is experienced as a destiny*."[12] According to Scheler, it is the existing discrepancies between the conceptual and the empirical levels of reality that tend to trigger the strongest *ressentiment* reaction. For example, Scheler notes that social *ressentiment* is strongest not in a social unit with a legal system condoning social inequality but rather in a society with sufficiently developed *concepts* of justice and equality, where the de jure status of a group may be at odds with its de facto powerlessness.[13] In other words, the likelihood of a *ressentiment* revolt is greater in a subject capable of *conceiving of* and even taught to *believe in* his own freedom and agency but repeatedly faced with factual powerlessness in reality.

It is precisely the painful discrepancy between what *should be* and *what is* that motivates and propels the *ressentiment*-like protest in Dostoevsky's *Notes from Underground*, without, however, leading the hero to organic *ressentiment* or plunging him into a full-blown *ressentiment* delusion. In somewhat simplified

---

[10] See Paolo Stellino, *Nietzsche and Dostoevsky: On the Verge of Nihilism* (Bern: Peter Lang AG, 2015), 45–56; and Charles Miller, "Nietzsche's 'Discovery' of Dostoevsky," *Nietzsche Studien*, vol. 2 (1973): 202–57.

[11] In my earlier analyses of *Notes from Underground*, which contain a partial application of the concept of *ressentiment* to the novella ("The Specter of Freedom" [2007], *The Gift of Active Empathy: Scheler, Bakhtin and Dostoevsky* [2016]), I also relate Nietzsche's *ressentiment* to several underground psychological and existential strategies but argue that Dostoevsky's hero *cannot* be fully equated with the man of *ressentiment*, which lends the Underground Man something akin to a surplus of vision in relation to Nietzsche's *ressentiment* persona. As will be shown below, this surplus of vision is importantly related to humor and comedic perspective taking, absent in *ressentiment*.

[12] Scheler, *Ressentiment*, 50. Here and throughout emphasis is added, unless otherwise indicated.

[13] Ibid.

terms, the key contradiction that perpetually frustrates the paradoxical hero, making him feel mocked by creation itself, can be formulated as a contradiction between man's innate desire for freedom and his rational realization of the impossibility of fully satisfying this God- or nature-given desire. This fundamental impasse can be defined in a social-historical context, as it has been done by Lev Shestov (as a conflict between the belief in individual freedom held by socialist idealists of the 1840s and the negation of individual will in the 1860s' materialist doctrines),[14] or in a wider, broadly philosophical way that constitutes an ontological dilemma, interpreted as "*онтологическая насмешка*"[15] by the hero.

"I probably would never be able to make use of my magnanimity," the Underground Man laments, explaining his impotence in responding to an insult under the paralyzing conditions of his deterministic universe, governed exclusively by the laws of nature, "neither to forgive, since the offender, perhaps, had slapped me in accordance with the laws of nature, and there's no way to forgive the laws of nature; nor to forget, because even if it is because of the laws of nature, it's offensive nevertheless."[16] Taking straightforward ethical action, like forgiveness, thus no longer makes sense to the befuddled hero because the anonymous *offender* possesses no personal agency, while the *offence* is seen as a painful but equally impersonal blow dealt by the fatalistic universe, as part of a universal joke at the hero's expense. Revenge, another ethically relevant

---

[14] I discuss this historical-philosophical explanation in *The Gift of Active Empathy*: "According to Shestov, the fundamental ideological inconsistency underlying the worldview of a progressive '*интеллигент*' of the 1860s, reflected in the Underground Man's dilemma, results from the simultaneous affirmation of two mutually exclusive ideas: (1) the proclamation of man's rights before society and (2) the whole-hearted acceptance of the laws of natural necessity (Shestov 13). The first postulate, championed by the utopian socialists of the 1840s and inherited by the succeeding socialist movements of the 1860s, came into a sharp contradiction with the central component of the materialist ideology—the belief in determinism. Thus, as Shestov puts it, the declaration of man's rights before humanity was negated by the simultaneous declaration of his lack of rights before the greater, ultimately, all-pervasive, authority of nature (13). Unrecognized by the myopic theoreticians of Russian socialist materialism, this profound contradiction was masterfully dramatized by Dostoevsky, Shestov argues." Alina Wyman, *The Gift of Active Empathy: Scheler, Bakhtin, and Dostoevsky* (Evanston, IL: Northwestern University Press, 2016), 75–6.

[15] To my knowledge this Russian term was coined by Boris Tikhomirov (see "'Kto zhe eto tak smeetsia nad chelovekom?'" op. cit.) but is based on the nouns "*насмешка*", "*усмешка*", "*смех*", and the verbs "*насмеяться*", "*насмехаться*", "*смеяться*", ("mockery", "sneer"/ "sneering smile", "laughter", "to deride", "to mock", "to laugh [at someone]") used in Dostoevsky in the context of what can be called existential or ontological mockery. In my own work and teaching I have used the following, largely synonymous, terms in English: "global joke"; "existential joke" or "jest"; "existential mockery".

[16] Fyodor Dostoevsky, *Notes from Underground*. Translated and edited by Michael R. Katz (New York and London: W. W. Norton & CO, 1989), 7; *PSS*, 5: 103. For quotations from *Notes from Underground* I use Michael Katz's Norton translation, occasionally modified by me for greater accuracy (*Notes*, page number), followed by the page numbers of the corresponding text in the Russian original in the 1972–90 collected writings edition (*PSS*). For other Dostoevsky works, I use my own translations followed by the volume and page numbers in *PSS*.

option, becomes equally absurd, as the culprit is simply nowhere to be found: "You look—and the object vanishes, the arguments evaporate, a guilty party can't be identified," the Underground Man exclaims, "*the offence ceases to be one and becomes a matter of fate*, something like a toothache for which no one's to blame [...]".[17]

This fateful or existential offence[18] corresponds closely to what Scheler describes as a perfect precondition for *ressentiment*, "[an] *injury [...] experienced as a destiny*" and is also a key precondition for the hero's conceptualization of himself as a victim of ontological mockery in Dostoevsky. While on the level of plot intrigue the Underground Man may be casually insulted by his former schoolmates or shrinking under the fist of the brutal "officer," on the higher, more abstract level of signification, relevant to the fundamental questions of Being, the hero is experiencing an intense *ontological injury*. In *Notes*, the offence issues from nature itself and from its omnipotent laws, thus affecting all of humanity, albeit now crystallized in the painfully lacerated, hypersensitive "I" of the underground hero. This injury is caused by man's and the world's allegedly faulty design ("why was I created [literally: *designed*] with such desires?") i.e. is ontological in nature.[19] The resulting internal conflict is then exacerbated by the fact that the hero is not simply conscious of this glaring ontological injustice (note the *consciousness* of the apparent injustice as the main precondition of the strongest *ressentiment* reaction in Scheler), but, in accordance with his underground temperament, he is *hyper*conscious of it.

Underground Resistance: Ontological Jest as a Value Dilemma in *Notes from Underground*

The hero's stubborn attempts to have a moral or at least morally relevant, *personal* response to the impersonal, mathematically rigid universe—a gesture that honors what he believes to be a worthy, but utterly antiquated and perhaps

---

[17] *Notes* 3; *PSS*, 5: 108–9

[18] "It's the laws of nature that *hurt / offended / insulted* me (*обижали*) the most my whole life," the Underground Man complains (*Notes*, 12; *PSS*, 5: 107). The choice of the verb *обижать / обидеть*,— which conveys a highly personal affront to the victim's ego—in relation to the emphatically impersonal injurer, the laws of nature, is deliberate and creates a strong comic effect, simultaneously conveying both the common-sense silliness and philosophical gravity of the Underground Man's dilemma.

[19] *PSS*, 5: 121.

unrealizable system of values—are paralleled by his refusal to surrender his high-minded vision of freedom in exchange for the sham "ideal" of sanctioned happiness in the Crystal Palace of socialist utopia. Instead of the "palatial chicken coop,"[20] merely masquerading as an authentic value choice, he demands the real Crystal Palace. "What do I care if it [the true Crystal Palace] is *impossible* and if I must settle for some apartments?" the hero asks emphatically, bracketing the common objection that an absolute value he longs for—an ideal ontological locus where supreme affirmation is compatible with individual freedom—is empirically impossible. "Then why was I designed with such desires? Can it be that I was made this way only in order to reach the conclusion that my entire way of being is a fraud [*одно надувание*]? Is that the whole purpose?"[21] All of this is likely part of some elaborate global joke, the hero concludes: "There must be some kind of pun [*каламбур*] concealed in all of this."[22]

The creation of human consciousness capable of conceptualizing and thus desiring the highest, absolute spiritual value, yet unable to realize or apprehend this value in practical terms, referenced here as one of the Underground Man's key existential grievances, is an important, if still somewhat embryonic, postulation of the ontological joke motif in what could be considered a philosophical introduction to all of Dostoevsky's post-Siberian novels. Despite tragic gravity of its consequences, illustrated by the Underground Man's dreary, painfully inactive existence in Part I, this global mockery is sufficiently light and playfully subtle to be likened to a pun, a witty and cruelly sophisticated comedic trope that becomes especially insulting to the hero in his ongoing confrontation with his tyrannical universe. Man's empirical inability to suspend the stone wall of natural laws to fully realize his ineffable individuality—a belief the freedom-worshiping hero is tragically unable to invalidate on the level of lived experience—results in the so-called underground protest, a series of paradoxical measures aimed at scandalizing his elusive and omnipotent offender. The Underground Man will

---

[20] This expression belongs to Joseph Frank, who brilliantly elucidates the idealistic underpinnings of the Underground Man's critique of rational egoism in Joseph Frank, *Dostoevsky: The Stir of Liberation, 1860–1865* (Princeton: Princeton University Press, 1986), 328.

[21] *Notes*, 26; *PSS*, 5: 120–1. In the preceding lines there is a telling reference to the idealism of the 1840s as the source of the character's irrational and uncompromising values, which addresses the sociopolitical and historical-philosophical explanation of the fundamental *impasse* underlying the underground revolt, discussed in note 5: "But let's say that [...] according to the laws of nature it [the Crystal Palace] shouldn't exist and that I've invented it only out of my own stupidity, *as a result of certain antiquated, irrational habits of my generation*" (*Notes* 25; *PSS*, 5: 120, italics added).

[22] *PSS*, 5: 119.

play the game but will do so on his own terms, intending to ridicule the global joker in the process.

Erupting with subversive laughter, the Underground Man sticks out his tongue and gives the Crystal Palace the finger, even if he does so in his pocket and later admits that, by its very definition, the "eternally indestructible" edifice would make such protest absolutely impossible, admitting that "it won't be possible to tease it [the Crystal Palace] either by sticking out one's tongue at it on the sly or by secretly giving it the finger in one's pocket."[23] He retaliates against nature and its pesky toothache by transforming an instinctual expression of pain into groans of such theatrical ingenuity that the resulting spectacle is anything but natural.[24]

By the hero's own admission his protest is tragically ineffective and steeped in despair, which makes it partially resemble a *ressentiment* revolt, a similarly negative enterprise, thoroughly dominated by the rejected values. Yet his spirited, usually satirical negation of the imposter ideals championed by the equally myopic "bulls" and the worshippers of "the sublime and the beautiful" is not without value in Dostoevsky's universe, even though no positive ideal is affirmed in the process. Furthermore, it is to the hero's credit that he himself recognizes the merely provisional, *relative* value of the underground: it is not "the best" (i.e., an absolute value), but merely "better" ("*лучше*" or "*выгоднее*") than the sham "ideal" of coerced bliss in the Crystal Palace or the complacent celebration of pure necessity as a moral choice.[25] The truly embraceable, if un-embraced, value ("the true Crystal Palace") remains unnamed and likely temperamentally and existentially unattainable for the ontologically homeless hero, but it is affirmed *in absentia*, unmistakably recognized by the reader as the absolute value of agapeistic love steeped in faith: "it is not the underground [that would be] better, but something different, something entirely different, something I long for but will never find [*вовсе не подполье лучше, а что-то другое, совсем другое, которого я жажду, но которого никак не найду!*]"[26]

The internally divided, often hilariously bilious and indignant Underground Man is able to perpetuate his caustic energy, fueled into endless negation, partly because this apophatic affirmation of the absolute value grants him a level of

---

[23] *Notes* 26, translation amended; *PSS*, 5: 120.
[24] *PSS*, 5: 106.
[25] *PSS*, 5: 120.
[26] *PSS*, 5: 121.

lucidity unknown to the man of *ressentiment*. The absolute value that torments the Underground Man continues to shimmer through the conditional value of the underground, making the latter, and the even lesser values of the "*homme de la nature et de la vérité*" and his followers ridiculous. It is thus the vital, if lacerating, energy of laughter—"*поджививляющая*" even in its sneering underground version—that protects the hero from lapsing into a full-fledged *ressentiment*, so feared by Scheler, with its most pernicious stage of "organic mendacity," where the subject is no longer aware of the substitution of values that has occurred in the process of *ressentiment* value renegotiation.

Humor's Spiritual Potential: Two Useful Theoretical Approaches

To further elucidate the spiritual relevance of humor in Dostoevsky's world, even in its darker, underground iterations, as well as the prominent place of the comedic in the author's ontology, I would like to turn to the theories of two kindred thinkers, both lifelong readers of Dostoevsky: Lev Pumpiansky and Vladimir Soloviev. Both connect laughter to liberation and to an ability to step outside of a consciousness dangerously locked within itself that tends toward totalitarian worldviews and dictatorial mandates. For both Soloviev and Pumpiansky, laughter provides a much-needed exterior space into which one can retreat in order to gain an external perspective on oneself; it protects us from dogmatism, teaches the value of otherness and may allow us to apprehend the quintessential diversity of Being more fully, an outcome arguably also celebrated in Dostoevsky's works.

In *La Sophia*, Vladimir Soloviev defines humans in their metaphysical capacity as "being[s] that laugh."[27] "An animal completely absorbed by reality at hand, cannot place itself in a critical and negative position toward that reality, and, for this reason, cannot laugh," Soloviev argues:

> Laugher supposes a state of freedom; a slave does not laugh. In natural laughter, in the laughter of a child or young girl, humanity's metaphysical freedom manifests itself unawares. It acquires consciousness of self [only] in the reflective laughter of a thinking person. Such a person has a clear understanding of another, ideal

---

[27] Soloviev, *La Sophia et les autres ecrits francais*. Edited by Francois Rouleau (Lausanne: L'Age D'Homme, 1978), 27, quoted in Judith Deutsch Kornblatt, "On Laughter and Vladimir Solov'ev's *Three Encounters*," *Slavic Review*, vol. 57, no. 3 (1998): 572.

world contrasted to this apparent reality [...]. He sees the contrast and he mocks the false reality: he laughs.[28]

In commenting on E.T.A. Hoffmann's use of fantasy, Soloviev again links ontological affirmation of multiple worlds, evident in Hoffmann's works, with both freedom and humor.[29] Because in Hoffmann's tales the fantastic realm is not only posited on equal footing with the mundane realm but is internally and organically linked with it, the poet and his poetically inclined heroes are truly free, never limited by or imprisoned in one, exclusive and uncontested reality.[30] The *given*, or mundane, reality thus cannot have a definitive, finalizing or dogmatically limiting "utterly *serious*" meaning, because the *posited* reality of the fantastic is always palpable behind or beside it as a possible corrective, Soloviev argues.[31] In this way, (romantic) humor becomes a source of ontological optimism in Soloviev's interpretation, for Hoffmann's (read: the Romantics') "dual freedom," clearly endorsed by Soloviev as a value also relevant for his own time, manifests itself precisely as a fundamentally life-affirming, if eccentric, sense of humor: "*свобода* [...] *выражается* [...] *в юморе*."[32]

A similar connection between the humorous and a crucial external space in relation to the realm of morose seriousness that can provide a sobering sideward perspective on one's (or an entire culture's) past goal-oriented activity ("*оглядка на цель*") is made by Lev Pumpiansky in his fascinating notes on Gogol and the culture of laughter.[33] Analyzing the pre-literary roots of Greek and Roman comedic genres the classicist Pumpiansky describes pre-Dionysian phallophoric

---

[28] Ibid. In her insightful discussion of Soloviev's philosophical and religious valuation of humor and comedy, Judith Deutsch Kornblatt also persuasively demonstrates that the philosopher consistently and skillfully uses humor in his own artistic and philosophical writings to convey the full complexity of his subjects and to avoid the impoverishing effects of that same morose seriousness which, in his view, was inherent in abstract moralism, false mysticism, facile spiritualism grounded in abstract "love" for the divine, and other lacking—*isms* of his time, which he tirelessly combated in his works as a personalist thinker. See Kornblatt, 575–8.

[29] V. S. Soloviev, "Predisloviie k skazke E.T.A. Gofmana 'Zolotoi gorshok,'" *Filosofiia iskusstva i literaturnaia kritika* (Moscow: Iskusstvo, 1991), 573.

[30] Soloviev makes a similar statement concerning the dismantling of the monological, narrowly realistic, of-this-world-only truths in A. K. Tolstoy's fantastic story "Vampire" ("Upyr'") in his forward to the tale but does not link this openness to alternative perspectives in literary fantasy to romantic humor in this piece. See V. S. Soloviev, *Sobranie Sochinenii Vladimira Sergeevicha Solov'eva*, 9 vols. (St. Petersburg: Obshchestvennaia Pol'za, 1901–7), 8: 410.

[31] Soloviev, *Filosofiia iskusstva*, 571.

[32] Ibid., 573.

[33] L. V. Pumpiansky, *Klassicheskaia traditisia. Sobranie trudov poistorii russkoi literatury*. Edited by A. P. Chudakov, E. M. Esserlin, and N. I. Nikolaev (Moscow: Iazyki russkoi literatury, 2000), 260.

processions performed as part of an ancient agricultural ritual cycle—a primal form of performance and, in his view, a predecessor of comedy—as strictly utilitarian, goal-oriented operations aimed at securing agricultural fertility. Pumpiansky concludes that the advent of laughter, which replaced this humorless form of performance during the Dionysian era and ultimately resulted in comedy, provided "*a sideward glance* at [a collective's] goal," resulting in historical consciousness which, in its turn, created a culture.[34]

Pumpiansky emphasizes the eccentric nature of the comedic, the necessity of an external perspective for the very act of laughter, which presupposes a debunking of some sorts, an exposure of a previous, limited point of view and a hostility toward *a priori* accepted, absolute truths. In its religious meaning, laughter for Pumpiansky may offer a temporary release from rigid moral constraints in order to free the laugher to embrace a new, spiritually informed ethics, an ethics that is not terminally locked within itself, i.e., within the realm of the strictly moral. The truly comical, which is always spiritually relevant in Pumpiansky, is opposed to the strict symmetry of ritualistic exchanges and, in our analysis of Dostoevsky, may be related to breaking up the cycle of being hurt-and-hurting-back and the corresponding chain of vengeful reciprocal ridicule prevalent in Dostoevsky's fictional world.

Together, these two relatable and in some ways complementary definitions of the comical may be helpful in explaining the spiritual—and potentially religious—relevance of humor and comedy in Dostoevsky's world and in probing the productivity of a comic response to the "global joke" by those characters who see themselves as objects of this particularly brutal form of ridicule. For instance, if the Underground Man possessed the full potency of Solovievian humor, he might be able to recognize himself as a citizen of multiple worlds, with the "dual freedom," resulting from this dual ontological citizenship, instead of thinking himself terminally confined to the cheerless tenement building of the immediately real. This, at once spiritually liberating and spiritually stabilizing, sense of humor would help him realize his fundamental non-coincidence with his vulgarly realistic, strictly natural or, as Bakhtin would put it, terminally finalized self-image, entirely defined by the laws of nature. If sufficiently powerful, humor in Soloviev's and Pumpiansky's definitions can be functionally analogous to a leap of faith, for in its vigorous abolition of assumed certainties,

---

[34] Ibid., 260–1.

a leap of laughter may suspend one's pedantic belief in the strictly real in order to make room for faith.

Although the Underground Man is temperamentally and spiritually incapable of a true leap of faith[35]—even as he wistfully contemplates faith as an impossible but spiritually preferable alternative to the underground—his several ingenious leaps of laughter shake up his seemingly immutable, rigid universe and effect a palpable change in its power dynamic. The ultimate tyrant of the Underground Man's world, "2 times 2 is 4," is omnipotent, deadly and anonymous, and yet "he" is portrayed laconically, and brilliantly, as simply a loser, a jerk, a bloody nuisance: he is a village drunk who "stands in your way, arms akimbo, and spits!"[36] When the initially ominous ontological joke is thus retold by the underground comedian, it becomes hilarious and strangely life-affirming. Crudely, scandalously, and irreverently the hero laughs at the dreaded laws of nature and at *himself* daring to laugh at this no longer impersonal or terrifying offender.

Thus finding himself on equal footing with his version of providence, engaged in yet another practically ineffective yet existentially and spiritually consequential bumping duel in the novella, the underground hero ultimately presents a much more personal and ontologically optimistic version of the universe than, say, Lermontov's utterly impersonal providence in "The Fatalist" or the morose vision of "icy boulders" as a metaphor for humanity's terminal end in Dostoevsky's *Adolescent*,[37] that novel's characteristically humorless version of the ontological dilemma. Although the Underground Man is not yet ready to "ride the [wave of the] ultimate laugh" of global communion that reconciles *what should be* with *what is*, together with Vladimir Soloviev and his wise-cracking Sophia,[38] his irreverent laughter in response to the providential pun may be a first step toward rewriting the sinister burlesque by significantly altering its meaning.

---

[35] I discuss this problem in greater detail in *The Gift of Active Empathy*, chapter 3, see esp. pp 77–84.
[36] *PSS*, 5: 119.
[37] See, for example, *PSS*, 13: 49.
[38] In her excellent discussion of the significance of laughter and humor in Soloviev's philosophy Judith Kornblatt explains how both the human person, that relates to both the physical and the metaphysical realms, and Sophia, an even higher form of synthesis or interpenetration between the divine and the organically human, essentially accomplish an act of supreme communion between the two fundamental realms through laughter. "Humanity, as we saw, links both worlds, and Sophia, as the 'all human organism, as the eternal body of God and eternal soul of the world' *must therefore ride the ultimate laugh*. As the soul of the 'laughing animal,' Sophia brings humor to the body of God as well, transfiguring matter and embodying the divine in a phenomenon as humble as Solov'ev's

Tragicomedy in *The Idiot*: Ippolit's Confrontation with the Ontological Joke

Subsequent underground types in *The Idiot, Demons* and *The Brothers Karamazov* do not sustain the Underground Man's lucidity and relative ideological flexibility evident in our analysis, and instead develop into ideologically rigid metaphysical rebels or even committed "god-fighters."[39] The characters who respond to the problem of ontological jest in Dostoevsky's subsequent novels—Ippolit, Kirillov, and Ivan Karamazov, all markedly less comically gifted than their underground predecessor—do so in ways that lead to a greater, and more debilitating, entrapment in *ressentiment*.

In these novels, the major conflict that in Scheler's terms creates a situation rich in *ressentiment* potential and that also underlies the grievances of Dostoevsky's god-fighting characters, making them suspect that they are the subject of ontological mockery, is once again between the magnitude of man's spiritual desires and the impossibility of their satisfactory fulfillment in the world as we know it. As the readers of *Notes from Underground* may have guessed, although the philosophically meandering narrator is curiously cryptic about it, the greatest "stone wall" among the dreaded laws of nature is death and

---

own 'hiccup-like high notes'" (Kornblatt 572). By quintessentially restating Ippolit's proposition to have the last laugh with an affirmative, instead of nihilistic meaning, Kornblatt's Soloviev-inspired metaphor ("to ride the ultimate laugh"), as it were, reaccentuates the ontological joke discourse to arrive at a radically different signification. This joyfully affirmative "rid[ing of] the ultimate laugh" could then be seen as a Solovievian positive, agapeistically inspired *rewriting* of the quintessential global joke narrative perpetuated by Dostoevsky's metaphysical rebels, which in practice could perhaps also be accomplished through a truly *comedic* response to the global joke even for those very same rebels. To respond to the global joke productively may simply mean to laugh at it wholeheartedly and "ride" the ultimate global laugh to a humbling and renewing revaluation of values. If the "leap of laughter" accomplished via the ride is powerful enough, it may ultimately lead to a cumulative leap of faith that would allow the ontologically uncertain Dostoevskian heroes to become confident in the existence of another, positively unfinalized, freedom-granting world.

[39] In his remarks on the difference between "the underground" as an existential position and the existential stance of the more typical Dostoevskian hero featured in the major works *after* "Notes from Underground," Lev Pumpiansky registers this fundamental change: according to Pumpiansky, the underground (*подполье*) as a psycho-existential stance is the state of "*anticipating* murder" or suicide (*предварение убийства*), which I interpret as an intermediate ideological space where the hero's existential despair is not yet channeled toward a commitment to murder, producing largely theoretical or potential violence. By contrast, the typical, read: post-underground, Dostoevskian hero "knows only murder and suicide." See Pumpiansky, *Klassicheskaia traditisia*, 521. I would argue that this indefinite suspension on the threshold of taking violent action against self or others is actually essential to the underground as a paradoxical, *a priori* conflicted system of values that results in a certain degree of ideological flexibility and alertness. This is in large part due to the caustic energy of underground wit that disables rigid mechanisms of progressive *ressentiment*, a condition that leads to organic mendacity, i.e. an atrophy of value recognition altogether.

it is man's finite existence, combined with his tormenting, usually misdirected, thirst for the infinite and the absolute, that becomes the essential grievance of Dostoevsky's metaphysical rebels—the stone wall of all stone walls.

As Boris Tikhomirov perceptively notes,[40] in Dostoevsky's post-Siberian novels the motif of the ontological jest is firmly linked to Christological themes, and I argue that it is the revelation of the highest spiritual ideal affirmed as a moral-spiritual *possibility* for humanity through Christ that becomes a source of ceaseless torment for those who both apprehend the beauty and necessity of the Christian ideal, often in spite of themselves, and see the demands it sets for its followers as impossible for man as we know him. This painful contradiction, which casts humanity in a comical light ("*человек устроен комически*"), becomes the essential content of the ontological joke that structures the Weltanschauung of such temperamentally different but ideologically similar characters as Ippolit Terentiev, Ivan Karamazov, and Aleksei Kirillov.[41] Here the low "comedy coefficient" of the former two and, arguably, the negative "comedy coefficient" of the latter signify the characters' inability to step outside of their rigid ideological position through comic perspective-taking, inherent in the eccentric nature of laughter. As a consequence, their dogmatism remains largely unchallenged, and they are unable to respond to the ontological dilemma comedically.[42]

---

[40] Tikhomirov, "Kto zhe eto tak smeetsia nad chelovekom," 73. See also "Khristos i Istina v poeme Ivana Karamazova 'Velikii inkvizitor'" (2012). In "Komicheskoe v proizvedeniiakh Dostoevskogo," I. I. Lapshin also briefly addresses the general phenomenon of ontological jest in Dostoevsky, without using this particular term, by registering the existence and fundamental importance of ontological comedy in the writer's oeuvre: it is not just society's imperfections that writers like Maupassant and Dostoevsky find funny, but "the very nature of things themselves," the fundamentally flawed structure of the world and the funny nature (натура) of the human person at its center, Lapshin observes. I. I. Lapshin, "Komicheskoe v proizvediniakh Dostoevskogo," *O Dostoevskom: Sbornik Statei*. Edited by A. L. Bem, 2 vols. (Prague: Petropolis, 1933), 2: 119.

[41] *PSS*, 5: 119.

[42] Kirillov's humorlessness (his "negative comedy coefficient," so to speak), which is linked to his inability to understand figures of speech, wordplay and idiomatic diction, is deeply significant, explaining his ideological rigidity and special vulnerability to "being eaten by an idea," a predicament that befalls several tragically "possessed" characters in *Devils*; Ippolit is capable of occasional witticisms and well-aimed spiteful mockery, but is thwarted in his comedic imagination by constantly taking offence at everyone and everything. Ivan comes across as morosely serious in most of the novel's conversations, and is consequently among the characters most vulnerable to *ressentiment* but is most likely no stranger to sarcasm and dry humor in his writings. He seems to have donated his funny bone to his devil, whose hilarious babble, allegedly consisting entirely of Ivan's own previously spoken (most likely written) words, estranges and bestranges Ivan's philosophical conclusions, paradoxically challenging him to reevaluate his ideological stance.

To reflect on Dostoevsky's use of comedy, and tragicomedy, with the purpose of highlighting a metaphysical rebel's inadequate reaction to the ontological dilemma, let us turn to Ippolit Terentiev in the context of the ontological jest motif. "If I had the power not to be born, I would not accept life under such insulting (literally, 'mocking'/'ridiculing') conditions," Ippolit exclaims at the end of his provocative farewell address to the world, delivered on the eve of his attempted suicide in chapter 7, part 3 ("*существования на таких **насмешливых** условиях*").[43] Unable to cancel his birth, Ippolit intends to use his power to alter the circumstances of his death. Ippolit's response to the ontological joke is to have the last laugh by beating the supreme comedian to the punch line. Ironically, he himself becomes embarrassingly, if not supremely, ridiculous instead.

Like the Underground Man, Ippolit blames the very structure of being ("*устройство мира*") for the comical incongruity between man's superior, divinely inspired powers of cognition and the ludicrous reality of his empirically limited, finite existence: "once I have been given the power to cognize that 'I am,' *what do I care* if the world was *designed* imperfectly and cannot stand otherwise [without the daily deaths of a myriad of creatures]?"; "*если уже раз мне дали сознать, что 'я есмь' то какое мне дело до того, что мир **устроен** с ошибками и что иначе он не может стоять?*"[44] Compare the almost identical diction in the Underground Man's indignant summary of ontological injustice, as he dismisses the empirical impossibility of a true Crystal Palace as an argument for tempering his lofty desire for the absolute, and not merely conditional, value: "*What do I care* if it's impossible to *design* it this way (*устроить*) and I have to be content with rented apartments. Then why was I *designed* (*устроен*) with such desires!"; "*Какое мне дело до того, что так невозможно **устроить**, и что надо довольствоваться квартирами. Зачем же я **устроен** с такими желаниями!*"[45]

Like the Underground Man, Ippolit rejects the argument that man's ignorance or incomprehension of the providential design in any way exonerates the global joker or allows for a possibility of a future just interpretation. On the contrary, man's lack of knowledge and ultimate inability to understand the providential punchline only makes the ontological insult more painful: "Fine! I'll accept that it's impossible to arrange the world in any other way, that is, without our continuous devouring of each other [...], *I am even ready to admit that I don't*

---

[43] *PSS*, 8: 344.
[44] *PSS*, 8: 344.
[45] *PSS*, 5: 121.

understand anything in this global arrangement (*устройстве*) [...] but, no matter what you say [...], it's unfair."⁴⁶ Compare this outburst to the Underground Man's: "in spite of all of these uncertainties and setups you are in pain, and *the less is known the more it hurts*."⁴⁷

The cruel "setup" cunningly prepared for humanity by the powers above consists in the glaring contradiction between man's seemingly limitless mental and spiritual capabilities and his radically limited empirical options, Ippolit concludes. While our intellect is designed for the infinite horizons of desire, our earthly life is an undignified tumble over the stumbling block of death. "I accept the possibility of eternal life and, perhaps, I've always accepted it," Ippolit exclaims:

> Let's admit that consciousness was ignited [within us] by the will of a higher power, and that it turned toward the world and said: "*I am!*" and let's say that this higher power suddenly mandated for it to be annihilated because it was necessary for something or other; fine, I accept all of this, but there still arises the eternal question: why do they also need my surrender? Couldn't they simply eat me without demanding praises to that which ate me?⁴⁸

In a similarly absurd and darkly comical fashion, "nature," read: providence, equated by Ippolit to an "enormous machine of the newest *design* (*громадн[ая] машин[а] новейшего устройства*)*,*" unfeelingly "devours (*поглотила в себя*)" the symbol of man's possibilities, the irreplaceable Christ, equally admired and pitied by Ippolit in His tragic but irredeemable demise.⁴⁹

In keeping with the consistently linked motifs of eating and laughing, the specter of Rogozhin, who appears a paragraph later as part of Ippolit's feverish dream inspired by these same reflections on man's fate in the comically designed universe, is described with a focus on the ominously opening mouth, pictured with nightmarish ambiguity: "At that moment, as if having guessed that I was frightened, Rogozhin retracted his hand ... straightened his shoulders *and started to slowly open his mouth, as if getting ready to laugh*; he was looking straight at me"; "*... выпрямился и стал раздвигать свой рот, точно готовясь смеяться.*"⁵⁰ Rogozhin, symbolically positioned in the novel as a chthonic deity

---

⁴⁶ *PSS*, 8: 344.
⁴⁷ *PSS*, 5: 106.
⁴⁸ *PSS*, 8: 343.
⁴⁹ *PSS*, 8: 339.
⁵⁰ *PSS*, 8: 341.

or perhaps a sinister executioner-priest in charge of un-Christian sacrifices—who, as it were, guards Christ's irredeemable corpse in his graveyard-like house and who will soon dispatch Nastasia Filippovna into the chthonic beyond, becomes directly associated with the "callous, dark and omnipotent being" mentioned half a page earlier.[51] His slowly opening mouth threatens to devour but may also signify laughter; the semiotic vagueness of the unfolding gesture points to both signifieds: the comically inclined demonic providence laughs at us as it devours us.

Like the hero of *Notes from Underground,* Ippolit thus finds himself an unwitting subject of a providential pun ("*каламбур*"), at the core of which is an infuriatingly clever semantic substitution ("*подмен*"): at the very moment he proudly proclaims that he IS ("*я есть*" in modern and nineteenth-century Russian), providence promptly EATS him ("*ест его*"). Indeed, in Ippolit's world, *to be is to be eaten.*[52] A similarly insulting semantic substitution can be traced in the lexical chain "*видение*" (a vision/an apparition), "*при-видение*" (a ghost), and, finally, "*про-видение*" (providence) that emerges in Ippolit's nightmarish, darkly caricatured descriptions of the evil, philosophically rejected divine Other, scattered throughout his "Necessary Explanation."

As Ippolit tries to rest after his emotionally exhausting visit to Rogozhin's house, with its haunting image of Holbein's "Dead Christ," a febrile hallucination becomes a way of processing his growing existential anxiety generated by this anti-iconic painting. Nature, the "mute" and merciless beast that, according to Ippolit, has callously ("*глухо*") "devoured […] the great and priceless Being [Christ]," now appears in the youth's tubercular nightmare as a terrifying tarantula. This panic-inducing progenitor of Kafka's absurd "Ungeziefer" paradoxically gives form to that same "callous, dark and mute" being of infinite

---

[51] *PSS*, 8: 340.

[52] The Church Slavonic "*Я есьмъ*" is uttered in the novel, but the modern-day "*есть*," with its identical forms in both first and third person, nearly homophonic with "*ест*," is on the reader's mind (the paronomasia of *есьм / ем*, if attributed to the Divine subject, also potentially evoked by the passage, is also suggestive and thought-provoking). Ippolit's metaphor of "our mutual devouring of each other" ("*поядени[е] друг друга*") as a fundamental part of the existing world order is literalized in Lebedev's hilarious lecture about monk-eating cannibals in the preceding chapter. While Ippolit uncompromisingly wants to break entirely free from the cycle of "eating and being eaten," Lebedev, in an underground fashion, defends the provisional, *relative value* of eating scrawny "secular babies" instead of the fat-bellied and thus vastly more nutritious monks, who, however, come with a higher price tag in terms of moral contrition (*PSS*, 8:314). In Lebedev's serio-comic narrative hunger emerges as a formidable law of nature and a force much more difficult to defy or resist than the Underground Man's paralyzing toothache.

power that is in principle shapeless and imageless—Ippolit's unquestionably evil version of providence.[53]

As Ippolit's hallucinations continue, it is a *vision* of Rogozhin (*видение*), subsequently called "apparition" or "ghost" (*привидение*), that replaces the tarantula in his haunted house of existential horrors, all representing the menacing "higher power" that has superseded the benevolent providential Other in the boy's world.[54] Both the tarantula and the spectral Rogozhin are illuminated by candlelight, Rogozhin suggestively appearing under "an icon lamp [*лампадка*]," as if replacing a revered icon. The unnamed "somebody" who takes Ippolit by the hand and shows him the tarantula, an anonymous dark priest supervising his sojourn with the sinister deity, *laughs* at his indignation; similarly, Rogozhin's "mockery [*насмешка*]" and inscrutable silence are profoundly insulting to Ippolit.[55]

Both Rogozhin-the-ghost and the tarantula are parodic versions of providence and both are apparitions or hallucinations: "this ghost [*привидение*] humiliated me"; "I cannot surrender to the dark power that takes the form of a tarantula."[56] In the conclusion of "The Necessary Explanation" Ippolit finally utters the word "providence [*провидение*]," the concept he had been referring to all along but by different, less attractive names. Although Ippolit seems to be using the word without palpable intonational quotation marks, now presumably referring to humanity's benevolent Other, and assumes the restrained tone of polite neutrality, positive value is not returned to the term that has been thoroughly reevaluated and discredited:

> We belittle providence too much by ascribing our own notions to it, just because we can't understand it. But, once again, if it's impossible to understand it in the first place, then, I repeat, it is hard to be responsible for that which is humanly impossible to understand; And if this is so, why would I be judged for not being able to understand the real will and laws of providence? No, let's put religion aside altogether.[57]

The malefic providence in "The Necessary Explanation" is thus represented by three structurally isomorphic lexical units with a shared root and provocatively

---

[53] PSS, 8: 339–40. "*темн[ая], нагл[а]я и бессмысленно вечн[ая] сил[а]*," PSS, 8: 349.
[54] PSS, 8: 340–1.
[55] PSS, 8: 340.
[56] PSS, 8: 341.
[57] PSS, 8: 344.

related but diverging meanings that form a linear sequence: *видение—привидение—провидение*.⁵⁸ Together with Ippolit, we become privy to an unfair and disappointing substitution (*"подмен"*; *"надувание"*). Instead of a vision-filled, potentially epiphanic *"видение,"* we are presented with a shabby *"привидение,"* itself a ludicrous version of *"провидение,"* whose malevolence Ippolit consistently exposes and whose reality he similarly makes suspect or irrelevant, yet does not deny altogether: "it's most likely that all of it [life after death and providence] exists but we understand nothing of life after death and its laws."⁵⁹

Structurally, the sequential use of these paronymous words may foreground the fraudulent substitution of values the Underground Man suspects underlies the foundation of our world: "[could it be] that my very design is *a fraud*?"; [*"неужели*] *все мое устройство одно надувание?"*⁶⁰ As a literary trope and a rhetorically justified "fraud" based on semantic substitution, the emerging pun importantly bridges the levels of content and form fused within the allegedly faulty "design [*устройство*]" of the underground characters' sabotaged universe. In Ippolit's philosophically provocative dream, providence is replaced by its inadequate substitute: a menacingly laughing, man-eating ghost, a chimeric and grotesque being whose very existence is refutable.⁶¹

Ippolit is thus teased, fooled, and ridiculed by the global Other: he may think that he *is*, but he is in fact annihilated into non-being, "eaten" by nature. He may have expected a just, kind, and ultimately real providence revealed through a serene vision, but has to make do with a ludicrous hallucination, an annoying consequence of his debilitating disease. Ippolit himself is likely only partly aware of this ominous wordplay (*"каламбур"*), whose philosophical implications are more clearly visible to the reader. Inherited from the Underground Man, Ippolit's suspicion that, unbeknownst to himself, he is part of an extended comedic trope authored by someone else, whose significance and logic he cannot fully understand, thus seems to be eerily justified within the frame of his own narrative.

---

⁵⁸ The use of each lexeme is consistent, confined to its particular section of the "Necessary Explanation" and uninterrupted by another term; *видение* is used once; *привидение*—six times and *провидение*—three times.

⁵⁹ *PSS*, 8: 344.

⁶⁰ *PSS*, 5: 121.

⁶¹ "*... я ни в какие привидения не верю*"; "... I don't believe in ghosts," Ippolit tells us in *PSS*, 8: 340.

In this context it is also important that the external narrative frame that contains the scene of Ippolit's reading of his "Necessary Explanation" is emphatically comical, alerting us to the consistent interpenetration between the comical and the serious in *The Idiot* and reminding us that Ippolit is living inside a very funny existential joke, not only telling us about one. Examples of this consistent serio-comic diction include Lebedev's hilariously grotesque, darkly Swiftian "lecture," praising the moral superiority of those eating human babies compared to opting for the vastly more nutritious Catholic monks, because, really, a human baby is "not nutritious, and I would even say tastes too treacly, so all you get for your trouble is the pangs of conscience, without any nutritional benefit"; Ptitsyn's keen and somewhat premature interest in Ippolit's skeleton promised to the Academy of Sciences, and, finally, the grotesque and scandalously funny scene following Ippolit's thwarted suicide, utterly lacking in solemnity: "Everyone's initial fright quickly turned into laughter; some even started laughing out loud, [...] Ippolit was weeping hysterically."[62]

Ivan Lapshin has noted the similarity of Ippolit's intended public suicide, preceded by an emotional and highly inappropriate lecture ("The Necessary Explanation"), to the Cynic Peregrinus's "pedagogical" suicide in front of his disciples and "all humanity" described by Lucian, with merciless derision, in his satire "The Passing of Peregrinus."[63] In the context of our inquiry, Lapshin's cursory but thought-provoking observations on the similarity of the two ideologically motivated suicides do not only highlight the comedic aspects of the narrated spectacles, but also remind us of the global context and scale of Ippolit's protest. The audience's unapologetically disparaging and, importantly, witty

---

[62] See *PSS*, 8: 314, 348, 349. The function of the audience's loud and unceremonious laughter in this scene can be generally categorized as public censure using the brief morphology of the functions of laughter in Dostoevsky developed in John Spiegel's *Dimensions of Laughter in Crime and Punishment*. Spiegel describes this type of laughter as "the laughter of negative sanction, exemplifying [...] the nonverbal equivalent of reprimand" in response to inappropriate or morally censured behavior, as when the townsfolk laugh at the jaywalking Raskolnikov, as it were, issuing a Greek-chorus-like response to his greater, future transgressions. See John Spiegel, *Dimensions of Laughter in Crime and Punishment* (London: Selingsgrove, 2000), 79. In *Dostoevskii i antichnost*, an essay based on his 1921 lecture, L. Pumpiansky mentions a similar chorus-like admonition of Dostoevsky's morally censured characters as a typical function of Dostoevskian laughter, linked to the ancient comical tradition: "taunting derision (*издевательство*) [in Dostoevsky] is always the task of the crowd that has gathered [around the character] and laughingly points to the unequivocally shameful that has been collectively acknowledged as ridiculous (laughable) (*смешное*)" Pumpiansky, *Dostoevskii i antichnost*, 520. In the Ippolit scene the expression of public sentiment in response to a violation of public decorum is, however, only one of the functions of group laughter.

[63] Lapshin, "Komicheskoe v proizvediniakh Dostoevskogo," 112.

reactions in both narratives foreground the glaring inadequacy of the heroes' response to perceived ontological injustice or challenge.[64]

The Cynic sect-leader Peregrinus announces and proceeds to perform an act of self-immolation in front of his disciples and other onlookers at the Olympic Games of 165 AD. Lucian, who claims to have witnessed the event, periodically interrupts his description of the spectacle with his own sneering laughter, in a sit-com fashion, as it were framing the tale by these irreverent and infectious chuckles:

> You can imagine, I expect, how I laughed: for it was not fitting to pity a man so desperately in love with glory beyond all others who are driven by the same Fury. Anyhow, he was being escorted by crowds and getting his fill of glory as he gazed at the number of his admirers, not knowing, poor wretch, that men on their way to the cross or in the grip of the executioner have many more at their heels.[65]

Lapshin argues that Dostoevsky's scene resembles Lucian's depiction of Peregrinus's pedagogical-turned-comical self-immolation in the crowd's bathetic

---

[64] The outlined similarities between Dostoevsky and Lucian are not intended as proof of Lucian's influence on Dostoevsky but as an example of analogous comedic situations that may help us better understand the role of laughter in a philosophical context. Although Mikhail Bakhtin famously suggested that Lucian, the "Voltaire of Antiquity," "well known in Russia beginning with the eighteenth century," was one of the likely sources of Dostoevsky's Menippean works, in particular, "Bobok," there is no evidence that Dostoevsky read Lucian. See Mikhail Bakhtin, *Sobranie sochinenii v semi tomakh*. Edited by S. G. Bocharov, et al., 7 vols. (Moscow: Russkie Slovari, 2002), 6:160, 162. Lucian's works are not attested for in Leonid Grossman's *Dostoevsky's Library* (*Biblioteka Dostoevskogo* [1919]); nor in the significantly expanded description of Dostoevsky's library compiled by Pushkinskii Dom in 2005 (*Biblioteka Dostoevskoko: Opyt rekonstruktsii, Nauchnoe opisanie*) and several Dostoevsky scholars conclude that Dostoevsky likely knew some *translations* of Lucian's texts by famous eighteenth-century Russian poets (such as Lomonosov and Sumarokov), which sometimes strayed rather far from the original, and it is this "mediated" Lucian that may have impacted the structure and content of "Bobok" (Khamitov, 32). Both M. Khamitov and N. Podosokorsky also emphasize Dostoevsky's likely familiarity with some of the numerous examples of the "Dialogues of the Dead" genre created by Russian writers in the eighteenth and nineteenth centuries as original, independent works (Kheraskov, Priklonsky, Sumarokov, etc.); nevertheless, Lucian is considered the progenitor and standard setter of this genre in the Russian tradition. See M. P. Khamitov, "Razgovory v tsarstve mertvykh: 'Bobok' F.M. Dostoevskogo," *Dostoevskii. Materialy iissledovaniia*, vol. 21 (2016): 31; and Nikolai Podosokorskii, "Zagrobnyi mir v rasskaze F. M. Dostoevskogo 'Bobok'," *Dostoevskii i mirovaiia kultura*, vol. 1 (2023): 76. In his analysis of "Bobok" S. Shul'ts draws a number of parallels between Dostoevsky and Lucian, noting, for example, both authors' active engagement with current events and topical issues of the day in their respective works (S. A Shul'ts, "Zhanrovaia traditsiia 'dialogov mertvykh' v rasskaze Dostoevskogo 'Bobok'," *Izvestiia RAN: Seriia literatury i iazyka*, vol. 72, no. 3 [2013]: 30). Whether or not Dostoevsky ever read "The Passing of Peregrinus," it is clear that he was at least aware of the general genre of antique "dialogues," saturated with rigorously debated philosophical content and infused with comedy, if not in its original expression, then through later imitators.

[65] Lucian of Samasota. *Lucian*. Translated by A. M. Harmon, 8 vols (Cambridge, MA: Harvard University Press, 1935–9) 5: 39.

reaction to the solemnly staged public suicide.⁶⁶ The Cynic Peregrinus proclaims that he will teach humanity to despise death by publically burning himself and calls his disciples to follow his example, but secretly expects those disciples to talk him out of the act instead, Lucian tells us mockingly.⁶⁷ In the context of his "Necessary Explanation," Ippolit's intended suicide is a similarly public expression of his ostensible disdain for life, a costly statement he too would secretly like to see interrupted by his involuntary audience, as Lapshin implicitly notes.⁶⁸ Not unlike Ippolit, Peregrinus is shocked that many of the spectators are joyfully calling his bluff, nudging him into the fire, as Lucian chuckles:

> I would swear a solemn oath that none of the gods will be upset if that rogue Peregrinus dies a rogue's death. [...] it's not easy for him to withdraw now, the surrounding cynics are egging him on and pushing him into the fire [...] If on his way into the flames he takes a couple of them with him, he will at least have one good deed to his credit!⁶⁹

In addition to the intriguing similarities noted by Lapshin, which also include the general tragicomic quality of both suicide scenes and the depiction of cynicism in the sense of "shamelessness" in both Lucian and Dostoevsky, there are additional parallels between the two scenes.⁷⁰ Peregrinus, who suffers from severe food poisoning nine days before his scheduled suicide, could simply let nature take its course; instead, he begs the doctors to treat him. When death is itself knocking at the door, why not simply follow her, without resorting to fire?, Lucian asks caustically.⁷¹ Echoing Lucian, not Peregrinus, and including this amusing irony in his own jocular response to the Global Joker, Ippolit tells us that he is aware that if he only waited two or three weeks, the same result would be reached quite naturally, so why go to all that trouble!⁷² The proposed timing of the two planned suicides also aligns. Peregrinus initially plans to pray to the

---

⁶⁶ Lapshin, "Komicheskoe v proizvediniakh Dostoevskogo," 112.
⁶⁷ Lucian, 5: 39.
⁶⁸ Lapshin, "Komicheskoe v proizvediniakh Dostoevskogo," 112.
⁶⁹ Lucian, 5: 31, translation modified.
⁷⁰ In another section of his essay, Lapshin notes the frequent and deliberate pairing of tragic and comic elements in Dostoevsky's prose, where "comedy is often tragicomedy," as Dostoevsky tends to "conclude[e] tragic situations with a spiteful satirical outburst." Some of these tragicomic and seriocomic moments result from the characters' cynical derision directed at their peers and the imperfect world around them, others are examples of Dostoevsky's post-romantic macabre humor, Lapshin concludes. See Lapshin, "Komicheskoe v proizvediniakh Dostoevskogo," 113–14.
⁷¹ Lucian, 5: 49.
⁷² PSS, 8: 343–4.

rising sun, and Ippolit plans to end his life at sunrise, addressing his rejection of life "to the source of power and life."[73]

The *tragic* inconsistency of Ippolit's stance comes to the fore through the *comic* incongruity of his actions, the glaring discrepancy between word and deed that his unsentimental audience finds positively annoying, as they all but kick him into the fire, quite like many spectators in Lucian's satire who shout, "Carry out your purpose!"[74] Lucian's Peregrinus presents himself as innocent and blameless, and thus markedly different because he *chooses* death, in contrast to those sentenced to the scaffold or the cross as punishment. Yet, Lucian contends that he deserves the fate of the latter as a rapist and murderer. Ippolit, too, considers murder instead of suicide as an alternative final joke of his life ("*для шутки*") and presents a real danger to others, not only to himself, as Evgenii Pavlovich reminds us.[75] The pretentiousness of Peregrinus's pose is exposed by Lucian, who calls him out for making his followers feel partly responsible for his death by forcibly including them in the unsavory spectacle. In *The Idiot*, this chastisement seems to be echoed by the outraged Lebedev, from whose property Ippolit is about to make his "private" exit into eternity: "Oh, so he thinks he won't bother anyone if he only takes three steps into the garden."[76]

The inadequacy of Ippolit's response to the global joker and the weakness of his own ontological laughter evident in this scene are caused by his fixation on his existential injury and retaliation. In these aspects his protest closely approximates a *ressentiment* rebellion, as it becomes utterly dominated by the negated values. Unlike Pumpiansky's liberating laughter that overcomes the tyranny of purpose, his performance becomes strictly goal-oriented and reactive in Nietzsche's terms, it is used merely as a weapon in the cycle of hurting and being hurt, of mocking others (and the Absolute Other) and being mocked in return. Instead of having the last laugh, he is becoming ever more painfully aware of his own ridiculousness in a solipsistic universe, where he is ontologically stranded. Unlike the spiritually freeing Solovievian laughter that provides a channel to other worlds, Ippolit's humor is too weak and fainthearted to unlatch his stifling universe of tyrannical natural laws, tragically locked within itself. This humbling revelation could eventually turn Ippolit toward the

---

[73] *PSS*, 8: 344.
[74] Lucian, 5: 39.
[75] *PSS*, 8: 342; 8: 350.
[76] *PSS*, 8: 347.

microcosm, leading to the apprehension of the Absolute Other in the human other (Christian neighbor, *ближний*), but his window of opportunity is closing. To rephrase Ivan Karamazov's observation, this final irony could be amusing, if it weren't so unbearably sad.

The question of a productive response to ontological mockery remains largely open in Dostoevsky's world, which places it firmly, if frustratingly, among the rest of his notorious "accursed questions" that inspire ceaseless debate. It yields no facile answer because, like Ivan Karamazov's grievances against God and His world, the confounding contradictions that comprise the searing content of ontological comedy cannot be easily dismissed. If we are to accept Scheler's recommended remedies for handling the "straining" *ressentiment*-inducing dilemmas, a thoroughly affirmative, active approach, via empathy, forgiveness, or even the less noble route of revenge, would be in order. But that would necessitate a belief in one's individual freedom, which is achievable, at times, through some version of a leap of faith in Dostoevsky's universe. Laughter, with its inherently visceral quality and irradicable, partly physiologically grounded, link to life-affirmation may be the next best thing for those heroes for whom the more direct pathways to affirmation, like faith and neighborly love, are not available. A surprisingly valid response to the ontological joke then may simply be to laugh at it and to witness the irreverent, authority-destroying energy of comedic probing envelop the global joker and his subjects alike. Laughing it off, as in the case of the Underground Man's rather embittered laughter at the ontological chicken coop and at himself *almost* daring to give it the finger, may not solve the tragic impasse behind the ontological joke on the intellectual level, but it temporarily strips the global stone wall of its formidable authority, dispelling fear—a major obstacle to love in Dostoevsky.

After all, if Lapshin is right in suggesting that it is "the very nature of things" that is funny to Dostoevsky and his hero,[77] then it is only logical that the latter should laugh vigorously and uproariously *at* "the nature of things," and that includes the dreaded "laws of nature" and other rigidly totalitarian forces that symbolize indomitable determinism in Dostoevsky's world. By doing so, the Dostoevskian comedian could move toward that Solovievian "metaphysical

---

[77] "It is not merely the imperfection of the social structure [that Maupassant and Dostoevsky find funny] but the very nature of things (*сама природа вещей*), [i.e. the world order]: ... egoism, lust and spite that is inherent in man's very nature." Lapshin, "Komicheskoe v proizvediniakh Dostoevskogo," 119.

freedom" that "manifests itself unawares" in laughter and opens our eyes to a higher, spiritually liberating reality but cannot be reached by a purely cerebral effort, without the crucial engagement of the vital sphere and the heart.[78]

Bibliography

Bakhtin, Mikhail. *Sobranie sochinenii v semi tomakh*. Edited by S. G. Bocharov, et al., 7 vols. vol. 6. Moscow: Russkie Slovari, 2002.

Budanova, N. F. (ed.). *Biblioteka F.M. Dostoevskogo: Opyt rekontruktsii. Nauchnoe opisanie*. Edited by N. F. Budanova. Saint Petersburg: Nauka, 2005.

Dostoevsky, Fyodor. *Notes from Underground*. Translated and Edited by Michael R. Katz. New York and London: W. W. Norton & CO, 1989.

Dostoevsky, Fyodor. *Polnoe sobranie sochinenii v tridtsati tomakh*, 30 vols. Leningrad: Nauka, 1972-90.

Frank, Joseph. *Dostoevsky: The Stir of Liberation, 1860-1865*. Princeton: Princeton University Press, 1986.

Grossman, L. P. *Biblioteka Dostoevskogo. Po neizdannym materialam s prilozheniem kataloga biblioteki Dostoevskogo*. Odessa: Knigoizdatelstvo Ivasenko, 1919.

Khamitov, M. P. "Razgovory v tsarstve mertvykh: 'Bobok' F. M. Dostoevskogo," *Dostoevskii. aterialy iissledovaniia*, vol. 21 (2016): 29-43.

Kornblatt, Judith Deutsch. "On Laughter and Vladimir Solov'ev *Three Encounters*," *Slavic Review*, vol. 57, no. 3 (1998): 563-84.

Lapshin, I. I. "Komicheskoe v proizvediniakh Dostoevskogo," *O Dostoevskom: Sbornik Statei*. Edited by A. L. Bem, vol. 2, Prague: Petropolis, 1933, 2: 102-20.

Lucian of Samasota. *Lucian*, 8 vols. Translated by A. M. Harmon. Cambridge, MA: Harvard University Press, 1935-9.

Miller, Charles A. "Nietzsche's 'Discovery of Dostoevsky,'" *Nietzsche Studien*, vol. 2 (1973): 202-57.

Nietzsche, Friedrich. *The Complete Works of Friedrich Nietzsche*. Edited by Oscar Levy. Translated by Horace B. Samuel, 18 vols. Edinburgh and London: T.N. Fouli, 1909-13.

Podosokorskii, Nikolai. "Zagrobnyi mir v rasskaze F. M. Dosotevskogo 'Bobok,'" *Dostoevskii i mirovaiia kultura*, vol. 1 (2023): 62-95.

Pumpiansky, L. V. *Klassicheskaia traditisia. Sobranie trudov po istorii russkoi literatury*. Edited by A. P. Chudakov, E. M. Esserlin, and N. I. Nikolaev. Moscow: Iazyki russkoi literatury, 2000.

---

[78] Soloviev, *La Sophia*, 27.

Scheler, Max. *Gesammelte Werke*, 15 vols. Edited by Maria Scheler and Manfred Frings. Bern: Francke Verlag, 1954–97.

Scheler, Max. *Ressentiment*. Edited by Lewis A. Coser. Translated by William W. Holdheim. New York: Free Press of Glencoe, 1961.

Shestov, Lev. "Dostoevsky and Nietzsche: The Philosophy of Tragedy," *Essays in Russian Literature. The Conservative View: Leontiev, Rozanov, Shestov*. Edited by Spencer E. Roberts, 3–183. Athens, OH: Ohio University Press, 1968.

Shul'ts, S. A. "Zhanrovaia traditsiia 'dialogov mertvykh' v rasskaze Dostoevskogo 'Bobok,'" *Izvestiia RAN: Seriia literatury i iazyka*, vol. 72, no. 3 (2013): 26–30.

Soloviev, V. S. *La Sophia et les autres ecrits francais*. Edited by Francois Rouleau. Lausanne: L'Age D'Homme, 1978.

Soloviev, V. S. "Predisloviie k skazke E.T.A. Gofmana 'Zolotoi gorshok,'" in *Filosofiia iskusstva i literaturnaia kritika*. Edited by R. Gal'tseva and I. Rodnianskaia, 571–3. Moscow: Iskusstvo, 1991.

Soloviev, V. S. *Sobranie Sochinenii Vladimira Sergeevicha Solov'eva*, 9 vols. St. Petersburg: Obshchestvennaia Pol'za, 1901–7.

Spiegel, John. *Dimensions of Laughter in Crime and Punishment*. London: Selingsgrove, 2000.

Stellino, Paolo. *Nietzsche and Dostoevsky: On the Verge of Nihilism*. Bern: Peter Lang, 2015.

Tikhomirov, Boris (B.N.). "Khristos i Istina v poeme Ivana Karamazova 'Velikii inkvizitor,'" in *"Ia zanimaius' etoi tainoi, ibo khochu byt' chelovekom": stat'i i esse o Dostoevskom*. Petersburg: Serebriannyi Vek, 2012, 92–124.

Tikhomirov, Boris (B.N.). "'Kto zhe eto tak smeetsia nad chelovekom?' Motif 'ontologicheskoi nasmeshki v tvorchestve Dostoevskogo,'" *Dostoevsky Studies*, vol. 17 (2013): 73–97.

Wyman, Alina. *The Gift of Active Empathy: Scheler, Bakhtin, and Dostoevsky*. Evanston, IL: Northwestern University Press, 2016.

Wyman, Alina. "The Specter of Freedom: *Ressentiment* and Dostoevsky's *Notes from Underground*," *Studies in East European Thought*, vol. 59 (2007): 119–40.

6

"Too Dragged Out, Can't Understand a Thing": The Impatience of Youth in *Demons*

Chloe Papadopoulos

Где спех, там и смех—"Where there is haste, there is laughter." *Поспешишь— людей насмешишь*—"If you hurry people will laugh." These Russian proverbs caution against impatience: haste provokes laughter and, even, makes the one who hurries the object of laughter. They capture, on the one hand, the lighthearted humor of an impatient blunder and the ridiculousness that inevitably accompanies a rushed endeavor, and, on the other, implicitly privilege forbearance and patience. This tension, between the serious and staid and the laughable and rushed, is fundamental to Fyodor Dostoevsky's *Demons* (1871), which represents one of the author's strongest critiques of sudden, sweeping social upheaval. The novel's revolutionaries are equated with demons and the plot is punctuated by murder, madness, arson, and suicides. The reader is transfixed by the onslaught of sensational plot devices, gasping and laughing in turn as Dostoevsky's proverbial fathers and children play out their roles in the author's fictional take on the grotesque, immoral underbelly of the 1869 Nechaev-Ivanov affair.

Demons' critical stance vis-à-vis revolutionary social movements hinges on its rendering of the affair's real-life radical youths, whose fictional doubles exhibit a thirst for change that manifests as boisterous impatience—impatience that, like the youths themselves, is both menacing and downright hilarious. In this chapter, I focus on the role that humor plays in Dostoevsky's critique of radicalism and depiction of youth. Specifically, I explore the comedic potential of impatience in *Demons*, arguing that the dissonance between the desire for immediate and sweeping change and the continual deferral of its enactment

---

* I would like to thank Irina Erman and Lynn Ellen Patyk for their generous feedback on this chapter from its earliest stages and for creating this forum for reflecting on the light side of Dostoevsky.

contributes to the novel's humor and to its critical depiction of the revolutionary movement's insidious plans. In the case of this novel, where there is haste, there is, often, laughter, but there is also the potential for something far more sinister.

When I discuss "youth" in this chapter, I do so with an eye to the "multifaceted and diverse" appearances to which Dostoevsky famously referred in his 1873 polemic, "One of the Modern Falsehoods" about the radicalism of the younger generation, while at the same time noting a certain overarching characteristic associated with the novel's radical youths: namely, their impatience.[1] Demonstrating the vital, though often overlooked role of impatience in *Demons*, I focus on one instance in the novel in which youthful impatience is terribly funny: the name-day party at the Virginskie's in "With Our People" ("У наших"). Reading this scene through the incongruity and relief theories of humor, I analyze the interplay between the guests' feelings of anticipation and uncertainty about the nature of the party and their thwarted expectations, and show that youthful impatience provokes laughter and, thereby, diminishes the solemnity of the would-be revolutionaries' meeting, or *заседание*. In my analysis of this scene, I focus especially on the young Miss (*девица*) Virginskaia, a female student and social activist, whose declaration "[t]oo dragged out, can't understand a thing [*слишком долго тянете, ничего не поймешь*]" serves as the title to this chapter precisely for its ability to capture the bellicosity and humor that I argue define the novel's representation of radical youths and allow us to situate and to better appreciate Dostoevsky's views about them within a broader field of cultural-historical studies of youth as a cultural category.[2]

Revolutionary Terrorism

Impatience is vital to the revolutionary movement's momentum in *Demons*, and to the novel's plot structure more broadly. Many of the novel's primary actors and episodes are defined by impatience, rashness, and pique. Take, for example, the dramatic and scandalous scene at Varvara Petrovna's in chapters four and

---

[1] Fyodor Dostoevsky, *PSS*, 21: 131.

[2] *PSS*, 10: 305; 394. Translations of *Demons* that are not mine are taken from Fyodor Dostoevsky, *Demons*. Translated by Richard Pevear and Larissa Volokhonsky (New York: Random House, 1994) and will appear directly following the pagination from Fyodor Dostoevsky, *PSS*, vol. 10 (Leningrad: Nauka, 1974) and a semicolon throughout.

five of Part One, during which some guests impatiently await a "catastrophe" and others rush to bring it to fruition.³ At times, it seems that the entire town is hastily jumping to conclusions, especially about the enigmatic Nikolai Stavrogin. When Stavrogin reappears in society after his duel with Gaganov, for instance, the novel's narrator-chronicler, G-v emphasizes that "all the eyes turned on [Stavrogin]" were filled with "impatient expectations [нетерпеливые ожидания]."⁴ Even the seemingly staid G-v doggedly rushes from place to place, trying to catch up on (and sometimes intervene in) town events that outpace and confound him. "With Our People," as I will show, is also characterized by a prevailing sense of anticipation that provokes impatience and gives way to confusion and unrestrained irritation.

The recurrent role of impatience in *Demons*' characterization and plot structure is undoubtedly linked to the novel's exploration of the causes and consequences of revolutionary terrorism and of the rapid social change occasioned by The Great Reforms of the 1860s and 1870s. In *Demons*, many who seek to bring about radical social change are depicted as young and impatient. These characters, in their desire to transform society, experience a temporal dissonance that is essential to impatience. This dissonance, discussed further below, might be best described as the desire to immediately see a goal that is presently unrealizable realized. The immediacy of the revolutionary upheaval that they desire is at odds with their stagnated reality, as well as with the gradual reform and the bureaucratic process that it entails. In this way, the impulse that underlies efforts to hasten social change is a fundamentally impatient one. Petr Verkhovensky emphasizes the problem of speed when he demands that the group of radicals assembled in "With Our People" declare whether they prefer the "slow route [...] or [a] quick solution," "a turtle's pace through the swamp, or full steam across it."⁵ Claudia Verhoeven writes that terrorism has frequently been treated as "an expression of political impatience" and that impatience is a trait that is often attributed not only to terrorists, but to all revolutionaries.⁶

³ *PSS*, 10: 127.
⁴ *PSS*, 10: 234.
⁵ *PSS*, 10: 315 and 316; 408, translation modified.
⁶ Claudia Verhoeven, "Time of Terror, Terror of Time: On the Impatience of Russian Revolutionary Terrorism (Early 1860s–Early 1880s)," *Jahrbücher für Geschichte Osteuropas*, vol. 58, no. H. 2 (2010): 254, 255. I am inclined to the classification of "revolutionaries" within the context of *Demons*. For consideration of and use of the term "terrorism" in relation to *Demons*, see Lynn Ellen Patyk, *Written in Blood: Revolutionary Terrorism and Russian Literary Culture, 1861-1881* (Madison: University of Wisconsin Press, 2017), 105–9.

The impatience that is ascribed to these figures, Verhoeven observes, presumes a violation of "the hegemony of bourgeois modernity's dominant regime of time."[7] Terrorists and revolutionaries, in other words, seek to accelerate the "natural or agreed-upon pace" of historical progress.[8]

Ilya Kliger identifies impatience as fundamental to one of *Crime and Punishment*'s emplotment scenarios. Kliger writes that Raskol'nikov has a "desire to know immediately" and "[to step] over stages in time."[9] His crime (or great deed), Kliger contends, represents a "radically accelerated time," which corresponds to "the time of revolution."[10] This temporal model very much resembles the temporal acceleration associated with *Demons*' radicals' activities, or emplotment scenarios. Miss Virginskaia's "[t]oo dragged out, can't understand a thing" is not simply an attempt to shut down her interlocutor, a high school boy with whom she verbally spars in "With Our People"; it is an indictment of protracted ideological progressivism that is embroiled in processes that defer the fulfilment of desired change. Miss Virginskaia's intensity and relentlessness read like an extreme reaction to "utter inertness" and "apathy," characteristics Nikolai Dobroliubov, in his 1859 review of Ivan Goncharov's *Oblomov* (1859), attributed not only to the novel's eponymous hero, but also to Russian society as a whole.[11] In his review, Dobroliubov saw Oblomov as something like a tipping point and, to quote Sarah Ruth Lorenz, "transform[ed] Goncharov's fabulously lazy protagonist into a sign of the coming revolution."[12]

Set almost one decade after *Oblomov*, *Demons* portrays the inverse of indifference and inaction by depicting a character type that Dobroliubov—himself a twenty-three-year-old at the time of writing his review—seems to have been craving as a remedy on the eve of the emancipation reform. Within the context of Dobroliubov's vision of revolutionary democracy, impatience is a virtue, whereas for Dostoevsky, whose novel was written in the wake of Ivanov's murder, it is associated with the demonic, which, as Val Vinokur has

---

[7] Verhoeven, "Time of Terror, Terror of Time," 254.

[8] Ibid.

[9] Ilya Kliger, "Shapes of History and the Enigmatic Hero in Dostoevsky: The Case of *Crime and Punishment*," *Comparative Literature*, vol. 62, no. 3 (Summer 2010): 236.

[10] Ibid., 229.

[11] Nikolai Dobroliubov, "Chto takoe Oblomovshchina?," *Sovremennik* LXXV otd. III (1859): 67.

[12] Sarah Ruth Lorenz, "Realist Convictions and Revolutionary Impatience in the Criticism of N. A. Dobroliubov," *SEEJ*, vol. 57, no. 1 (Spring 2013): 81.

persuasively argued, accommodates and amplifies the comic in Dostoevsky.[13] It is no coincidence that G-v, upon first meeting Verkhovensky, characterizes him in the following way:

> He speaks rapidly, hurriedly [скоро, торопливо], but at the same time self-confidently, and is never at a loss for words. His thoughts are calm, despite his hurried look [торопливый вид], distinct and final—and that is especially noticeable. His enunciation is remarkably clear; his words spill out like big, uniform grains, always choice and always ready to be at your service. You like it at first, but later it will become repulsive, and precisely because of this all too clear enunciation, this string of ever ready words. You somehow begin to imagine that the tongue in his mouth must be of some special form, somehow unusually long and this, terribly red, and with an extremely sharp, constantly and involuntarily wriggling tip.[14]

Verkhovensky's speech is rushed, but it is also deliberate and always oriented toward a goal. In this way, his communicative style does not accommodate discourse.[15] Instead, it functions in service of his ambitions; and, through it, the revolutionary ringleader seeks to tempt and to manipulate his interlocutor, just as the serpent (Nachash), with whom Verkhovensky is equated in this excerpt, did in the Garden of Eden. As David Bethea and Victoria Thorstensson have shown, however, Dostoevsky's comparison was not merely a biblical allusion, but also drew on contemporary anti-nihilist rhetoric, which frequently compared nihilists to animals in order to criticize their misapplication of Darwinist theories about evolution in nature.[16] *Demons*' representation of Verkhovensky as a serpent gestures to critical debates concerning the nihilist's desire to forcibly speed up the pace of historical and evolutionary time; it suggests that "demonic suddenness," as Vinokur refers to it, can be just as ineffectual as the apathy of Goncharov's bedridden aristocrat.[17] In notes dating between 1860 and 1862,

---

[13] Val Vinokur, "All of a Sudden: Dostoevsky's Demonologies of Terror," in *Just Assassins: The Culture of Terrorism in Russia*. Edited by Anthony Anemone (Evanston: Northwestern University Press, 2010), 53–72.

[14] *PSS*, 10: 143; 180.

[15] For more on this topic, see Adam Weiner, "Narrative Possession in *The Devils*," in *By Authors Possessed: The Demonic Novel in Russia* (Evanston: Northwestern University Press, 1998), 93–137.

[16] David Bethea and Victoria Thorstensson, "Darwin, Dostoevsky, and Russia's Radical Youth," in *Dostoevsky beyond Dostoevsky: Science, Philosophy, Religion*. Edited by Svetlana Evdokimova and Vladimir Golstein (Boston: Academic Studies Press, 2016), 55–6.

[17] Vinokur, "All of a Sudden: Dostoevsky's Demonologies of Terror," 65.

Dostoevsky wrote that society was not ready for the kind of social change that was then being proposed by thinkers such as Chernyshevsky, an imaginary interlocutor in the notes to whom Dostoevsky, evoking Nikolai Gogol, addresses the question, "[w]here are you hurrying [*торопитесь*]?"[18]

Impatience

Impatience in *Demons* is associated with eagerness, restlessness, discomfort, and, above all, the inability to wait. For example, upon first meeting Stepan Trofimovich, Kirillov listens to him "with awkward impatience."[19] Captain Lebyadkin is in a "frenzied fit of impatience [*нетерпения*]" when he fumblingly attempts to pay Varvara Petrovna twenty rubles in "The Wise Serpent."[20] G-v states that Varvara Petrovna receives the "new people" in St. Petersburg, "expecting" much of them, with "all of a woman's hysterical impatience [*нетерпением*]."[21] Men of the "previous generation" who followed the likes of "Chaadaev, Belinsky, Granovsky, and Herzen" are dubbed "hurrying [*торопившимися*] people."[22] Stepan Trofimovich refers to the Russian people as "hurried [*торопливые*]" when discussing the emancipation of the serfs.[23] Liza's speech and movements are described as "hurried" four times in quick succession when she proposes her prospective book project to Shatov.[24]

Two Russian terms that appear in the text to signal impatience most distinctly are *нетерпение* (impatience) and *торопиться* (to rush), and derivations of its root, *-тороп-*, like *торопливо* (hastily) and *торопливый* (hasty). *Нетерпение* is particularly important for *Demons* because, unlike *торопиться*, this form of impatience accommodates the expression of affect. While not an emotion itself, impatience certainly has an affective dimension (it frequently evokes or is coupled with an affective state). For example, impatience can convey positive affect when experienced in conjunction with excitement (take, for

---

[18] *PSS*, 20: 153.
[19] *PSS*, 10: 75; 92.
[20] *PSS*, 10: 138; 173.
[21] *PSS*, 10: 22; 23.
[22] *PSS*, 10: 8; 8.
[23] *PSS*, 10: 31; 35.
[24] For example: "*торопливо прибавила она*"; "*торопливо схватила* [...] *пачку газет*"; "*торопилась Лиза*"; "*покраснев и торопясь стала объяснять нам Лиза*" in *PSS*, 10: 105 and 106.

instance, the sentiment that underlies phrases like, "I cannot wait to see your play!"). More often, it is associated with negative affect: namely, with irritation and "its close relations," described by Sianne Ngai as "bother, annoyance, vexation, aggravation, [and] pique."[25] Vladimir Dal' denoted the affective side of *нетерпение* by equating the term with hatred (*ненависть к чему*).[26] In the context of the novel, *нетерпение*'s affective connotation is markedly negative and can be best conveyed by the English phrase, "I have absolutely no patience for so-and-so."

Broadly speaking, we might trace the progress of impatience as follows: an individual has a desire that he or she would like to see realized; when the desire is not achieved within an expected or an acceptable timeframe, the individual grows impatient; the longer the desire remains unsatisfied, the more impatient he or she will grow. The goal toward which the individual strives must feel imminent and achievable, but, like Tantalus's fruit, just beyond reach. Indeed, the philosopher and literary critic Maurice Blanchot wrote that impatience implies a belief that "the goal is close or that one is coming nearer to it."[27] Impatience is contingent upon this temporal dissonance and, often, upon an external circumstance that is beyond the control of the individual who experiences impatience. As the individual waits for his or her desire to come to fruition, he or she may attempt to exhibit agency, or to usurp control of that which is preventing the achievement of his or her goal. The individual may act unpredictably and unexpectedly.

In *Demons*, the unexpected becomes inextricably bound up with the experience of impatience, which is indicated through the frequent use of adverbs of time, such as "suddenly" (*вдруг*), "instantly" (*мигом*), and "quickly" (*скоро*), and the description of rushed movements, signaled by verbs like "to twitch" (*дернуться*), "to jump up" (*подскакивать, привскочить*), and "to fly in" (*влететь*). In the words of Greta Matzner-Gore, "[I]n Dostoevsky's fiction, the unexpected rules."[28] Its prominence in Dostoevsky's poetics has been the subject of scholarly interest for the better part of a century. Vladimir Toporov famously recognized the

---

[25] Sianne Ngai, *Ugly Feelings* (Cambridge: Harvard University Press, 2005), 181.

[26] Vladimir Dal', *Tolkovyi slovar' zhivogo velikorusskogo iazyka*, vol. 2 (Saint Petersburg-Moscow: M.O. Vol'f, 1905), 1398.

[27] Maurice Blanchot, *The Space of Literature*. Translated by Ann Smock (Lincoln: University of Nebraska Press, 1982), 79.

[28] Greta Matzner-Gore, "The Improbable Poetics of *Crime and Punishment*," in *Dostoevsky at 200: The Novel in Modernity*. Edited by Katherine Bowers and Kate Holland (Toronto: University of Toronto Press, 2021), 166.

frequency with which "suddenly" appears in *Crime and Punishment* (560 times) and identified a connection between sudden occurrences, moments of transition, and emotional transformation.[29] More recently, the significance of suddenness has informed scholarship on Dostoevsky's engagement with contemporary statistical analysis and scientific discovery.[30] Jerky and hurried movements have likewise been considered within the context of the unexpected, being characteristic of many of Dostoevsky's troubled protagonists. Eric Naiman, for example, observes that "starting involuntarily is a hallmark of Dostoevskian motor response."[31] In his analysis of "The Double," Naiman considers Golyadkin's jarring movements as signs of authorial intervention, showing that the fractured protagonist's physicality reflects the lack of control he exerts over his own life. In *Demons*, startling, abrupt, and unexpected movements are similarly linked to loss of control; the experience of impatience is dominated by a recognition of such a loss and, in the case of this novel, motivates a desire to bend time to one's will, compressing it in order to (suddenly) bring an intangible goal to fruition.

Impatience can also emerge as an obstinate refusal to surrender to another's pace or to time itself, as an assertion of one will over another. In this case, impatience may lead to rash action. Philip Fisher writes that rashness is a feature of an inflamed will that "translates" a vehement state into action.[32] Rashness stands in contrast to reflection and its thoughtful conversion into deliberate action: to act rashly is to act suddenly and unthinkingly and, for this reason, "the rash act and the premeditated act are nearly antipodal."[33] For Fisher, rashness is to the passions as deliberation is to the rational will.[34] It takes place "within the narrow time frame of the immediate past and the imminent future."[35] If we consider this temporal definition within the context of impatience, then, for the impatient individual, rash action offers an outlet and reprieve from the

---

[29] V. N. Toporov, "O strukture romana Dostoevskogo v sviazi s arkhaichnymi skhemami mifologicheskogo myshleniia," in *Structure of Texts and Semiotics of Culture*. Edited by Jan van der Eng and Mojmir Grygar (The Hague: Mouton, 1973), 233–6.

[30] See especially Matzner-Gore; Alexey Vdovin, "Dostoevsky, Sechenov, and the Reflexes of the Brain: Towards a Stylistic Genealogy of *Notes from Underground*," in *Dostoevsky at 200: The Novel in Modernity*. Edited by Bowers and Holland; and "Introduction: Fiction beyond Fiction: Dostoevsky's Quest for Realism," in *Dostoevsky Beyond Dostoevsky*. Edited by Evdokimova and Golstein, 1–34.

[31] Eric Naiman, "What If Nabokov Had Written 'Dvoinik'? Reading Literature Preposterously," *The Russian Review*, vol. 64, no. 4 (October 2005): 580.

[32] Philip Fisher, *The Vehement Passions* (Princeton: Princeton University Press, 2009), 102.

[33] Ibid., 101.

[34] Ibid., 102.

[35] Ibid.

seemingly inexorable present of impatience, but does not guarantee an escape from it. Impatience and rashness do not, however, always "translate" into action. According to Aristotle's *Nicomachean Ethics*, the rash person acts impulsively, but, being fundamentally uncourageous, is unlikely to act out their impulse when faced with a dangerous situation.[36] In a similar vein, if impatience is affective and provokes irritation, then it might not actually occasion any action at all. According to Ngai, irritation is among the "weakest, mildest, and most politically effete" forms of negative and dysphoric affect and is therefore unlikely to contribute significantly to "any oppositional praxis or ideological struggle."[37] The outcome of impatience is, in other words, unpredictable; it may provoke rash, passionate action or it may come to absolutely nothing. In *Demons*, impatience represents potential, and this potential invites the unexpected, the power of which is fundamental to the execution of the revolutionaries' plans.

Youth

If revolutionary temporality is fundamentally impatient, then it seems only natural that those who seek to bring about revolution can also be characterized as impatient. Impatience in *Demons* is associated particularly strongly with recent social change, and, equally so, with the youths who seek such change, among whom are included Verkhovensky, Shatov, and Kirillov (despite the fact that they are about twenty-seven, they are introduced as young men).[38] In the novel, as well as in essays like "Something about Youth" (1876) and "Isolated Phenomena" (1876), Dostoevsky conceived of Russian youths within collective terms. *Demons*' youths are portrayed as a population at the helm of revolutionary activity in the capitals and the provinces. At one point, G-v states that the "old [greybeard]" Karamzinov was deeply concerned about his relations with "the progressive young men of both capitals": "The great writer trembled morbidly before the newest revolutionary young men."[39] In "Filibusters," Andrei Antonovich von Lembke responds to Stepan Trofimovich's admission that he delivered lectures to "the youth" by exclaiming "'[y]o-o-outh!' [*ю-но-шеству!*] [...] 'That, my very

---

[36] Aristotle, *Nicomachean Ethics*. Translated by Joe Sachs (Newburyport: Focus Publishing, 2002), 50.
[37] Ngai, *Ugly Feelings*, 181.
[38] Each is called a *молодой человек* in the original, see *PSS*, 10: 54, 28, 75; 65, 30, 91.
[39] *PSS*, 10: 69; 85 and *PSS*, 10: 170; 213.

dear sir, I will not allow,' [...] 'I do not allow youth. It's all these tracts. It's a raid [*наскок*] upon society, my dear sir, a sea raid, filibusterism ...'"⁴⁰ Lembke imagines "youth" not as an age category, but as an ideological position that one can forbid from existing and as an attack to be fended off—the sudden and jumpy nature of which is clear in the Russian *наскок*, with its relation to the verb "to jump" (*наскочить, наскакивать*).

The notion of youth in *Demons* does not represent a clearly delimited or culturally cohesive category, at least as it has been understood in Europe and the United States since the Second World War.⁴¹ There was, nonetheless, a recognition of discreet age categories during the historical moment that the novel depicts. For example, the age of majority for criminal cases was seventeen and the age of full majority was twenty-one; under Catherine II's 1785 law, one could own property at seventeen, but could not engage in property transactions (such as mortgaging or selling) without the permission of a parent or guardian until twenty-one.⁴² Such legal boundaries are represented in the novel's rendering of Stepan Trofimovich's mishandled stewardship of his son's land. Attempting to ease his guilty conscience when explaining to Varvara Petrovna that he, effectively, stole from his son, Stepan emphasizes the then-palpable generational gap between the men of the forties and sixties; he imagines a scenario in which he "would show former fathers and former people generally in such a disinterested and magnanimous light, as compared with the new frivolous and social youth."⁴³ His son may be of legal age, but he, nevertheless, belongs to the "new" youth.

The former people, among whom Stepan counts himself, imagine themselves to be dignified and magnanimous, and, therefore, superior to the new youth. Indeed, as von Lembke's outcry demonstrates, the term "youth" is used pejoratively by the old guard, who are averse to the generational transition taking place amid the reforms. In the words of Yulia Mikhailovna, the youth are being pushed into an "abyss" by the "intolerance of all these old codgers

---

⁴⁰ *PSS*, 10: 344–5; 447.

⁴¹ Notably, Richard Ivan Jobs, *Riding the New Wave: Youth and the Rejuvenation of France after the Second World War* (Stanford: Stanford University Press, 2007).

⁴² For more on this particular law in the nineteenth century, see Sergei Antonov, *Bankrupts and Usurers of Imperial Russia: Debt, Property, and the Law in the Age of Dostoevsky and Tolstoy* (Cambridge: Harvard University Press, 2016), especially "Usurer's Tales"; and N. C. Tagantsev, *Issledovaniia ob otvestvennosti maloletnikh prestupnikov po russkomu pravu i proekt zakonopolozhenii ob etom voprose* (Saint Petersburg: Tipografiia A.M. Kotomina, 1871). Many thanks to Sergei Antonov for his valuable reading suggestions on this topic.

⁴³ *PSS*, 10: 63; 76.

[*старикашек*]."⁴⁴ The older generation's views on the youth are made especially clear on the day following Stavrogin's duel with Gaganov, when certain members of the town gather in celebration of Yulia Mikhailovna. At the event, the townspeople come to the conclusion that Stavrogin did not challenge Shatov for his slap not because of some intrigue, as they had believed, but because he would not deign to challenge his former serf. Those present are delighted by this revelation; one old man (*старичок*) suggests that Stavrogin is now not a member of the "youth" (*молодежь*), he is, on the contrary, a "star."⁴⁵ In other words, when his behavior confounded society and flouted its conventions, Stavrogin was a part of the youth and ought to be derided; when it is discovered that he, on the contrary, supposedly respects pre-reform hierarchy, he becomes a star precisely because, despite being young, he behaves in the old way.

A character's impatience, regardless of his or her age, often gestures to youthful naiveté, impetuosity, capriciousness, and an inclination to radical thinking.⁴⁶ There is a quixotic volatility to youth that favors movement between extremes. Stavrogin's character trajectory certainly traces a path from one extreme state to another: he begins the novel (in its prehistory) as a spontaneous rebel, who goes about biting ears and pulling noses, only to transform into a mannequin-like shell. Speaking of Shatov's convictions, Stepan Trofimovich says: "[T]he man changed his former, perhaps too youthful, but still correct ideas too abruptly."⁴⁷ Shatov is likewise described as "one of those ideal Russian beings who can suddenly be so struck by some strong idea that it seems to crush them."⁴⁸ Miss Virginskaia shares this quality, exemplifying extreme, almost performative impatience. Her behavior at the name-day party is one of the most obvious examples of how age, impatience, and subversive ideas coalesce in the world of the novel. She has been overcome by a passion for decrying the plight of the

---

⁴⁴ *PSS*, 10: 236.

⁴⁵ *PSS*, 10: 233.

⁴⁶ Impatience is not solely exhibited by the novel's young characters, but also by the novel's parents (intellectual and biological). This is especially true of Stepan Trofimovich, whose impatience is often described as hysterical and sentimental. Stepan's ceaseless letter writing is a symptom of compulsive impatience and insecurity; he obsessively attempts to anticipate his interlocutor's reactions to his admissions of inadequacy, and his expressions of his desires and fears. Stepan's adverse impact upon the development of his former students is implied throughout the novel, as well as in Dostoevsky's explanatory essays. In "One of the Modern Falsehoods," the author likewise condemns the generation of liberal fathers for infecting the youths with their cynicism and lack of patriotic feeling. In so doing, Dostoevsky writes the fathers into the developmental trajectory of the contemporary youths and invites his reader to imagine their culpability.

⁴⁷ *PSS*, 10: 76; 94.

⁴⁸ *PSS*, 10: 27; 30.

students before all of Russia, beginning with the guests at her relatives' name-day party, which one might define as a comical series of miscommunications that arise as a result of rushed and disordered exchanges and to which I now turn with the aim of examining how impatience, youth, and ambiguity combine to create a truly hilarious series of events.

"With Our People"

At the name-day party, a ramshackle group of would-be radicals and out-of-place relatives gather around the table to assemble politically under the guise of a celebration. What ensues is a disorderly series of debates about approaches to public issues and the enigmatic cause. It is during this scene that Shigalev articulates his infamous social system, referred to jestingly by the guests as "Shigalev's despair."[49] In my analysis of the Virginskie's gathering, rather than focus on the gravity of the Shigalevian future, however, I analyze the levity of the scene's comedic timing. Nowhere is the funny side of impatience clearer than in the case of the acerbic "student and nihilist," Miss Virginskaia, who represents a rare instance of female-led activism in Dostoevsky, but who is also a cultural-historical parody of women nihilists of the 1860s.[50] Recently returned from the capital with the hope of instigating a student protest, she shouts at, pounces upon, and eviscerates her meandering male interlocutors, but, ironically, never manages to get to her point.

Setting out to describe the party, G-v notes that around fifteen guests, "almost all men," representing "the flower of the brightest red liberalism" had assembled around two tables in the middle of a large, blue-wallpapered drawing room.[51] The drawn-together tables, covered with a "not quite clean" tablecloth, were set with twenty-five glasses, two samovars, and a basket of sliced bread.[52] G-v writes that the scene, especially the table setting, was reminiscent of "upper-class male and female children's boarding schools."[53] Only three women are present: the hostess, Arina Prokhorovna and her "browless," "venomous"

---

[49] *PSS*, 10: 311.
[50] *PSS*, 10: 302; 390.
[51] *PSS*, 10: 302.
[52] *PSS*, 10: 301; 389.
[53] Ibid.

sister, as well as Miss Virginskaia.⁵⁴ The party's overall tenor is as if designed to provoke a fit of impatience in its guests; everyone sits in expectation, biding time until the arrival of the group's ringleader, Verkhovensky and the aloof, mysterious Stavrogin: "obviously they were all waiting for something [*все чего-то ждали*], and, while waiting [*в ожидании*], engaged each other in loud but as if irrelevant conversation."⁵⁵ Arina looks upon her guests silently, "with a dauntless gaze"; her sister silently pours tea; her husband, unwell, is sunk in an armchair. Miss Virginskaia, sitting next to her aunt, is also silent, "studying the guests with impatient, leaping eyes [*разглядывала гостей нетерпеливыми прыгающими глазами*]."⁵⁶ The guests have been informed that they will learn "something especially curious" at the gathering.⁵⁷ All of the attendees, including Verkhovensky's hand-picked revolutionary cell, have been kept in the dark about the nature of the meeting. The withholding of this coveted information has everyone on edge; not only do they not know what to expect, they do not know who is "theirs" (viz., ours/*наши*, as per the chapter's title) and who is not: "in the end all of those gathered suspected each other, and assumed various postures in front of each other, which indeed lent the whole gathering a rather incoherent and even partly romantic appearance."⁵⁸ Because almost everyone present is on tenterhooks, there is an intense sense of urgency in the room.

In this scene, and throughout the novel, expectation and impatience go hand in hand. One need only think of the general atmosphere of expectation that is reflected in titles like, "All in Expectation" ("*Все в ожидании*") and in episodes like the much-anticipated Fete, which fills von Lembke with "strange and sinister forebodings."⁵⁹ The longer the characters are forced to wait for something to be revealed or accomplished, the more impatient, rash, and affected they seem to become. This tense relationship is echoed in G-v's narrative sequencing, in which the sharing of information is continually deferred and in which the pacing exponentially accelerates as the state of affairs in the town rapidly unravels.⁶⁰

---

[54] *PSS*, 10: 301; 390.
[55] *PSS*, 10: 302; 390.
[56] Ibid.
[57] Ibid.
[58] *PSS*, 10: 303; 392.
[59] *PSS*, 10: 267; 343.
[60] The convention of deferral is exploited by G-v, who frequently introduces new information, only to postpone explicating its significance, using phrases like, "of which we shall speak later" and "of that later." See, for example, *PSS*, 10: 241, 245, 248, 394.

Verkhovensky plays on the guests' impatient expectations: in calling the meeting, he erects a symbolic podium and then, while forcing everyone to wait for his arrival and for him to address the elephant in the room, leaves it enticingly unoccupied. By implicitly inviting ideological exchange (by calling together the sham party), and then refusing to engage in meaningful discourse, Verkhovensky baits his guests into airing their grievances and announcing their ideological positions, into compromising themselves in a public setting. The keen Miss Virginskaia takes the bait and seizes the opportunity to speak, using Verkhovensky's exaggerated condescension as a pretext for engaging in a debate. Already riled up from a "spat with her uncle over their views on the woman question" and eager to debunk the merit of tradition and "prejudices," she seizes on the very first thing uttered by Verkhovensky, who, at that moment, is sprawled in a chair, scolding the hostess for her low-quality tea service: "'You always serve such vileness instead of tea—and for a name-day party at that.' 'What, you also recognize name days?' the girl student suddenly laughed [*засмеялась вдруг*]."[61] Instead of intellectually sparring with her elder, who does not even acknowledge her challenge, she launches an attack on her younger adversary, a character identified as the high school boy [*гимназист*], whose responses she characterizes as "maundering."[62] To his responses, she dismissively shouts: "Too dragged out, can't understand a thing," and "If you don't know how to talk, shut up."[63] The abrupt outburst and Miss Virginskaia's downright derisive barbs heighten the tension in the room. This is an extreme manifestation of youthful impatience; specifically, an intolerant impatience that impedes effective communication.

This brief exchange points to the primary problem at the heart of this gathering: ambiguity. Verkhovensky's refusal to call the gathering what it really is piques the guests' curiosity, but also engenders doubt. What role does this man really play in the revolutionary movement? In the end, ambiguity invites miscommunication and results in chaos, which manifests in the guests' confused soliloquys and confrontational inquiries. In this scene, and in *Demons* more broadly, ambiguity impedes the younger generation's desire for change, which seems stifled at every turn by unreliable communication, shadowy dealings, and secrets. The opacity of the revolutionary cell's de facto leaders Verkhovensky

---

[61] *PSS*, 10: 304; 393 and *PSS*, 10: 305; 394.
[62] *PSS*, 10: 305; 395.
[63] Ibid.

and Stavrogin is, after all, one of the novel's primary plot devices. What is the narrator-chronicler G-v's text if not an exposition of all that they have hidden from their followers and from each other? Describing the whirlwind of events that he chronicles, G-v says: "Now, when everything is past and I am writing my chronicle, we know what it was all about; but then we still knew nothing."[64] The youth's lack of transparency, however, does more than motivate narrative suspense; it also introduces impatience into the plot. The tension created by the interplay of suspense and impatience heightens the drama that plays out in the provincial town, and also makes for some of the novel's most humorous episodes.

After Miss Virginskaia's outburst, the hostess, embarrassed by the trite nature of her relative's debate and the impression that it is making upon her guests, attempts to take control of the meeting. But, before she can do so, it turns out that, before it can proceed, the meeting *must* be defined as a meeting. After all the waiting and mystery, the guests finally want to know what the gathering constitutes: a party or a meeting. "Are we a meeting or not?" asks Arina, quickly insisting that Lyamshin play the piano, for the sake of secrecy.[65] This is where the guests' eagerness and curiosity collide to create a parody of politics, the absurdity of which prefigures the zemstvo elections that Lev Tolstoy would later represent in *Anna Karenina* (1878).[66] Lyamshin, unwilling to play, assures the hostess that no one is eavesdropping and that even if someone were, they wouldn't understand a thing that was happening. He is quickly seconded by an unnamed guest, who remarks that even those in attendance have no idea what is going on. A hilarious vote ensues, only no one can quite figure out which hand to raise in order to vote yes or no. Moreover, people keep raising and lowering their hands, unsure of how to vote. No one can count the votes. Some shout that they can't understand; others shout that it is all very simple:

- No, I understand, a third one shouted, hand up if it's *yes*.
- Yes, but what does *yes* mean?
- It means a meeting.
- No, not a meeting.
- I voted a meeting, the high-school boy shouted, addressing Madame Virginsky.
- Then why didn't you raise your hand?

[64] *PSS*, 10: 166; 209.
[65] *PSS*, 10: 308; 398.
[66] Many thanks to Kate Holland for suggesting this comparison.

– I kept looking at you, you didn't raise yours, so I didn't either.
– How stupid, it's because I made the suggestion, that's why I didn't raise mine.[67]

After they vote *for* a meeting, they demand a more precise definition, then a president, and so on. Finally, everyone turns to Verkhovensky and Stavrogin. Given the floor, Verkhovensky states that he would like some cognac, but has nothing to say otherwise; Stavrogin declares that he doesn't drink and also has nothing to say. And, so, the two much anticipated figures decline to speak and the meeting, now a total mockery, offers no definitive information about the "cause" and is up for grabs. Miss Virginskaia again seizes the opportunity to speak: "The girl student stood up. She had already tried to jump up [*подскакивала*] several times. 'I came to declare about the sufferings of the unfortunate students and about arousing them everywhere to protest ….'"[68] She is, of course, interrupted by Shigalev, whose dystopian theory is both fiercely debated and the source of much laughter for the "young" (*молодые*) and "less initiated" guests, who seem eager to minimize the despotic consequences of "unlimited freedom."[69] Stavrogin and Verkhovensky ultimately exit, shrouded in mystery and somewhat compromised in the eyes of the guests.

After all the anticipation, confusion, and caustic declarations, it is difficult not to laugh at the lack of clarity offered by the scene's conclusion. The discrepancy between the guests' expectations for the party and its reality (a dissonance that is exploited today on the internet in myriad comical "expectations vs. reality" memes) considerably contributes to the scene's humor and can be interpreted through the incongruity theory of humor, which holds that humor arises from incompatible combinations or from situations that deviate from habitual customs.[70] The incongruity theory generally understands an incongruity to be a thing or an event that violates our expectations.[71] According to Immanuel Kant, when our expectation "suddenly dissipate[s] into nothing," we laugh: "Laughter is an affectation arising from the sudden transformation of a strained expectation into nothing."[72] Not only the guests', but also the reader's expectations are violated

---

[67] *PSS*, 10: 309; 399–400. Translation modified.
[68] *PSS*, 10: 310; 401.
[69] *PSS*, 10: 311.
[70] For more on incongruity theory, see John Morreall, *Comic Relief: A Comprehensive Philosophy of Humor* (Malden: Wiley-Blackwell, 2009) and Patricia Keith-Spiegel, "Early Conceptions of Humor: Varieties and Issues," in *The Psychology of Humor: Theoretical Perspectives and Empirical Issues*. Edited by Jeffrey H. Goldstein and Paul E. McGhee (New York: Academic Press, 1972), 7–9.
[71] Morreall, *Comic Relief*, 10–11.
[72] Immanuel Kant, *Critique of Judgement* (Oxford: Oxford University Press, 2007), 161.

when, upon arriving at the "party," Verkhovensky and Stavrogin decline a big reveal and, instead, assume a passive role in the proceedings, allowing themselves to be overshadowed by the young Miss Virginskaia and the nameless high school boy. As in Kant's formula, the guests expect some definitive information about the revolutionary movement; they spend a considerable amount of time in expectation; finally, their expectations are violated, and they learn absolutely nothing.

Unlike the reader, however, the party guests do not seem to appreciate the humorous aspect of their informal hosts' prevarication and evasion. Indeed, they are (understandably) outraged when the meeting comes to naught. The guests are unable to perceive the discordance of the two schemata suggested by the novel: one being an illuminating plot point, through which the reader comes to understand the revolutionary movement obliquely referred to throughout the novel up to this point; the other being a farcical enactment of such a plot point. In the latter variant, the reader's laughter is elicited by the recognition of the situation's absurdity, but also by his position outside of the text. According to Jerry M. Suls's understanding of incongruity theory, "humor derives from experiencing a sudden incongruity which is then made congruous."[73] The punchline, for Suls, is the incongruity (or the first stage necessary for the appreciation of the joke), which is "made congruous" through identifying a cognitive rule that "follow[s] from the main part of the joke" (the second stage).[74] The disordered and anticlimactic non-meeting of confused and indignant would-be radicals seems incongruous with the aims that such individuals would ostensibly pursue: to organize a plan for overturning the social order. Conversely, there is something rather comical about a group of radicals and nihilists, many of whom claim to reject traditional customs, attempting to stage a meeting that relies on conventional ceremony. Here, Henri Bergson would identify the source of the reader's laughter in the clash between the guests' "rigidity" and the "suppleness of life."[75] The "mechanical inelasticity" of the guests is at odds with the reality to which they ought to be adapting themselves, for example,

---

[73] Jerry M. Suls, "A Two-Stage Model for the Appreciation of Jokes and Cartoons: An Information-Processing Analysis," in *The Psychology of Humor: Theoretical Perspectives and Empirical Issues*. Edited by Jeffrey H. Goldstein and Paul E. McGhee (New York: Academic Press, 1972), 82. For a cognitive approach to laughter and incongruity theory, see Arthur Koestler, *The Act of Creation* (New York: Macmillan, 1967).

[74] Suls, "A Two-Stage Model," 82.

[75] Henri Bergson, *An Essay on the Meaning of the Comic*. Translated by Cloudesley Brereton and Fred Rothwell (New York: Macmillan and Co., 1911), 44.

when the high school boy mechanically votes *not* to hold a meeting when he really meant to do the opposite.[76]

The reader, in contrast to the party guest, understands that the reorganization of society cannot be successfully achieved by a group of individuals who are unable to do something as simple as decide whether or not they, already in the middle of a meeting, are meeting. And so, the reader laughs, while the diegetic figures grow disappointed, confused, and weary of each other. The young Miss Virginskaia is, of all the guests, particularly unaware of her role in the joke. By far the most fervent, active character in the scene, she amplifies its absurdity and signals to the reader that he will learn absolutely nothing definitive about Verkhovensky's plans. She is, in some ways, a mere punchline, as the notion is understood by Suls: she provokes laughter by virtue of the fact that, subverting typical gender and age hierarchies, she rejects the conventions that might have made it possible for the group to hold a successful meeting.

Perhaps most importantly, the vehement student offers a means for releasing all the tension that has been building up to this point in the reader through laughter. This is laughter that, to quote John Dewey, "marks the ending [...] of a period of suspense, or expectation."[77] It can best be understood within a relief theory of humor, in which laughter functions as a discharge of (nervous) energy.[78] In this way, it is tempting to interpret the reader's laughter within the context of Mikhail Bakhtin's carnivalistic laughter, as laughter that, as Caryl Emerson writes, represents a "moment of relief and joy."[79] Despite being born of such a moment, the reader's laughter is not the virtuous laughter of Bakhtin's carnival, primarily because it is neither reciprocal, nor reciprocated. (After all, it is only experienced by and serves the reader.) As Lynn Ellen Patyk observes, Dostoevsky's satirical caricature of the revolutionaries demonstrates the "bankruptcy of abstract ideas by exposing their disastrous, rather than regenerative effects on the individuals

---

[76] Ibid., 10, 11.

[77] John Dewey, "The Theory of Emotion. (I) Emotional Attitudes," *Psychological Review*, vol. 1, no. 6 (1894): 558. See also, Herbert Spencer, "The Physiology of Laughter," *Macmillan's Magazine*, 1860: 395–402. https://wellcomecollection.org/works/agb23fva.

[78] My use of relief theory in this article is predicated upon John Dewey's above-cited formulation, rather than Sigmund Freud's understanding of humor as the release of repressed energy, which he developed in *Jokes and Their Relation to the Unconscious* (1905).

[79] Caryl Emerson, "Coming to Terms with Bakhtin's Carnival: Ancient, Modern, Sub Specie Aeternitatis," in *Bakhtin and the Classics*. Edited by R. Bracht Branham (Evanston: Northwestern University Press, 2002), 7.

who embrace them."⁸⁰ The reader may laugh, but within the *diegetic world*, relief is not achieved through laughter. Among the party guests, laughter is not the means through which pent-up energy is released and it does not succeed in "deflating the genuinely corrosive emotions" experienced by characters like Miss Virginskaia.⁸¹ When the young guests laugh at Shigalev, it is impudent and mean-spirited laughter, which merely serves to escalate division among the group.

The tension that gradually builds in the scene is, ultimately, discharged. Indeed, it blows up, and it does so where the social body is at its most volatile, in Miss (*девица*) Virginskaia, who, seeming to stand in for all female nihilists of the early reform era, is brusque, commandeering, and impatient. Her utterances are accompanied by the jarring adverbs of time discussed above, like "suddenly" ("suddenly laughed"), "instantly" ("instantly declared").⁸² She is, moreover, continually, literally lunging at everyone's words: "simply lunging forward from her chair [*дернувшись вперед со стула*]," "the girl student lunged forward [*дернулась вперед*]."⁸³ She is embodied impatience, an externalization of youthful fervor. Her gender and age are also impactful here, with her other major interlocutor, her uncle Kapiton Maximovich, stating that her physicality is inadmissible precisely because she is a young woman: "And you shouldn't pop up [*выскакивай*]! [...] You are a young lady, you should behave modestly, and it's as if you're sitting on pins."⁸⁴ Her entire demeanor is at odds with the implied humility of her gendered title, *девица* (maiden). Miss Virginskaia's extremism and impetuosity impede the meeting's progress, but also remind us of the grave potential of impatience with an ideological tendency. The time of revolution is, to harken back to Kliger's reading of *Crime and Punishment*, an impatient temporal mode. The incongruity between the hotheaded, rash young woman and the calm and collected Verkhovensky and Stavrogin likewise provokes the reader's laughter. Within the diegesis, her persistent effort to commandeer the conversation distracts from the blasé Verkhovensky and his fabricated messiah and explodes the conspiring radicals' illusion (and delusion) of gravitas.

---

⁸⁰ Lynn Ellen Patyk, "By the Double-Edged Sword of Word and Deed: Revolutionary Terrorism and Russian Literary Culture, 1871–1917" (Ph.D. diss., Stanford University, 2006), 30–1. Quoted in Vinokur, "All of a Sudden: Dostoevsky's Demonologies of Terror," 56.

⁸¹ Emerson, "Coming to Terms with Bakhtin's Carnival," 7.

⁸² *PSS*, 10: 305.

⁸³ *PSS*, 10: 305; 394 and *PSS*, 10: 306; 395.

⁸⁴ *PSS*, 10: 306; 396.

At the same time, if we recall Ngai's assertion that irritation plays an insubstantial role in political activism, then Miss Virginskaia's irritability signals the potential inefficaciousness of her impatience.

This scene is marvelously funny. It highlights the town radicals' total lack of knowledge and shows that keeping these people in a state of confusion and ignorance creates utter chaos. This chaos has the potential to be very entertaining, but also disastrous. After all, the spread of misinformation through rumors, hearsay, and gossip are imperative to the success of Verkhovensky, whose discourse is, notably, rushed throughout the work. He says, "so I finally decided that it would be best [...] to be in a great rush [*очень торопиться*] to prove something, and towards the end to get tangled up in one's own proofs, so that the listener throws up his hands, or, best of all, just spits and walks away without any end."[85] In "With Our People," Verkhovensky, with his serpent-like tongue, does just that. Using Fisher's distinction between the rash and premeditated act, we observe a fundamental difference between the impatience of Miss Virginskaia and Verkhovensky: whereas Virginskaia's rash impatience does little more than impede the productivity of an event that was doomed from the outset, Verkhovensky's premeditated impatience aids him in committing murder.

"With Our People" is defined first by tense expectation, then by tense debate (which is actually rather funny), then by confusion (also funny), then by Shigalev's solemnness, and finally by confusion again (this time foreboding in nature). The scene is most entertaining when the characters are inhabiting some kind of exaggerated state, be it extreme disdain, anger, apathy, or perplexity. The coexistence of these various zealous states is fundamental to the party's funniness, but the interplay of the young generation's impatient extremism and shammed indifference enhances the scene's comedic potential. All revved up, ready to show off her learning with a prepared, impassioned speech for these supposedly important people, Miss Virginskaia is thwarted not by Verkhovensky's or Stavrogin's superior political or theoretical knowledge, but by their total indifference. Miss Virginskaia is ready to fly off the handle; Stavrogin is ready to fall asleep. The juxtaposition of this youthful fanatic and the more reserved and affected elder radicals demonstrates the "multifaceted and diverse" breadth of Dostoevsky's vision of inefficacious "youth" in the work. The author certainly seems to be laughing at this generation, while also taking seriously their lofty, but alarming ambitions.

---

[85] *PSS*, 10: 176; 221.

Bibliography

Antonov, Sergei. *Bankrupts and Usurers of Imperial Russia: Debt, Property, and the Law in the Age of Dostoevsky and Tolstoy*. Cambridge, MA: Harvard University Press, 2016.

Aristotle. *Nicomachean Ethics*. Translated by Joe Sachs. Newburyport: Focus Publishing, 2002.

Bergson, Henri. *An Essay on the Meaning of the Comic*. Translated by Cloudesley Brereton and Fred Rothwell. New York: Macmillan and Co., 1911.

Blanchot, Maurice. *The Space of Literature*. Translated by Ann Smock. Lincoln: University of Nebraska Press, 1982.

Bowers, Katherine and Kate Holland (eds.). *Dostoevsky at 200: The Novel in Modernity*. Toronto: University of Toronto Press, 2021.

Dal', Vladimir. *Tolkovyi slovar' zhivogo velikorusskogo iazyka*, vol. 2. Saint Petersburg-Moscow: M. O. Vol'f, 1905.

Dewey, John. "The Theory of Emotion. (I) Emotional Attitudes," *Psychological Review*, vol. 1, no. 6 (1894): 553–69.

Dobroliubov, Nikolai. "Chto takoe Oblomovshchina?," *Sovremennik*, vol. LXXV otd. III (1859): 59–98.

Dostoevsky, Fyodor. *Demons*. Translated by Richard Pevear and Larissa Volokhonsky. New York: Random House, 1994.

Dostoevsky, Fyodor. *Polnoe sobranie sochinenii v tridtsati tomakh*. Leningrad: Nauka, 1972–90.

Emerson, Caryl. "Coming to Terms with Bakhtin's Carnival: Ancient, Modern, Sub Specie Aeternitatis," in *Bakhtin and the Classics*. Edited by R. Bracht Branham, 5–26. Evanston: Northwestern University Press, 2002.

Evdokimova, Svetlana and Vladimir Golstein (eds.). *Dostoevsky beyond Dostoevsky: Science, Philosophy, Religion*. Boston: Academic Studies Press, 2016.

Fisher, Philip. *The Vehement Passions*. Princeton: Princeton University Press, 2009.

Goldstein, Jeffrey H. and Paul E. McGhee. *The Psychology of Humor: Theoretical Perspectives and Empirical Issues*. New York: Academic Press, 1972.

Jobs, Richard Ivan. *Riding the New Wave: Youth and the Rejuvenation of France after the Second World War*. Stanford: Stanford University Press, 2007.

Kant, Immanuel. *Critique of Judgement*. Oxford: Oxford University Press, 2007.

Kliger, Ilya. "Shapes of History and the Enigmatic Hero in Dostoevsky: The Case of *Crime and Punishment*," *Comparative Literature*, vol. 62, no. 3 (Summer 2010): 228–45.

Koestler, Arthur. *The Act of Creation*. New York: Macmillan, 1967.

Lorenz, Sarah Ruth. "Realist Convictions and Revolutionary Impatience in the Criticism of N. A. Dobroliubov," *SEEJ*, vol. 57, no. 1 (Spring 2013): 67–88.

Morreall, John. *Comic Relief: A Comprehensive Philosophy of Humor*. Malden: Wiley-Blackwell, 2009.

Naiman, Eric. "What if Nabokov Had Written 'Dvoinik'? Reading Literature Preposterously," *The Russian Review*, vol. 64, no. 4 (October 2005): 575–89.

Ngai, Sianne. *Ugly Feelings*. Cambridge, MA: Harvard University Press, 2005.

Patyk, Lynn Ellen. "By the Double-Edged Sword of Word and Deed: Revolutionary Terrorism and Russian Literary Culture, 1871–1917," Ph.D. diss., Stanford University, 2006.

Patyk, Lynn Ellen. *Written in Blood: Revolutionary Terrorism and Russian Literary Culture, 1861–1881*. Madison: University of Wisconsin Press, 2017.

Spencer, Herbert. "The Physiology of Laughter," *Macmillan's Magazine* (March 1860): 395–402, https://wellcomecollection.org/works/agb23fva.

Tagantsev, N. C. *Issledovaniia ob otvestvennosti maloletnikh prestupnikov po russkomu pravu i proekt zakonopolozhenii ob etom voprose*. Saint Petersburg: Tipografiia A.M. Kotomina, 1871.

Toporov, V. N. "O strukture romana Dostoevskogo v sviazi s arkhaichnymi skhemami mifologicheskogo myshleniia," in *Structure of Texts and Semiotics of Culture*. Edited by Jan van der Eng and Mojmir Grygar, 225–302. The Hague: Mouton, 1973.

Verhoeven, Claudia. "Time of Terror, Terror of Time: On the Impatience of Russian Revolutionary Terrorism (Early 1860s–Early 1880s)," *Jahrbücher für Geschichte Osteuropas*, vol. 58, no. H. 2 (2010): 254–73.

Vinokur, Val. "All of a Sudden: Dostoevsky's Demonologies of Terror," in *Just Assassins: The Culture of Terrorism in Russia*. Edited by Anthony Anemone, 53–72. Evanston: Northwestern University Press, 2010.

Weiner, Adam. *By Authors Possessed: The Demonic Novel in Russia*. Evanston: Northwestern University Press, 1998.

7

Restorative Parody from *Devils* to *Hamilton*

Susanne Fusso

The first time I became fully aware of the funny side of Dostoevsky was at the end of a graduate seminar on Turgenev taught by Robert Louis Jackson at Yale. After guiding us through a thoroughly serious and characteristically profound analysis of Turgenev's "Phantoms" and "Enough," Jackson ended the session by reading the passage in Dostoevsky's novel *Devils* that describes the literary festival at which the pompous Westernizing writer Karmazinov presents his latest work "*Merci*," a ruthless parody of those two stories by Turgenev. By the end of the passage, the entire class was laughing out loud, and Jackson was in tears and almost unable to read. Yes, although *Devils* deals with the darkest impulses of the human spirit and includes multiple murders and suicides, it is devastatingly funny, in large part because of Dostoevsky's mastery of parody. But Dostoevsky's parody requires an initiated reader to grasp its full effect. A roomful of nervous graduate students, not to mention one of the foremost Slavic scholars in the world, would not have been laughing so spontaneously and unselfconsciously at Dostoevsky's text had we not just devoted sustained attention to the works that form the target of the parody. It may be an axiom of the mechanism of parody that the better informed the audience about the target texts, the funnier or more effective the parody. I add "more effective" because along with Yuri Tynianov, Linda Hutcheon, and other theorists of parody, I do not believe that humor is necessarily the main aim of all parody, although it tends to be present even in the most serious parodies, if only by virtue of the incongruity inherent in parodic discourse.

In his pioneering 1921 essay on parody, Yuri Tynianov writes, "The comic is a coloration [*okraska*] that usually accompanies parody, but it is not by any means the coloration of parody itself."¹ Linda Hutcheon, whose approach to parody is the closest to my own, similarly declines to use humor as the defining criterion for parody: "What I am calling parody here is not just that ridiculing imitation mentioned in the standard dictionary definitions ... Parody ... is a form of imitation, but imitation characterized by ironic inversion, not always at the expense of the parodied text."² Hutcheon's definition provides a space in which to think about parody in more complex terms than the narrow understanding of it as a purely humorous and mocking genre. Nevertheless, humor can intensify the effect of parody, even in cases where the major aim of the parody is something different from pure humor.

The complex and multifarious referentiality of Dostoevsky's novels, particularly *Devils*, bears a kinship with the postmodern art of the late twentieth and early twenty-first centuries. In this regard, Dostoevsky's novels seem to be more in tune with the highly parodic and referential discourse in Russian journals of his time than with the novels of Tolstoy or Turgenev, and Dostoevsky's deep involvement in journalism as both editor and polemicist probably plays a major role in shaping the parodic and intertextual nature of his art, as well as our sense of his novels as eternally new, eternally relevant. In this chapter, I would like to consider a particular form of parody that appears in *Devils* and that also lies at the heart of Lin-Manuel Miranda's *Hamilton: An American Musical* (2015). Both these works deal with revolution, with "sons" rebelling against "fathers," although in Dostoevsky's case, unlike Miranda's, the rebels are not heroicized. Nevertheless, both works employ parody in a way that revivifies values and symbols that had been mummified in their respective cultures, drained of vital significance by both attackers and worshipers. This kind of parody, which in a 1995 article I termed "restorative parody," operates in *Devils* and in *Hamilton* to

---

[1] Iurii Tynianov, "Dostoevskii i Gogol'" (1921), in *Arkhaisty i novatory* (Leningrad: Priboi, 1929; Ardis reprint, May 1985), 455. This has been translated in Victor Erlich's edition as "The comic often accompanies parody, but the former is not coextensive with the latter" (Victor Erlich, ed., *Twentieth-Century Russian Literary Criticism* [New Haven: Yale University Press, 1975], 116). In the more recent translation by Ainsley Morse and Philip Redko, this passage reads, "The comic is a connotation that ordinarily accompanies parody, but it is in no way a connotation of the parodic per se" (Yuri Tynianov, *Permanent Evolution: Essays on Literature, Theory and Film*. Edited and Translated by Ainsley Morse and Philip Redko [Boston: Academic Studies Press, 2019], 63). I would like to thank the editors of this volume, Irina Erman and Lynn Patyk, for their helpful suggestions for developing this chapter. I would also like to thank the students in my course on Parody at Wesleyan University for stimulating discussions that have informed my work.

[2] Linda Hutcheon, *A Theory of Parody: The Teachings of Twentieth-Century Art Forms* (Urbana and Chicago: University of Illinois Press, 2000), 5, 6.

renew petrified symbols, with the effect of the renewal given enhanced power by the humorous effect of the parody's incongruity.

Restorative parody does not fit neatly into the general conception of parody as an adversarial genre, the major aim of which is a humorous attack on its target. Dostoevsky certainly deployed the ridiculing or attacking mode of parody throughout *Devils*, as in the assault on Turgenev referenced above. But *Devils* also includes another, more unusual but perhaps more interesting variety of parody, which seeks not to assert its own authority but to preserve, revivify, and draw strength from the authority of its original.[3] The world depicted in *Devils*, published in 1871–2, is one in which both art and faith are under attack by the new generation of radicals, and Raphael's Sistine Madonna is a convenient target embodying both. None of the novel's characters has a living, vital perception of Raphael's painting of the Madonna; it is irrevocably mediated through the countless analyses and appreciations by poets and travelers.[4] As I will discuss later in this chapter, the "Founding Fathers" occupy a similar position in the artistic scheme of *Hamilton*.

In *Devils*, the key scene in which restorative parody operates is the fifth chapter of the third and final part of the novel, titled "A Woman Traveler." Although the first word of the chapter is "catastrophe," and it is preceded by the murders of Marya and Ignat Lebyadkin and followed by the murder of Ivan Shatov by the radicals led by Pyotr Verkhovensky, the chapter is suffused with humor. Three years before the time of the action, Shatov had "lived matrimonially in Geneva two weeks and a few days" with Marya Ignatievna Shatova, a free-thinking governess. The couple had then parted "as free people not bound by anything; of course, also because of poverty."[5] In "A Woman Traveler," Ivan Shatov is awakened by the sudden appearance of Marya pounding at his gate in the middle of the night, at a moment when he was seriously contemplating going to the authorities to denounce his former revolutionary colleagues. There is slapstick humor in Shatov's unsuccessful fumbling search for matches and his dropping of

---

[3] In an approach that contrasts with that of Hutcheon, Gary Saul Morson's definition of parody requires that the parodic text assert a "higher semantic authority" than the target text. Gary Saul Morson, *The Boundaries of Genre: Dostoevskii's "Diary of a Writer" and the Traditions of Literary Utopia* (Austin: University of Texas Press, 1981), 110. I am using Hutcheon's more expansive definition here.

[4] Susanne Fusso, "Maidens in Childbirth: The Sistine Madonna in Dostoevskii's *Devils*," *Slavic Review*, vol. 54, no. 2 (summer 1995): 264. My analysis here revisits key points from this article but has been expanded and refocused.

[5] Fyodor Dostoevsky, *Devils* in *Polnoe sobranie sochinenii v tridtsati tomakh* (Leningrad: Nauka, 1974), 10: 434, 27. Translations are mine. For anglophone readers, I recommend the translation by Michael R. Katz, *Devils* (Oxford: Oxford University Press, 2008).

his candlestick, so that he and Marya must ascend the steps in the dark. Marya's conversation with her cabbie displays an almost Gogolian logic. She has told him to take her to Voznesenskaya (Assumption) Street rather than the correct Bogoyavlenskaya (Epiphany) Street, but she blames the cabbie: "Assumption, Epiphany—you should know all these stupid names better than I do, since you are a local inhabitant."[6] Marya's discourse is permeated with incongruous nihilist jargon; she explains to Shatov her plans to open "a bookbinding shop on rational principles" as she lies on his bed, obviously quite ill.[7] After Marya falls asleep, her skirt hikes up to her knee, and chaste Shatov, "almost in fright," covers her leg with his coat "trying not to look at the bared spot."[8] Shatov comically misinterprets Marya's symptoms: Dostoevsky offers a detailed description of her physical discomfort as she goes into labor, but she has to explicitly tell the naive Shatov what is taking place: "You are an abstract, useless chatterbox [...] Do you really, finally, not see that I am having labor pains?"[9]

Shatov's neighbor and former revolutionary colleague Kirillov supplies verbal humor, as Dostoevsky takes advantage of the strange way Kirillov speaks Russian (an aspect of the novel that is confounding for translators). When Shatov informs him that his wife has returned and asks for a samovar so he can make her tea, Kirillov says, "If wife, then a samovar is needed."[10] Later, when Shatov tells him that Marya is in labor, he says, "It's really too bad that I don't know how to give birth [...] that is, not that I don't know how to give birth, but to make it so that somebody gives birth, I don't know how ... or ... No, I don't know how to say it."[11] The midwife Arina Prokhorovna Virginskaya, who spouts nihilist jargon along with Marya, joins her in caustic, malicious laughter at Shatov's fatherly distress. The main source of Arina's laughter is Shatov's status as a cuckolded husband, since the baby Marya is giving birth to must be another man's son, probably Stavrogin's. After the baby is born, Arina asks Shatov if he is adopting him, and he replies with simple dignity, "He is already my son."[12] Arina is highly amused by Shatov's selfless and loving behavior: "You've made me laugh for my whole life long. I'm not going to take any money from you; I'm

---

[6] Dostoevsky, *Devils*, *PSS*, 10: 433.
[7] *PSS*, 10: 441.
[8] *PSS*, 10: 440.
[9] *PSS*, 10: 442, 443.
[10] *PSS*, 10: 436.
[11] *PSS*, 10: 444.
[12] *PSS*, 10: 452.

going to break out laughing in my sleep. I have never seen anything funnier than you this night."[13]

Unlike Arina, Marya is transformed by the birth. She ceases her nihilistic cursing and mockery and expresses her love for Shatov through eloquent looks and gestures: "Everything seemed to have been reborn."[14] Shatov himself expresses the deep significance of the birth: "There were two, and suddenly a third person, a new spirit, integral, finished, of a kind human hands do not make; a new thought and a new love, it's even terrifying … And there is nothing higher on earth!"[15] A passage near the beginning of the scene, when Marya enters Shatov's apartment, provides a clue to the significance of this detailed scene of childbirth followed by renewal. The narrator gives a parenthetical description of Marya that is an ekphrasis of Raphael's Madonna: "It was a woman of about twenty-five years old, of a rather strong build, taller than average height … with dark-blond luxuriant hair, a pale oval face, and big dark eyes." The detailed description of her traveling bag "of Dresden workmanship" also directs the reader to the Sistine Madonna, the painting located in the Gemäldegalerie in Dresden, where it was the site of aesthetic and religious pilgrimage.[16]

In *Devils*, both the hidebound defenders of Raphael as the exemplar of "art for art's sake," like Stepan Trofimovich Verkhovensky, and attackers like the governor's wife Julie von Lembke, who blindly follow radical-chic fashion, are discredited and lampooned. But thanks to the divine power of art, embodied in Marya Shatova as a walking, breathing, birth-giving Sistine Madonna, through the Shatov family trio Dostoevsky is able to recover "the primordial sense of awe before the mystery of the human image and of human artistic creation."[17] The operation of what I have called restorative parody, as exemplified by the scene of the Shatov family's apotheosis, has been concisely described by Adam Gopnik in an article on the Victorian nonsense poetry of Edward Lear: "Parody can be a vehicle for the renewal of feeling …. Mockery cleanses clichés, and then restores emotion."[18] The comic nature of the Marya Shatova scene helps to lighten the mood of "catastrophe" and prepare the reader for the eloquently moving culmination of the episode.

---

[13] *PSS*, 10: 453.
[14] Ibid.
[15] *PSS*, 10: 452.
[16] *PSS*, 10: 435, 433.
[17] Fusso, "Maidens in Childbirth," 271, 274.
[18] Adam Gopnik, "Knowing Mr. Lear," *New Yorker*, April 23, 2018, 81.

In thinking about restorative parody, it is important to note the difference between what happens within the narrative and what happens for readers of the narrative. It is true, as Yuri Corrigan pointed out in his response to my paper at the "Funny Dostoevsky" conference, that in the case of the Shatov family as a parodic embodiment of the Holy Family, "Joseph is murdered, the baby dies, Mary dies. Nothing is being restored."[19] But we as readers see Shatov freely accept another man's child as his own son, exalt the mystery of that child's birth and join in a loving union with the estranged wife who had entered his room cursing only hours before. This moment, in which the sacred significance of Raphael's Madonna is brought to life and restored, is a fleeting one for the characters within the novel, but it is there for readers to access again and again, as long as Dostoevsky's novel is read. Here we might turn to Vasily Zhukovsky, whose 1824 essay on the Sistine Madonna gave rise to the Russian fashion, alluded to in *Devils*, for visiting Dresden to view the masterpiece. In a diary entry of February 1821, Zhukovsky writes:

> Rousseau says: *il n'y a de beau que ce qui n'est pas!* The beautiful is only that which is not! This does not mean *only that which does not exist*. The beautiful exists, but it is not, for *in a sense it appears to us* solely in order to manifest itself to us, to revive and *elevate the soul*, but we can neither retain it, nor discern it, nor *comprehend* it; *it has neither name nor image*; it is perceptible and incomprehensible. It visits us *at the best moments of life*.[20]

The brevity of the Shatov family's beautiful moment in their own story does not negate the lasting power of this moment for Dostoevsky's readers. In a similar fashion in *Hamilton*, the audience witnesses the untimely deaths of both Alexander Hamilton and his son in senseless duels, but the musical ends with a celebration of Hamilton's far-reaching legacy, as perpetuated by his wife Eliza.

Zhukovsky's insight about beauty could be extended to refer to faith in Dostoevsky's created world. Moments of certainty in faith, like Shatov's epiphany, are similarly fleeting and cannot be retained, discerned, or comprehended, to use Zhukovsky's terms. One of the things that is hardest for my twenty-first-century students to understand is that faith is not a simple binary, that it is possible for

---

[19] Yuri Corrigan, respondent's notes shared with me.

[20] Cited in O. B. Lebedeva and A. S. Ianushkevich, "V. A. Zhukovskii i A. V. Nikitenko o Sikstinskoi madonne Rafaelia: Tipologiia ekfrasisa kak reprezentant esteticheskogo soznaniia," *Vestnik Tomskogo gosudarstvennogo universiteta. Filologiia*, no. 46 (2017): 131. Emphasis in Zhukovsky's original. Zhukovsky's essay on the Sistine Madonna is "Rafaeleva 'Madonna,'" in his *Estetika i kritika*. Edited by F. Z. Kanunova, et al. (Moscow: Iskusstvo, 1985), 307–11.

Ivan Karamazov to be an "atheist" at the outset of *The Brothers Karamazov* and then to assert his faith in God later in the novel, only to lose it again. Faith is not a constant but an ongoing struggle for moments of clarity like the one that Shatov has in the presence of his "Sistine Madonna."

The twentieth-century philosopher Vasily Rozanov discusses the scene of Marya Shatova's childbirth at length (or, more precisely, quotes it at length) in his 1903 book *The Family Question in Russia*, in a section titled "The Boundaries of Our Era." Rozanov's concluding note on the scene is in line with my interpretation of this passage as a moment of resurrection: "We have expressed our opinion that *birth* and *everything surrounding birth is religious*; and now we have introduced an illustration of the fact that it *resurrects*, and even resurrects from such a desert of negation as our nihilism."[21] The midwife's mockery and Marya's pre-birth cursing of her own child do not withstand the sacred mystery of birth that the former nihilist Shatov recognizes and illuminates for the reader. Restorative parody in *Hamilton* similarly works against deadening, dogmatic ideology that fetishizes the Founding Fathers as either idols or villains.

For the past twenty years, I have offered an undergraduate course on the theory and practice of parody that has Dostoevsky's *Devils* as an anchoring text. The last three times I taught the course, in 2016, 2018, and 2022, I included Miranda's *Hamilton* alongside other literary, cinematic, and theatrical texts that embody the many aspects of parody, from pure humor to artistic evolution to *parodia sacra* (the medieval practice of parodying the most sacred rites of the church) and restorative parody. Lin-Manuel Miranda graduated from Wesleyan University, where I teach, but I do not know him and to my knowledge he never took any courses in Russian literature. Thus, I am not claiming that his use of restorative parody derives from Dostoevsky. Rather, his teacher seems to have been Weird Al Yankovic. In a recent profile of Yankovic published in the *New York Times Magazine*, Miranda defines Yankovic's art in a way that is consistent with the concept of restorative parody: "'Weird Al is a perfectionist,' Miranda said. 'Every bit as much as Michael Jackson or Kurt Cobain or Madonna or any artist he has ever spoofed. So you get the musical power of the original along with this incredible twist of Weird Al's voice and Weird Al's brain. *The original*

---

[21] V. V. Rozanov, *Semeinyi vopros v Rossii*, in his *Sobranie sochinenii*. Edited by A. N. Nikoliukin, et al. (Moscow: Respublika, 2004), 18: 59. See the discussion by Irina Erman, "Autobiography of a 'Living Plagiary': Vasilii Rozanov's Secret Dostoevskian Genealogy," *AutobiografiYA*, no. 7 (2018): 171–90, especially 181–4. I would like to thank Irina Erman for bringing this passage in Rozanov to my attention.

songs lose none of their power, even when they're on a polka with burping sound effects in the background. In fact, it accelerates their power.'"[22] This definition is consistent with Olga Freidenberg's discussion of the operation of *parodia sacra* as "intensification of content, the intensification of the nature of the gods."[23]

In *Hamilton*, it is not art and Christian faith, as embodied in Raphael's Madonna, that are in need of restoration and rescue from both their slavish admirers and their mindless attackers. The "Founding Fathers," white males in powdered wigs and eighteenth-century clothing, occupy a position in American culture similar to that of Raphael's Madonna in nineteenth-century Russia: a convenient shorthand, as idol or target, for conservative or radical politics.[24] A few years before the creation of *Hamilton*, the Tea Party movement, born out of a 2009 tirade by a CNBC business commentator about President Barack Obama's housing plan and financially supported by powerful right-wing organizations, used tricorn hats and knee breeches as visual props in their demonstrations against every aspect of the policies of our first Black president.[25]

In *Hamilton*, Miranda uses classic techniques of parody, like incongruity and decontextualization, to restore the deeper meaning of the origins of the United States, revitalizing the conception of the "Founding Fathers" as Dostoevsky restored the deeper meaning of the Sistine Madonna, which transcends the sterile adoration of the "fathers" and the cynical mockery of the "sons." In Miranda's play, Alexander Hamilton, George Washington, Thomas Jefferson, and others are embodied by Black and brown performers and express themselves in modern musical genres, especially hip-hop. A song cut from *Hamilton* (but included in the later *Hamilton Mixtape*) asserts that "what you're about to witness is no John Trumbull," referring to the static poses of the all-white men in John Trumbull's 1818 painting *Declaration of Independence* (which now hangs in the Rotunda of the US Capitol).[26] At the end of the 1969 musical

---

[22] Sam Anderson, "The Weirdly Enduring Appeal of Weird Al Yankovic," *New York Times Magazine*, April 9, 2020, https://www.nytimes.com/2020/04/09/magazine/weird-al-yankovic.html; emphasis mine.

[23] Olga Freidenberg, "The Origin of Parody," in *Semiotics and Structuralism: Readings from the Soviet Union*. Edited by Henryk Baran (White Plains: International Arts and Sciences Press, 1976), 282.

[24] For a discussion of how the ethos of *Hamilton* can be seen as supporting conservative values, see Elizabeth Titrington Craft, "Headfirst into an Abyss: The Politics and Political Reception of *Hamilton*," *American Music*, vol. 36, no. 4 (Winter 2018; special issue on *Hamilton*), 429–47.

[25] On the origins of the Tea Party and the racist overtones of the movement, see Barack Obama, *A Promised Land* (New York: Crown, 2020), 272–4, 403.

[26] The Roots, "No John Trumbull," SongMeanings, https://songmeanings.com/songs/view/3530822107859582613/.

1776, the cast freezes to represent "the familiar Pine-Savage engraving" of the signing of the Declaration of Independence. This refers to Edward Savage's 1801 completion and engraving of Robert Edge Pine's unfinished 1784–8 painting *Congress Voting Independence*, another white male tableau of the same genre as Trumbull's painting. In *1776*, the authors recommend adherence to the appearance of the Founders as reflected in historical accounts, as the "Historical Note by the Authors" indicates, in contrast to the intentionally nonhistorical casting of *Hamilton*.[27]

Hamilton does not present a *tableau vivant* of a classic painting or a historically accurate depiction of the physical traits of the Founding Fathers. Instead, the frozen white figures of our national iconography are transformed and revivified, as diverse young performers rap and dance to Andy Blankenbuehler's dynamic choreography, bringing back to life the ideal of the equality of all humans that our Founders asserted but did not live by. The process is reminiscent of the process by which the often reproduced, seemingly petrified beauty of Raphael's Madonna is transformed in *Devils* into an angry, irritable, cursing young radical woman, whose life-creating labor pains and regeneration by love happen before the reader's eyes. This is a deeper and more complex process than just "making the founders cool and relatable," as one critic calls it.[28] Like the parody of the Sistine Madonna in *Devils*, the transformation of the Founders in *Hamilton* is a reclamation of a core set of values that have been damaged by both idolatry and profanation.

As with the Marya Shatova scene in *Devils*, the deployment of restorative parody in *Hamilton* has a comic element that enhances the effect of the parody. This comic element was evident at an early stage in the creation of *Hamilton*, when Miranda performed a version of the opening song at the White House in May 2009, with President Barack Obama and First Lady Michelle Obama in the audience. In introducing his performance, Miranda says, "I'm thrilled the White House called me tonight, because I'm actually working on a hip-hop album. It's a concept album about the life of someone I think embodies hip-hop: Treasury Secretary Alexander Hamilton."[29] The audience erupts in laughter at

---

[27] *1776: A Musical Play*, book by Peter Stone, music and lyrics by Sherman Edwards (New York: Viking, 1970), 141, 155. On the modern political resonances of *1776*, see Elissa Harbert, "'Ever to the Right'? The Political Life of *1776* in the Nixon Era," *American Music*, vol. 35, no. 2 (summer 2017): 237–70.

[28] Craft, "Headfirst into an Abyss," 439.

[29] "An Evening of Poetry, Music, and the Spoken Word," YouTube, https://www.youtube.com/watch?v=WNFf7nMIGnE.

the incongruous juxtaposition. This comic element also permeates the play in its finished version, as King George III sings a Beatles-style breakup song, George Washington raps about hearing "the British cannons go Boom!," and Thomas Jefferson appears in a foppish purple velvet suit to sing in a 1950s jazz style.[30]

Henry Louis Gates, Jr., has explored the ways in which parody, and in particular Mikhail Bakhtin's concept of the "double-voiced word," is central to a particular kind of Black discourse known as "signifying."[31] The reappropriation and reinterpretation of hallowed white signifiers is a recurrent phenomenon in this process. The art of Robert Colescott (1925–2009), with paintings such as *George Washington Carver Crossing the Delaware: Page from an American History Textbook* (1975), is a salient example of this phenomenon. This painting "transforms Emanuel Leutze's depiction of George Washington, heading for victory, into a Black achievement, paying homage to one of America's great educators."[32] Colescott's own comment on this painting exemplifies the ethos and technique of restorative parody as used by both Dostoevsky and Miranda: "Subversion of this icon, a quasi-religious image that everyone bows to and believes in—but nobody thinks about—seemed like a good idea, a new life for an old shoe."[33] Miranda's use of the Black-created genre of rap for much of the music in *Hamilton* is aptly complemented by his deployment of the double-voiced word of parody.

Hamilton has been criticized for erasing the experience of Black people by putting the white Founding Fathers at the center of the narrative, even if they are portrayed by people of various ethnicities. As Lyra Monteiro writes, "The idea that this musical 'looks like America looks now' in contrast to 'then' … is misleading and actively erases the presence and role of black and brown people

---

[30] Lin-Manuel Miranda, "Right Hand Man," in Lin-Manuel Miranda and Jeremy McCarter, *Hamilton the Revolution* (New York: Grand Central Publishing, 2016), 61.

[31] Henry Louis Gates, Jr., *The Signifying Monkey: A Theory of African-American Literary Criticism* (New York: Oxford University Press, 1988), *passim*. See the discussions of parody in Mikhail Bakhtin, *Problems of Dostoevsky's Poetics*. Edited and Translated by Caryl Emerson (Minneapolis: University of Minnesota Press, 1984). Bakhtin has a more consistently adversarial conception of parody than that of Hutcheon. Dale Peterson takes his cue from Gates in using Bakhtin as a framework for analyzing the parallels between Russian and African American literary culture. See Dale E. Peterson, *Up from Bondage: The Literatures of Russian and African American Soul* (Durham: Duke University Press, 2000).

[32] Roberta Smith, "Robert Colescott Throws down the Gauntlet," *New York Times*, July 7, 2022, https://www.nytimes.com/2022/07/07/arts/design/robert-colescott-new-museum-painter-race.html.

[33] Quoted in Smith, "Robert Colescott Throws Down the Gauntlet."

in Revolutionary America, as well as before and since."³⁴ But a play about "black and brown people in Revolutionary America" would be a different play, one that would not deal with the central events of the nation's founding and would not reclaim the significance of "all men are created equal" for people living today, as *Hamilton* has. What critics like Monteiro apparently fail to take into consideration is the layer of meaning provided by many of the specific rap songs that are referenced in *Hamilton*. The experience of Black people in the eighteenth century may be largely absent from the play (despite its numerous references to slavery), but the experience of Black people in contemporary America is vividly present to anyone who investigates the lyrics of the raps that are referenced.³⁵

Central to both *Devils* and *Hamilton* is the use of what Mandelstam scholars Kiril Taranovsky and Omry Ronen call subtext, "an already existing text (or texts) reflected in a new one."³⁶ As Taranovsky explains, "If an investigator finds a subtitle ['Pindaric fragment'] in the first printing of [Mandelstam's poem 'The One Who Has Found a Horseshoe'], *it means that he has to reread Pindar's odes*. And I would like to emphasize that such reading is fascinating indeed."³⁷ Knowing the subtext expands and deepens one's understanding of the text, adding multiple layers of meaning. Although Taranovsky and Ronen are dealing with modernist poetry, their method of reading can be fruitfully applied to Dostoevsky's works. In reading *Devils*, it is important not just to laugh at the parodic poems of Captain Lebyadkin, but to revisit his sources in Afanasy Fet's love lyrics and especially Gavrila

---

[34] Lyra D. Monteiro, "Race-Conscious Casting and the Erasure of the Black Past in Lin-Manuel Miranda's *Hamilton*," *The Public Historian*, vol. 38, no. 1 (February 2016): 93. The article has been reprinted in *Historians on* Hamilton: *How a Blockbuster Musical Is Restaging America's Past*, ed. Renee C. Romano and Claire Bond Potter (New Brunswick, NJ: Rutgers University Press, 2018), 58–70. Probably the most prominent critic of *Hamilton* is the writer Ishmael Reed (see Julian Lucas, "I Ain't Been Mean Enough," *New Yorker*, July 26, 2021).

[35] An analysis that is close to mine in acknowledging *Hamilton*'s engagement with Black American life through intertextuality is Loren Kajikawa, "'Young, Scrappy, and Hungry': *Hamilton*, Hip Hop, and Race," *American Music*, Hamilton issue, 467–86, especially 473–4. The generally accepted understanding of the terms rap and hip-hop is that rap music is a subset of the larger cultural phenomenon of hip-hop, which includes rapping, Djing, graffiti, and breakdancing. See Justin Williams, *Rhymin' and Stealin': Musical Borrowing in Hip-Hop* (Ann Arbor: University of Michigan Press, 2013), 5–6.

[36] Taranovsky cited by Omry Ronen, *An Approach to Mandel'štam* (Jerusalem: The Magnes Press/The Hebrew University, 1983), xi.

[37] Kiril Taranovsky, *Essays on Mandel'štam* (Cambridge, MA: Harvard University Press, 1976), 4, emphasis mine. My focus in this article is on textual referentiality, which is of course inadequate to encompass all the dimensions of a work of musical theater like *Hamilton*. For a discussion of the musical referentiality of the work, see Kajikawa, "*Hamilton*, Hip Hop, and Race." For a very interesting analysis of the referentiality of the choreography, see Anne Searcy, "Bringing Dance Back to the Center in *Hamilton*," *American Music*, Hamilton issue, 448–66. Hip-hop is a quintessentially referential form. See Justin Williams, *Rhymin' and Stealin': Musical Borrowing in Hip-Hop*.

Derzhavin's ode "God," because these works add a deeper meaning to Dostoevsky's text and lead us to an important counternarrative to the nihilists' desecrations. For *Hamilton*, rap is not just a stylistic frill or gimmick, as it has sometimes been treated, but a serious subtextual layer, one that adds a parallel, more contemporary narrative to the story of the historical Hamilton, Jefferson, and Burr.

Probably the most important and prominent song in Act 1 of *Hamilton* is "My Shot," in which Hamilton meets his revolutionary comrades Lafayette, John Laurens, and Hercules Mulligan. Hamilton raps, "I gotta holler just to be heard," a reference to Tupac Shakur's "Holler if Ya' Hear Me" (1993). In this song, the lyric speaker describes a situation of poverty ("How long will it last 'til the po' get mo' cash"), police killings of Black men (the main plot of the song's narrative as dramatized in the official video), incarceration ("Much love to my brothers in the pen / See ya when I free ya if not when they shove me in"), and a desire for revolution ("Raise up! / Tell my young black males / Blaze up!"). This call is also echoed in "My Shot": "Rise up / When you're living on your knees, / You rise up. / Tell your brother that he's gotta rise up. / Tell your sister that she's gotta rise up."[38] The subtextual presence of Shakur's rap makes it clear that the revolution being referenced here is not confined to the past, the world of eighteenth-century characters, but is also a possibility for the future, for the world the twenty-first-century audience is living in. This is appropriate for both levels of the text; in his study of Shakur, Michael Eric Dyson stresses the revolutionary ethos of his upbringing in a Black Panther milieu.[39] Juxtaposing the revolution called for by Shakur with the one implemented by Hamilton and Lafayette elevates the former to a status of higher legitimacy.

Hamilton's line "Only nineteen but my mind is older" references Mobb Deep, "Shook Ones (Part II)" (1995), which deals with gang warfare in the projects and the awareness of the nearness of death: "Thirteen years in the projects—my mentality is what, kid? / You talk a good one, but you don't want it / Sometimes I wonder, do I deserve to live? / Or am I gonna burn in Hell for all the things I did?"[40] As Loren Kajikawa writes, "Miranda's borrowing of this line equates the

---

[38] Tupac Shakur, "Holler If Ya' Hear Me," Genius, https://genius.com/2pac-holler-if-ya-hear-me-lyrics. Miranda, "My Shot," in *Hamilton the Revolution*, 28. On the echoes of both the Civil Rights movement and the Black Lives Matter movement in "My Shot," see Craft, "Headfirst into an Abyss," 432–3.

[39] Michael Eric Dyson, *Holler If You Hear Me: Searching for Tupac Shakur* (New York: Basic Civitas Books, 2001).

[40] Mobb Deep, "Shook Ones (Part II)," Genius, https://genius.com/Mobb-deep-shook-ones-part-ii-lyrics.

struggle of inner-city youth with biographer Ron Chernow's description of Alexander Hamilton as a remarkably strong individual who overcame poverty, abandonment, and the death of his mother at an early age."[41] This theme is apposite to another area in which *Hamilton* has been subject to criticism. Kajikawa discusses the critique of *Hamilton*'s reinforcement of the narrative common to both Chernow's biography and the mythos of the rap star, "stories about great men whose innate talents led to upward mobility and acclaim."[42] A similar critique appears in a *Vanity Fair* profile of rapper and producer Sean Combs:

> Before financial bubbles started bursting in rapid succession in the 2000s, hustling felt democratic. Anyone with the right dream and the right grind could make it out of the hood, sometimes literally but usually metaphorically … It isn't that the hustle is dead, but that valorization of the hustle culture is surely on the ropes. Hip-hop's core constituency wants to debate the veracity of hustling when predatory mortgages, student loan debt, rising rent, flat wages, and surveillance police states choke the very life out of Black lives, Black hopes, and Black hustle.[43]

Another important rap subtext involves the song "Ten Duel Commandments." Both *Devils* and *Hamilton* include prominent scenes of dueling. In her book on dueling in Russian culture, Irina Reyfman has aptly called the practice, which originated in Renaissance Italy and spread throughout Europe and the Americas, "ritualized violence."[44] In Russian literature, beginning with Alexander Pushkin's *Eugene Onegin* (1825–33), literary treatments of dueling have used striking departures from the ritual for dramatic effect. *Hamilton* does something similar, using Hamilton's decision to "throw away his shot" and fire into the air during his duel with Aaron Burr as part of his martyrology.[45] In a brilliantly funny scene in *Devils*, Stavrogin enrages and decisively demoralizes his adversary Gaganov by "throwing away his shot" three times, the third time contemptuously firing into

---

[41] Kajikawa, "*Hamilton*, Hip Hop, and Race," 473–4. See Ron Chernow, *Alexander Hamilton* (New York: Penguin, 2004).

[42] Kajikawa, "*Hamilton*, Hip Hop, and Race," 481.

[43] Tressie McMillan Cottom, "With Love, Sean Combs," *Vanity Fair*, September 2021, 97. Combs was an associate of The Notorious B.I.G., Shakur's nemesis and another major subtextual source for *Hamilton* (see below).

[44] Irina Reyfman, *Ritualized Violence Russian Style: The Duel in Russian Culture and Literature* (Stanford: Stanford University Press, 1999).

[45] Miranda, "The World Was Wide Enough," in *Hamilton the Revolution*, 273.

a grove of trees.⁴⁶ In *Hamilton*, the song "Ten Duel Commandments" outlines the steps in the ritual of dueling. "Ten Duel Commandments" is modeled on "Ten Crack Commandments" (1997) by The Notorious B.I.G., Christopher Wallace, also known as Biggie Smalls. In this rap, detailed advice is given for how to succeed as a drug dealer, and premature death is as imminent a possibility as it is in the ritual of the duel. "Duel commandment No. 6" in *Hamilton* is "Leave a note for your next of kin. Tell 'em where you been. Pray that hell or heaven lets you in." Biggie Smalls raps: "Follow these rules you'll have mad bread to break up / If not, twenty-four years on the wake up / Slug hit your temple, watch your frame shake up / Caretaker did your makeup, when you passed."⁴⁷

Perhaps the most telling subtext in *Hamilton* is the classic 1982 rap "The Message" by Grandmaster Flash and the Furious Five, which is referenced in "Cabinet Battle #1."⁴⁸ Thomas Jefferson's line "Such a blunder sometimes it makes me wonder why I even bring the thunder" is a reference to the despairing refrain in "The Message": "It's like a jungle sometimes / It makes me wonder how I keep from going under."⁴⁹ This rap presents a vivid picture of Black urban poverty, with broken glass, rats, drug addicts, the homeless, prostitutes, broken families, bad education, prison, and death: "You'll grow in the ghetto living second rate / And your eyes will sing a song of deep hate." The other half of the refrain in "The Message," "Don't push me 'cause I'm close to the edge," like Shakur's later call to "Raise up," offers a potential response to despair by resorting to violence and revolution. Nevertheless, *Hamilton* ultimately affirms the democratic system that was created by the founders, despite its flaws.

My examples are by no means exhaustive, but I hope they help to demonstrate that it is unfair to claim that the Black American experience is erased in *Hamilton*.

---

46 Dostoevsky, *Devils*, *PSS*, 10: 227.

47 Miranda, "Ten Duel Commandments," in *Hamilton the Revolution*, 99. The Notorious B.I.G., "Ten Crack Commandments," Genius, https://genius.com/The-notorious-big-ten-crack-commandments-lyrics. See also Glenn Harlan Reynolds, "Hamilton, Hip-Hop, and the Culture of Dueling in America," in *Hamilton and the Law: Reading Today's Most Contentious Legal Issues through the Hit Musical*. Edited by Lisa A. Tucker (Ithaca: Cornell University Press, 2020), 145–53.

48 Although "The Message" was credited to Grandmaster Flash and the Furious Five, it was co-written by Melvin Glover (Melle Mel) and Edward Fletcher, known as Duke Bootee, who received a B.A. in English from Dickinson College in 1973. Alex Traub, "Duke Bootee, 69, Whose 'Message' Educated Hip-Hop," *New York Times*, January 31, 2021, https://www.nytimes.com/2021/01/29/arts/music/duke-bootee-dead.html.

49 Miranda, "Cabinet Battle #1," in *Hamilton the Revolution*, 162. Grandmaster Flash & the Furious Five, "The Message," Genius, https://genius.com/Grandmaster-flash-and-the-furious-five-the-message-lyrics.

Hamilton is a brilliant example of Bakhtin's concept of the double-voiced word. The intertextual references incorporate the oppressions of modern American life, particularly for Black citizens, as a counterpoint to the silk dresses and minuets and heroic battles in the show. Through the rap subtexts, the eighteenth-century duels in *Hamilton* in which both Hamilton and his son die are paralleled by twentieth-century feuds among young Black men, like the one waged between Tupac Shakur and Biggie Smalls in the violent years before they each died a few months apart in gun murders that remain unsolved to this day, although in September 2023, an arrest was made in the killing of Shakur. The revolutionary fervor that is acted out on stage may be directed not just against King George III in the eighteenth century but also against targets closer to home in our own day. The "double-voiced word" demands that we keep all these possibilities alive in our perception of *Hamilton*. Tynianov famously wondered how many "undiscovered parodies" still await understanding.[50] Most of the raps referenced in *Hamilton* are from the 1990s, thus they are historical documents that may be as difficult to access for today's listener as Washington's Farewell Address. Not every reader of Mandelstam's poetry rereads all of Pindar's odes; not every viewer of *Hamilton* is aware of the larger meanings of its rap references. But they are a vital part of the texture and meaning of the work.

Critic Monteiro asks, "Is it necessarily a good thing to feel ownership over a celebratory, white narrative of the American past? Is it a good thing for people of color to feel connected to the story of Hamilton, Washington, Jefferson, Madison, and Burr?"[51] There may be various answers to that question, affirmative or negative, but in essence Miranda seems to be an artist like Dostoevsky, who would rather restore the ideal than explode it or negate it, whether it is Dostoevsky's ideal of art and faith in the materialistic 1870s or Miranda's ideal of equality in the inequitable twenty-first century. The striving to make the Founders' ideal live up to reality is affirmed in Frederick Douglass's "What, to the Slave, Is the Fourth of July" (1852) as well as in Martin Luther King Jr.'s *Letter from Birmingham Jail* (1963). The failure of an ideal is not an excuse to give up on it, for either Dostoevsky (the ideal of the transcendent power of art and faith) or Miranda (the ideal of equality).

---

[50] Tynianov, "Dostoevskii i Gogol'," 455.
[51] Monteiro, "Race-Conscious Casting," 97; in Romano and Potter (eds.), *Historians on* Hamilton, 67.

Daveed Diggs, who created the roles of Lafayette and Jefferson, gives an answer to Monteiro's question that focuses on action to make the ideal closer to reality:

> What is implied to me now when I watch the show is that, if you get this sense of patriotism that I do from watching it, if you are filled up and prideful about America, and we are the bodies you see performing America, you then have a responsibility to go make that America exist. Because it doesn't. And it didn't then, and it still doesn't.[52]

It is the double-voiced word of parody in *Hamilton* that makes the modern experience of people of color in America present in the narrative of the founding and ensures that the ideal of equality does not remain static like Trumbull's painting but moves dynamically and summons all of us to action. As legal scholar Christina Mulligan writes, "In order for America, its Founding, and its Constitution to be redeemed, we have to commit ourselves to the project … America is in a constant state of becoming. It will become different Americas, depending on whether we, as individuals, choose to commit to it or not."[53]

"America is in a constant state of becoming," and democracy needs to be constantly nurtured if it is to survive. The most recent cooptation of the imagery and rhetoric of "1776" has been by the MAGA movement, most strikingly in the January 6, 2021, storming of the US Capitol by a mob seeking to overturn the results of the 2020 presidential election. Far-right Rep. Lauren Boebert of Colorado tweeted "Today is 1776" the morning of the attack, and members of the mob chanted "1776" as they broke into the Capitol. A document later found by federal prosecutors that contained a detailed plan for storming government buildings on January 6 was called "1776 Returns." As legal scholar Franita Tolson writes, "Some Americans have, throughout the course of our history, romanticized the revolutionaries of 1776, selectively using that moment to justify violent behavior that is inconsistent with the democratic ideals that we have committed to as a nation. Not coincidentally, the language of revolution reemerges when whites feel threatened by the rise of minority political power."[54]

---

[52] Daveed Diggs in "*Hamilton*: History Has Its Eyes on You," Disney+.

[53] Christina Mulligan, "Finding Constitutional Redemption through *Hamilton*," in *Hamilton and the Law*, 74.

[54] Franita Tolston, "Why the mob thought attacking the Capitol was their '1776 moment,'" *Los Angeles Times*, January 21, 2021, https://www.latimes.com/opinion/story/2021-01-21/insurrection-capitol-attack-patriotism-1776. See also Alan Feuer, "Document in Jan. 6 Case Shows Plan to Storm Government Buildings," *New York Times*, March 14, 2022, https://www.nytimes.com/2022/03/14/

The struggle over the iconography of the Revolutionary War has not ended with *Hamilton* and its new vision of the founders, but, as Diggs says, we have "a responsibility to go make that America exist."

In 1995 I argued that Dostoevsky's use of restorative parody in *Devils* was part of his quest for an approach to the art of the past that would represent "not naive, sterile imitation but historically informed enthusiasm."[55] Miranda's transformation of the facts of Hamilton's biography into a joyous musical is a prime example of historically informed enthusiasm. It is a truism that comedy is serious business. The deployment of restorative parody and of subtextual reference by both Dostoevsky and Miranda (and by Weird Al Yankovic, for that matter) requires virtuosity, perfectionism, and adeptness at both imitation and creation. Although parody transcends funniness, there is something funny about Raphael's Madonna reborn as a cursing nihilist; there is something funny about a rapping George Washington. And that humor is central to the vital power of restorative parody in Dostoevsky's novel and Miranda's play.

Bibliography

Anderson, Sam. "The Weirdly Enduring Appeal of Weird Al Yankovic," *New York Times Magazine*, April 9, 2020, https://www.nytimes.com/2020/04/09/magazine/weird-al-yankovic.html.

Bakhtin, Mikhail. *Problems of Dostoevsky's Poetics*. Edited and translated by Caryl Emerson. Minneapolis: University of Minnesota Press, 1984.

Chernow, Ron. *Alexander Hamilton*. New York: Penguin, 2004.

Cohen, Marshall. "January 6 Was Opposite of 1776, Judge Tells Rioter Who Carried Revolutionary Flag into Capitol," *CNN Politics*, December 2, 2021, https://www.cnn.com/2021/12/02/politics/january-6-andrew-wrigley/index.html.

Cottom, Tressie McMillan. "With Love, Sean Combs," *Vanity Fair*, September 2021.

---

us/politics/enrique-tarrio-jan-6-document.html; "Identifying far-right symbols that appeared at the U.S. Capitol riot," *The Washington Post*, January 15, 2021, https://www.washingtonpost.com/nation/interactive/2021/far-right-symbols-capitol-riot/; Marshall Cohen, "January 6 was opposite of 1776, judge tells rioter who carried revolutionary flag into Capitol," CNN Politics, December 2, 2021, https://www.cnn.com/2021/12/02/politics/january-6-andrew-wrigley/index.html; and Quentin Young, "What I learned from watching more than 500 Jan. 6 videos," *Virginia Mercury*, February 11, 2022, https://www.virginiamercury.com/2022/02/11/what-i-learned-from-watching-more-than-500-jan-6-videos/.

55 Fusso, "Maidens in Childbirth," 262.

Craft, Elizabeth Titrington. "Headfirst into an Abyss: The Politics and Political Reception of *Hamilton*," *American Music*, vol. 36, no. 4 (Winter 2018; special issue on *Hamilton*): 429–47.

Dostoevsky, Fyodor. *Devils*. Translated by Michael R. Katz. Oxford: Oxford University Press, 2008.

Dostoevsky, Fyodor [Dostoevskii, F. M.]. *Polnoe sobranie sochinenii*, 30 vols. Leningrad: Nauka, 1972–88.

Dyson, Michael Eric. *Holler if You Hear Me: Searching for Tupac Shakur*. New York: Basic Civitas Books, 2001.

Erman, Irina. "Autobiography of a 'Living Plagiary': Vasilii Rozanov's Secret Dostoevskian Genealogy," *AutobiografiYA*, no. 7 (2018): 171–90.

"An Evening of Poetry, Music, and the Spoken Word," *YouTube*, https://www.youtube.com/watch?v=WNFf7nMIGnE.

Feuer, Alan. "Document in Jan. 6 Case Shows Plan to Storm Government Buildings," *New York Times*, March 14, 2022, https://www.nytimes.com/2022/03/14/us/politics/enrique-tarrio-jan-6-document.html.

Freidenberg, Olga. "The Origin of Parody," in *Semiotics and Structuralism: Readings from the Soviet Union*. Edited by Henryk Baran, 269–83. White Plains: International Arts and Sciences Press, 1976.

Fusso, Susanne. "Maidens in Childbirth: The Sistine Madonna in Dostoevskii's *Devils*," *Slavic Review*, vol. 54, no. 2 (summer 1995): 261–75.

Gates, Henry Louis, Jr. *The Signifying Monkey: A Theory of African-American Literary Criticism*. New York: Oxford University Press, 1988.

Gopnik, Adam. "Knowing Mr. Lear," *New Yorker*, April 23, 2018.

Grandmaster Flash and the Furious Five. "The Message," *Genius*, https://genius.com/Grandmaster-flash-and-the-furious-five-the-message-lyrics.

"*Hamilton*: History Has Its Eyes on You," *Disney+*.

Harbert, Elissa. "'Ever to the Right'? The Political Life of *1776* in the Nixon Era," *American Music*, vol. 35, no. 2 (summer 2017): 237–70.

Hutcheon, Linda. *A Theory of Parody: The Teachings of Twentieth-Century Art Forms*. Urbana and Chicago: University of Illinois Press, 2000.

"Identifying Far-Right Symbols That Appeared at the U.S. Capitol Riot," *Washington Post*, January 15, 2021, https://www.washingtonpost.com/nation/interactive/2021/far-right-symbols-capitol-riot/.

Kajikawa, Loren. "'Young, Scrappy, and Hungry': *Hamilton*, Hip Hop, and Race," *American Music*, vol. 36, no. 4 (Winter 2018; special issue on *Hamilton*): 467–86.

Lebedeva, O. B. and A. S. Ianushkevich. "V. A. Zhukovskii i A. V. Nikitenko o Sikstinskoi madonne Rafaelia: Tipologiia ekfrasisa kak reprezentant esteticheskogo soznaniia," *Vestnik Tomskogo gosudarstvennogo universiteta. Filologiia*, no. 46 (2017): 124–51.

Lucas, Julian. "I Ain't Been Mean Enough," *New Yorker*, July 26, 2021.

Miranda, Lin-Manuel, and Jeremy McCarter. *Hamilton the Revolution*. New York: Grand Central Publishing, 2016.

Mobb Deep. "Shook Ones (Part II)," *Genius*, https://genius.com/Mobb-deep-shook-ones-part-ii-lyrics.

Monteiro, Lyra D. "Race-Conscious Casting and the Erasure of the Black Past in Lin-Manuel Miranda's *Hamilton*," *The Public Historian*, vol. 38, no. 1 (February 2016): 89–98. Reprinted in *Historians on Hamilton: How a Blockbuster Musical Is Restaging America's Past*. Edited by Renee C. Romano and Claire Bond Potter, 58–70. New Brunswick, NJ: Rutgers University Press, 2018.

Morson, Gary Saul. *The Boundaries of Genre: Dostoevskii's "Diary of a Writer" and the Traditions of Literary Utopia*. Austin: University of Texas Press, 1981.

Mulligan, Christina. "Finding Constitutional Redemption through *Hamilton*," in *Hamilton and the Law: Reading Today's Most Contentious Legal Issues through the Hit Musical*. Edited by Lisa A. Tucker, 69–74. Ithaca: Cornell University Press, 2020.

The Notorious B.I.G. "Ten Crack Commandments," *Genius*, https://genius.com/The-notorious-big-ten-crack-commandments-lyrics.

Obama, Barack. *A Promised Land*. New York: Crown, 2020.

Peterson, Dale. *Up from Bondage: The Literatures of Russian and African American Soul*. Durham: Duke University Press, 2000.

Reyfman, Irina. *Ritualized Violence Russian Style: The Duel in Russian Culture and Literature*. Stanford: Stanford University Press, 1999.

Reynolds, Glenn Harlan. "*Hamilton*, Hip-Hop, and the Culture of Dueling in America," in *Hamilton and the Law: Reading Today's Most Contentious Legal Issues through the Hit Musical*. Edited by Lisa A. Tucker, 145–53. Ithaca: Cornell University Press, 2020.

Ronen, Omry. *An Approach to Mandel'štam*. Jerusalem: The Magnes Press/The Hebrew University, 1983.

The Roots. "No John Trumbull," *SongMeanings*, https://songmeanings.com/songs/view/3530822107859582613/.

Rozanov, Vasily. *Semeinyi vopros v Rossii*. In his *Sobranie sochinenii*, vol. 18. Edited by A. N. Nikoliukin, et al. Moscow: Respublika, 2004.

Searcy, Anne. "Bringing Dance Back to the Center in *Hamilton*," *American Music*, vol. 36, no. 4 (Winter 2018; special issue on *Hamilton*): 448–66.

Shakur, Tupac. "Holler If Ya' Hear Me," *Genius*, https://genius.com/2pac-holler-if-ya-hear-me-lyrics.

Smith, Roberta. "Robert Colescott Throws down the Gauntlet," *New York Times*, July 7, 2022, https://www.nytimes.com/2022/07/07/arts/design/robert-colescott-new-museum-painter-race.html.

Stone, Peter and Sherman Edwards. *1776: A Musical Play*. Book by Peter Stone. Music and Lyrics by Sherman Edwards. New York: Viking, 1970.

Taranovsky, Kiril. *Essays on Mandel'štam*. Cambridge, MA: Harvard University Press, 1976.

Tolson, Franita. "Why the Mob Thought Attacking the Capitol Was Their '1776 Moment,'" *Los Angeles Times*, January 21, 2021, https://www.latimes.com/opinion/story/2021-01-21/insurrection-capitol-attack-patriotism–1776.

Traub, Alex. "Duke Bootee, 69, Whose 'Message' Educated Hip-Hop," *New York Times*, January 31, 2021, https://www.nytimes.com/2021/01/29/arts/music/duke-bootee-dead.html.

Tynianov, Yuri [Tynianov, Iurii]. *Arkhaisty i novatory*. Leningrad: Priboi, 1929; Ardis reprint, 1985.

Tynianov, Yuri [Tynjanov, Jurij]. "Dostoevsky and Gogol," in *Twentieth-Century Russian Literary Criticism*. Edited by Victor Erlich, 102–16. New Haven: Yale University Press, 1975.

Tynianov, Yuri. *Permanent Evolution: Essays on Literature, Theory and Film*. Edited and translated by Ainsley Morse and Philip Redko. Boston: Academic Studies Press, 2019.

Williams, Justin. *Rhymin' and Stealin': Musical Borrowing in Hip-Hop*. Ann Arbor: University of Michigan Press, 2013.

Young, Quentin. "What I Learned from Watching More than 500 Jan. 6 Videos," *Virginia Mercury*, February 11, 2022, https://www.virginiamercury.com/2022/02/11/what-i-learned-from-watching-more-than-500-jan-6-videos/.

Zhukovsky, V. A. [Zhukovskii]. "Rafaeleva 'Madonna,'" in *Estetika i kritika*. Edited by F. Z. Kanunova, et al., 307–11. Moscow: Iskusstvo, 1985.

8

The Funny and the Furious: Laughter and Gender in Dostoevsky

Irina Erman

Men are afraid that women will laugh at them.
Women are afraid that men will kill them.

—attributed to Margaret Atwood

Fyodor Dostoevsky spent the summer of 1866 in the warm and boisterous company of his sister Vera Ivanova's family in Liublino near Moscow. He took up residence near their dacha and spent the days with the Ivanov kids and their numerous visitors. One of the family's servants was assigned to stay with Dostoevsky at night to make sure he was not alone in case of an epileptic attack. His niece Maria Ivanova reports that one day, the servant categorically refused to go back to the writer's house. Terrified, he said that Dostoevsky was planning to kill someone. Dostoevsky would pace his room late at night and talk to himself about his murderous plans. He was, of course, composing *Crime and Punishment*. As had become his method, he would act out his ideas and test scenes aloud before committing them to paper.

While he was unwittingly terrorizing the Ivanovs' poor servant at night with his dark materials, Dostoevsky was filling his days with games, practical jokes, and amateur theatricals, of which he was apparently the "leading instigator."[1] Memoirs written by family and friends record the writer's indefatigable creativity in staging planned and impromptu performances and his enthusiasm for organizing games. At one point, Dostoevsky masterminded the "rescue" of three sisters at the neighboring dacha from their too-strict German governess for a

---

[1] Maria [Mariia] Aleksandrovna Ivanova, "Vospominaniia," in *F. M. Dostoevskii v vospominaniiakh sovremennikov v dvukh tomakh*, vol. 2. Edited by K. Tiunkin (Moscow: Khudozhestvennaia Literatura, 1990), 41. Translations from the Russian are my own unless otherwise noted.

night-time walk. Dostoevsky referred to this detested governess as a "chicken leg in crinoline."[2] He would kindly lend a version of this hilarious moniker to Katerina Ivanovna to throw at her German landlady in *Crime and Punishment*. His niece noticed the incredible reciprocity between Dostoevsky at play and at work, as he would suddenly turn serious and depart a game to write down an idea, before rejoining his young companions with renewed energy:

> Fyodor Mikhailovich would lead in all the games and promenades. It would sometimes happen that during a game he would leave the others and go to his dacha to write something down for his work. In these instances, he would ask for someone to come get him in about ten minutes. But when they came to get him, he would be so consumed by his work that he would get irritated and chase them out. After some time, he would come back on his own, cheerful, and once again ready to continue the game.[3]

Maria Ivanova's recollections from the summer of 1866 help to visualize Dostoevsky's creative process, wherein play interweaves with even his most somber thematics, while comic theatricality offers paths for subversion and survival from tragic despair.

Once we get over our shock at the idea of the man, whose novels feature murder and abuse with the same constancy with which his portraits feature a long beard and drawn face, playing practical jokes on his nieces and nephews and staging elaborate comic improvisations, we are bound to ask: what, then, does Dostoevsky laugh at and who does he laugh with? The all-female line-up of authors in the present collection invites yet another intriguing question about who laughs along with Dostoevsky today and why. This chapter attempts to address these questions in five sections, each of which explores a different aspect of the nexus of laughter and gender in Dostoevsky. The first section draws on contemporaneous memoirs to consider what Dostoevsky laughs at as he is composing a novel about the murder of two women and the abuse of many others. The next section analyzes *Crime and Punishment* to reveal Dostoevsky's emphatically feminized comic counterpoint to misogynist violence, which champions communal responsibility over egoism and isolation. The third section explains the pathologization of Dostoevsky's comedy by his contemporary critics by demonstrating its fundamentally subversive perspective, which flips patriarchy's gendered script via the vaudeville and its stock types. The following

---

[2] Ibid., 43.
[3] Ibid., 42.

section turns to his explicitly comic and theatrically inflected "Uncle's Dream," with a focus on its obnoxious and hilarious heroine, whom—like the other unruly women who dominate their scenes in his texts—Dostoevsky endows with his own improvisational abilities and the spirit of his comedy. And, finally, the concluding section briefly extends this analysis to *The Idiot*, wherein Dostoevsky's unruly woman type matures. By tracing this trajectory, I aim to demonstrate how Dostoevsky addresses problematic gender relations through dimensions of laughter, transforming the immediate world around him with the power of play and inflecting his fictional worlds with humor that defies patriarchy's deadening power structures.

The Polar Bear Ate Him: Laughing at Misogyny

During the summer of 1866, Dostoevsky singled out Aleksandr Karepin, the son of his younger sister Varvara, as the favorite subject for his pranks and comic compositions due to the twenty-five-year-old doctor's retrograde attitude toward "the woman question." "Karepin was single, but always fantasized about his ideal fiancé, who would be no older than 16 or 17 and on whose account he was already terribly jealous. He hated emancipated women and said that his wife will be far removed from all the contemporary ideas about women's equality and work."[4] In response to his nephew's fantasy of a submissive teenage bride, Dostoevsky would frighten Karepin with the plot of Nikolai Chernyshevsky's then wildly popular novel *What Is To Be Done?*, telling him that she would inevitably run away from his oppression and join a sewing collective, following Chernyshevsky's emancipated heroine. Dostoevsky's mockery culminated in the writer's staging of an elaborate "trial" to adjudicate between the viewpoints of Karepin and his runaway bride, wherein Dostoevsky played both the judge and executioner in a bear suit. Maria Ivanova writes,

> Fyodor Mikhailovich played the judge wearing his sister's red cardigan, paper glasses and a bucket on his head. Next to him sat the secretary, Sof'ia Aleskandrovna Ivanova, and the accused Karepins—husband and wife. Fyodor Mikhailovich makes a brilliant speech in defense of the wife, who wants to run away to St. Petersburg to learn to sew on a sewing machine.

---

[4] Ibid., 45.

In the end he finds the husband guilty and sentences him to exile at the North Pole. Karepin gets mad and throws himself at Dostoevsky. The curtain falls, the first Act concludes. The second Act takes place at the North Pole. There is snow all around made from sheets and cotton balls. Karepin sits and complains about his fate. Dostoevsky in the guise of a polar bear sneaks up on him and eats him.

Such plays were put on quite often.[5]

In another hilarious episode, Dostoevsky spoke at length to convince his nephew that he was too good for the modest profession of doctor and needed to try his hand at a grander title. In the end, Dostoevsky suggested declaring Karepin the second prophet Muhammed. During the raucous procession staged in the new prophet's honor, Karepin apparently said something impertinent to one of the ladies and was immediately sentenced to "hanging" from a tree by his armpits. Tellingly, the women in the family remember Karepin with more than a hint of irritation. In her recollections, Maria Ivanova acknowledges Karepin's impressive scholarly abilities, but claims that "in life he was almost an idiot."[6] Dostoevsky's daughter Liubov' echoes this sentiment to write, "The son of my aunt Varvara was so stupid that his stupidity bordered on idiocy."[7] Aleksandr Andreevich Dostoevsky is kinder to his cousin than his female relatives, noting that "A. P. Karepin really did suffer from a mental abnormality for which medicine probably has a specialized term, but this was not stupidity, and certainly not idiocy. I personally remember Aleksandr Petrovich very well, and we—the kids together with the adults—did joke about his, so to speak 'verbal incontinence,' but no one ever brought up his being stupid."[8]

I suspect that, in some part, Fyodor Dostoevsky's teasing of Aleksandr Petrovich Karepin—especially where "the woman question" was concerned—also had to do with the writer's dislike of his father. Pyotr Karepin was by all accounts a decent, hard-working man, practical, and good with money. He married Dostoevsky's younger sister Varvara when he was forty-four and she was seventeen years old. Fyodor Dostoevsky did not approve of the match and came to resent Karepin even more when he had to repeatedly beg him for

---

[5] Ibid.
[6] Ibid., 44.
[7] Liubov' Fyodorovna Dostoevskaia in M. V. Volotskoi. *Khronika roda Dostoevskogo, 1506–1933* (Moscow: Sever, 1933), 165.
[8] Aleksandr Andreevich Dostoevsky in M. V. Volotskoi, *Khronika roda Dostoevskogo*, 165.

money, since Pyotr Karepin served as the guardian of the Dostoevsky estate after Mikhail Dostoevsky's death in 1839. Some of the tensest correspondence between Dostoevsky and the elder Karepin—dripping with sarcasm on Dostoevsky's side—dates to the period when the financially struggling young writer was composing *Poor Folk*, and he seems to have associated Karepin with Bykov when he gave the novella's abused heroine his younger sister's name. Pyotr Karepin is also unfairly caricatured in the figure of Pyotr Petrovich Luzhin in *Crime and Punishment*, a forty-five-year-old businessman who dreams of a helpless young bride to dominate, and whom the brother of the potential bride considers practically illiterate.[9]

It is worth noting, though, that Fyodor Dostoevsky's disapproval of the age difference in his sister's marriage did not prevent him from marrying Anna Snitkina when he was forty-six and she was twenty-one. He was apparently uncomfortable enough with it, however, to repeatedly make fun of his own hypocrisy by putting on lengthy improvised performances in the exaggerated comic role of the elderly husband, much to the chagrin of his wife who reported:

> I would get very annoyed ... when Fyodor Mikhailovich would play the role of "the old man trying to appear younger" ["*молодящегося старичка*"]. He could spend hours relaying the words and thoughts of his hero, the old prince from his "Uncle's Dream." He expressed extremely original and surprising thoughts, spoke humorously and brilliantly, but I would be bothered by these stories from the point of view of a good for nothing old man who was trying to appear younger.[10]

Dostoevsky is clearly not afraid to laugh at himself. Meanwhile, the men in his novels who are particularly abusive to women—such as Raskolnikov, Akulka's husband, Totsky from *The Idiot*, just to name a few—are as a rule terrified of being laughed at because they see social relations as merely a struggle for

---

[9] For more on Fyodor Dostoevsky's relationship with Pyotr Karepin and its transposition into his art, see Konstantin Mochulsky, *Dostoevsky: His Life and Work* (Princeton: Princeton University Press, 1967), 18–22.
Raskolnikov thinks that Luzhin "writes like an illiterate [*безграмотно пишет*]." See Fyodor Dostoevsky, *Crime and Punishment, PSS* (Leningrad: Nauka, 1973), 6: 180.

[10] Anna Dostoevskaia, *Vospominaniia* (Moscow: Khudozhestvannaia Literatura, 1971), 88, quoted in Tatiana Rodina, *Dostoevskii: Povestvovanie i drama* (Moscow: Nauka, 1984), 102. Rodina's chapter on Dostoevsky's satire, which also touches on Dostoevsky's penchant for improvisations, makes for exceptionally worthwhile reading for those interested in the subject of Dostoevsky, comedy, and theater.

dominance. Those who desire to dominate and objectify others become Dostoevsky's favorite comic targets. But even as he holds would-be tyrants up for ridicule, Dostoevsky looks toward more positive uses of laugher, which he associates with the feminine: namely, comedy's leveling potential that uplifts the social over the individual and empathy over destructive egoism.

Crime and Punishment and the Gender of Comedy

Dostoevsky may seem a strange champion of "the woman question," given that his fictional worlds are so replete with gendered violence that he has been accused of "heroine abuse."[11] Beginning with *Poor Folk*, the sexual abuse of a young woman or a girl by an older man functions as the fulcrum on which entire plots hinge.[12] This scenario appears so fundamental to Dostoevsky's writing that Harriet Murav astutely wonders, whether "Dostoevsky's narratives in general, or indeed, narrative in general, require a (female) victim."[13] Even when the violence is not explicitly sexual in nature, it is typically gendered and motivated by a problematic version of masculinity that takes its insecurities out on women. Consider, for example, the disturbing confession of "Akulka's Husband" embedded exactly half-way through *Notes from the Dead House*. Another notable example is Raskolnikov's abuse of the women in his life, which includes, in addition to the obvious murder of the pawnbroker and her sister, his appalling treatment of his mother, sister, and Sonya.[14] While the divide in "Akulka's Husband" lies between two men—one who remains an unrepentant murderer and the second who asks forgiveness for his sins against the tormented

---

[11] See Thomas Gaiton Marullo, *Heroine Abuse: Dostoevsky's Netochka Nezvanova and the Poetics of Codependency* (Dekalb, IL: Northern Illinois University Press, 2015). Marullo's title evocatively renders the obsessive repetition of scenarios of the abuse of young women and girls in Dostoevsky's works as addiction, suggesting his narratives' dependence on "heroine abuse."

[12] The centrality of this topic has long been recognized by Dostoevsky's critics and biographers. For instance, Victor Terras notes that it is "obviously present and prominent" in his earliest texts no less than in the mature novels. See Victor Terras, *The Young Dostoevsky (1846-1849). A Critical Study* (Paris: Mouton, 1969), 76.

[13] Harriet Murav, "Reading Woman in Dostoevsky," in *A Plot of Her Own: The Female Protagonist in Russian Literature*. Edited by Sona Stephan Hoisington (Evanston: Northwestern University Press, 1995), 46.

[14] For example, Raskolnikov's aggressive behavior toward Sonya culminates in the Bible reading scene, when Raskolnikov coerces a reluctant Sonya into reading Lazarus aloud to him. This interaction is narrated using vocabulary that evokes sexual coercion, which leads Eric Naiman to memorably expose it as "gospel rape." See Eric Naiman, "Gospel Rape," *Dostoevsky Studies*, vol. 22 (2018): 9–38.

young woman—Raskolnikov's split is internal. Yet his *raskol*, or schism, also primarily manifests in his behavior toward women. The actions of a radicalized young loner, whose insecurities and desires for grandeur materialize in violence against women, are punctuated by moments of unmediated empathy and a sense of communal responsibility, as, for example, he tries to save the young girl on the street from a predator, whom he calls Svidrigailov after his sister's harasser.

Raskolnikov takes himself way too seriously. But astute readers notice that everyone in the novel—including even his murder victim in his nightmare—is laughing at Raskolnikov. Indeed, *Crime and Punishment* presents a systematic undressing of the young man in the clown suit.[15] Dostoevsky ridicules Raskolnikov's delusions of grandeur with the help of the weirdly feminized detective Porfiry Petrovich, who reminds the narrator of "a peasant woman" as he regularly outmatches Raskolnikov in wit and humor.[16] Further comic relief is provided by a real peasant woman, the kindly cook Nastasya who pities and charitably feeds Raskolnikov while he lays around pondering his superiority, and erupts in bubbling, irrepressible laughter at how seriously he takes himself.

Nastasya stands out in a novel where laughter tends to be either derisive or deeply disturbing, as it is in the numerous scenes of crowds entertained by suffering. It makes sense that derisive laughter, which adheres to the superiority theory of humor and displays of a lack of empathy, would dominate *Crime and Punishment* given how intently it resonates with Raskolnikov's "great man" theory wherein the absence of empathy is construed as superiority. Nastasya, however, offers an alternative to detached observation or disdain by combining laughter with active compassion. She shares the tea from her cracked kettle with Raskolnikov and asks a series of questions that deliver the most positively comic and down-to-earth scene in the novel:

- I'm doing ...—Raskolnikov said reluctantly and sternly.
- What are you doing?
- Work ...

---

[15] For a discussion of Raskolnikov's clownish aspects, see Fiona Bell's chapter in this volume. For a discussion of his ridiculous clothing and what it says about him, see Boris Christa, "Raskolnikov's Wardrobe: Dostoevsky's Use of Vestimentary Markers for Literary Communication in *Crime and Punishment*," in *Dostoevsky on the Threshold of Other Worlds: Essays in Honor of Malcolm V. Jones*. Edited by Sarah Young and Lesley Milne (Ilkeston: Bramcote Press, 2006), 14–20.

[16] Dostoevsky, *Crime and Punishment*, *PSS*, 6: 192.

- What kind of work?
- Thinking—he answered seriously after a pause.
Nastasya was overcome with laughter. She was a jovial type and, when moved to laughter, she laughed silently, her whole body shaking and shuddering until she was nearly bursting.
- Have you thought up a lot of money then?—she finally managed to get out.[17]

Nastasya might be nearly bursting, but it is Raskolnikov who is deflated. He speaks "sternly" and "seriously," while Nastasya's charitable compassion and simple questions expose his egoism as ridiculous. She appears as the very spirit of comedy, echoing Erasmus's feminine Folly from *In Praise of Folly* and prefiguring George Meredith's conception of comedy as "a sweet cook" who "proposes the correcting of pretentiousness, of inflation, of dulness [sic], and of the vestiges of rawness and grossness to be found among us" in the preface to his 1879 novel *The Egoist*.[18]

Raskolnikov's tragic isolation and hubris are countered by a fundamentally comic vision of communal responsibility that underpins Dostoevsky's entire philosophical outlook. This contrast in genre is potentially engendered. "Comedy's interest in the social, as opposed to tragedy's in the individual, aligns it with values that are conventionally associated with the feminine: community over separation, and the preservation of life rather than its sacrifice for principle, power, or a Faustian knowledge that oversteps proper limits."[19] Some feminist thinkers even go so far as to suggest, "If tragic form is associated with a specifically male psychological experience, might comedy be an affirmation of female experience?"[20] Although such a reductive distinction is perhaps too extreme, there is a suggestive correspondence in way that comedy has been historically denigrated in parallel to women's stories by patriarchal discourse. Taking stock of this correspondence in the history of Dostoevsky criticism, I would suggest a more productive discussion of Dostoevsky's feminism or lack thereof can be had by first locating it within the comic strains in his work.

---

[17] *PSS*, 6: 26–7.

[18] George Meredith, *The Egoist: A Comedy in Narrative* (London: Archibald Constable & Co, 1909), 8.

[19] Kathleen Rowe, *The Unruly Woman: Gender and the Genres of Laugher* (Austin: The University of Texas Press, 1995), 103.

[20] Lisa Merrill, "Feminist Humor: Rebellious and Self-Affirming," in *Last Laughs: Perspectives on Women and Comedy*. Edited by Regina Barrecca (New York: Gordon and Breach, 1988), 272.

Flipping the Script: The Vaudeville's Victim

Critical distaste for Dostoevsky's lighter side can be traced back to Vissarion Belinsky's negative reaction to *The Double*, which rendered comedy as pathology. Dostoevsky took this criticism so much to heart that he eventually rewrote *The Double* to cut down on comic repetition and take out the novella's explicitly comic genre markers: the mock-heroic chapter subheadings that hailed from picaresque novels, such as Cervantes' *Don Quixote* and Fielding's *Tom Jones*. In the history of Dostoevsky criticism, however, Nikolai Mikhailovsky's "A Cruel Talent" remains the most famous pathologization of the writer, rivaled only by Freud's "Dostoevsky and Parricide" in influence. It might come as a shock to readers of "A Cruel Talent" that the essay originated as a review of the author's most comic works, including *The Double*, "Uncle's Dream," and *The Village of Stepanchikovo and Its Inhabitants*.[21] Unsurprisingly, Mikhailovsky does not find Dostoevsky funny, and instead famously proclaims him to be the unparalleled poet of sadism who has "analyzed the feelings of a wolf devouring a sheep with such detail, depth, and with such, one might say, love" as no one else in Russian literature.[22] To be slightly fairer to Mikhailovsky than he is to Dostoevsky, the critic does acknowledge the Underground Man's terrible treatment of Liza in his discussion of *Notes from the Underground*. However, the other "sheep" whose suffering Mikhailovsky bemoans tend to be rather surprising. Rather than focus on the serial abuse of women behind socially acceptable façades exposed by Dostoevsky's narratives, Mikhailovsky takes issue with the suffering inflicted on Dostoevsky's men.

Spare a thought for Nastasya Filippovna's victims in *The Idiot*. She is an exemplar of a "tyrannical to the point of cruelty, unhinged, yet captivating" type that Mikhailovsky also identifies in Polina from *The Gambler* and Grushenka from *The Brothers Karamazov*.[23] Mikhailovsky's erasure of the suffering

---

[21] Mikhailovsky's essay was intended to review Volumes 2 and 3 of Dostoevsky's collected works. Volume 2 consisted of *Poor Folk*, *The Double*, "Mr. Prokharchin," "A Novel in Nine Letters," "The Landlady," "A Weak Heart," "The Other Man's Wife and the Husband Under the Bed," "The Honest Thief," "A Christmas Tree and a Wedding," "White Nights," *Netochka Nezvanova*, and "The Little Hero." Volume 3 included "Uncle's Dream," *The Village of Stepanchikovo and Its Inhabitants*, "A Nasty Story," "Winter Notes of Summer Impressions," *Notes from the Underground*, "The Crocodile," and *The Gambler*. While not all these texts are comic, the comic predominates in this list, and the ones Mikhailovsky spends the most time on (the parodic *Notes from the Underground*, the vaudeville-inspired "The Other Man's Wife and the Husband Under the Bed" and the uproariously hilarious *The Village of Stepanchikovo*) are.

[22] Nikolai Mikhailovsky, "Zhestokii talant," in *Literaturnaia kritika: Stat'i o russkoi literature XIX-nachala XX veka*. Edited by V. Averin (Leningrad: Khudozhestvennaia Literatura, 1989), 158.

[23] Mikhailovsky, "Zhestokii talant," 167.

endured by Dostoevsky's so-called "infernal women" is caricaturishly funny in combination with the suffering he locates in the unlikeliest of places. Peeking "under the bed" into the realm of Dostoevsky's comedy, Mikhailovsky emerges horrified. According to him, Dostoevsky's "The Other Man's Wife and the Husband Under the Bed"—two early vaudeville-inspired stories ("The Jealous Husband" and "The Other Man's Wife") from 1848 that the author combined into the two-part tale for his first collected works—contains all of Dostoevsky's cruelty in embryonic form. It takes Mikhailovsky two pages to summarize the story, which, he says, "would have looked like the most run-of-the-mill vaudeville of the most talentless of such products' purveyors had it not been for this drawn-out excessiveness of the hero's torments."[24] The hero's torments consist of his increasingly more and more ridiculous attempts to catch his wife, whom he rightly suspects of adultery, in the act, while simultaneously claiming that he is anything but that most humiliating of comic stock types: a cuckold. Mikhailovsky turns the husband's humiliation into a metaphorical barrage of physical violence on the part of the author:

> Was it really necessary to beat, drag him about by his hair and spit on foolish Ivan Andreevich so much for the sake of such a lesson? Is this really anything but a bullfight put on solely for the sake of unnecessary cruelty? Let us allow that Ivan Andreevich is a very funny bull, but that only makes this arsenal of misfortunes aimed at him, this lineup of bandeliers, picadors and matadors that aggravate, stab, and kill him all the more uncalled for.[25]

To be clear, no one beats, stabs, spits on Ivan Andreevich or drags him by his hair. He is bitten on the nose by a tiny dog while he is hiding under the bed of a general's wife, into whose bedroom he mistakenly charged during his hunt. (And he strangles the dog, losing any chances he had for my sympathy, at least.) Mikhailovsky's reconfiguration of Ivan Andreevich's humiliation into an onslaught of physical attacks presents a striking illustration of the aphorism, which serves as the epigraph to this essay: "Men are afraid women will laugh at them. Women are afraid men will kill them." As women well know, laughter's harm to an insecure man's ego risks triggering violence.

In Dostoevsky's take on the vaudeville, this violence is transposed onto the dog. The adulterous wife, Glafira Petrovna, does not emerge merely unscathed

---

[24] Ibid., 197.
[25] Ibid., 196–7.

but, in fact, triumphant. At the end of "The Jealous Husband," Ivan Andreevich, together with a young man he does not realize is also her lover, catches Glafira Petrovna emerging from a rendezvous with yet a third man, but she adroitly maneuvers all three, and packs her befuddled husband into a carriage while setting a date for later with lover number two. Punctuated by role reversals, Dostoevsky's story literalizes the husband's debasement, while offering a comedic antidote to patriarchy's assigned roles, wherein a woman emerges on top. I can only guess as to what really bothered Mikhailovsky so much about a narrative that refuses to punish a shameless, clever woman who will continue to run circles around the men in her life. Contrary to Mikhailovsky's assertion that Dostoevsky's vaudeville goes against the genre's grain, Natalie Zemon Davis' influential study of "Women on Top" asserts that the clever adulteress is a rather common comic type and reports that, in fact, "Husband-dominators are everywhere in popular literature."[26]

However, a disturbing yet familiar story also lurks in the background of "The Other Man's Wife and the Husband Under the Bed" that connects it to Dostoevsky's weightier narratives. Susanne Fusso examines it alongside two other short tales of the same period, "A Petersburg Chronicle" (1847) and "A Christmas Party and a Wedding" (1848), to connect Ivan Andreevich's marriage with the much younger Glafira Petrovna with the motif of "pedophilic marriage" evident across these texts. In "A Christmas Party and a Wedding," for example, an older gentleman sees an eleven-year-old girl at a Christmas party and learns that she is set to inherit a significant sum of money. He resolves to marry her when she turns sixteen. Despite his intention to wait until she reaches that still young but more socially acceptable age, he spends the rest of the Christmas party trying to insinuate himself into the children's games to be close to the object of his desire. Noting the connections between the weddings portrayed in the stories, Fusso convincingly links "The Husband Under the Bed" with the "pedophilic impulse" that connects Dostoevsky's many sinners and which "lies behind the socially approved marriage of a couple like Ivan Andreevich and Glafira Petrovna."[27]

---

[26] Natalie Zemon Davis, "Women on Top," in *Society and Culture in Early Modern France: Eight Essays* (Stanford: Stanford University Press, 1975), 134.

[27] Susanne Fusso, "Husbands and Lovers: Vaudeville Conventions in 'Another Man's Wife,' 'The Jealous Husband,' and *The Eternal Husband*," in *Before They Were Titans: Essays on the Early Works of Dostoevsky and Tolstoy*. Edited by Elizabeth Cheresh Allen (Brighton: Academic Studies Press, 2015), 73.

Christine Froula's well-known feminist essay, "The Daughter's Seduction: Sexual Violence and Literary History," argues that fictions which depend on violence against women also inevitably perpetrate violence against their female readers. Froula does not discuss Dostoevsky specifically but makes the argument about the dominant literary tradition as such, suggesting that "Metaphysically, the woman reader of a literary tradition that inscribes violence against women is an abused daughter. Like physical abuse, literary violence against women works to privilege the cultural father's voice and story over those of women, the cultural daughters, and indeed to silence women's voices."[28] Given his sustained focus on the victimization of women and young girls, Dostoevsky should be infuriating or, at the very least, extremely troubling for a woman reader, and he has certainly given plenty of gender trouble to feminist critics.[29] However, I benefit from locating this essay as the concluding chapter to *Funny Dostoevsky*, which in itself testifies to Dostoevsky's ability to engage women readers and, especially, to make them laugh. In part this is because no other nineteenth-century author has so thoroughly worked to deconstruct and break apart authoritative discourses as Dostoevsky. Mikhail Bakhtin's *Problems of Dostoevsky's Poetics* foregrounds this accomplishment by crediting Dostoevsky with the creation of the polyphonic novel, in which no single voice is able to dominate, no matter how much would-be authoritarians would love to impose their will on others.

Dostoevsky deconstructs what Froula terms the "cultural father's voice" by exposing violence against women as systemic. In *Crime and Punishment*, which Nina Pelikan Straus has identified as "a text in which Dostoevsky discovers the politics of gender, a text in which Raskolnikov's crime and punishment are engendered," Porfiry Petrovich understands not only Raskolnikov's misguided motivations, but also the role of "the environment" in shaping his crime.[30] During their discussion of criminality, Razumikhin challenges Porfiry: "so tell me then: a forty-year-old man dishonors a ten-year-old girl,—did the environment make

---

[28] Christine Froula, "The Daughter's Seduction: Sexual Violence and Literary History," *Signs*, vol. 11, no. 4 (Summer, 1986): 633.

[29] To quote from Connor Doak's excellent summary of feminist approaches to Dostoevsky: "There remains significant disagreement about the gender politics of Dostoevskii's work. Heldt and Andrew, for example, see misogyny in Dostoevskii's works, whereas Briggs offers a much more positive assessment of his representation of women. Straus sees the emergence of a proto-feminist consciousness in Dostoevskii." See Connor Doak, "Myshkin's Queer Failure: (Mis)Reading Masculinity in Dostoevskii's *The Idiot*," *Slavic and East European Journal*, vol. 63, no. 1 (2019): 16 n. 25.

[30] Nina Pelikan Straus, "'Why Did I Say Women?' Raskolnikov Reimagined," *Diacritics*, vol. 23, no. 1 (Spring 1993): 56.

him do it?" "With surprising gravity" Porfiry answers that "in a strict sense we can indeed say it is the environment ... the crime against the little girl can be explained by 'the environment' all too well."[31] This answer drives Razumikhin berserk because he does not recognize the significance of Porfiry's shift in tone. This is the only serious statement Porfiry makes in a conversation that is otherwise punctuated by his laughter, playful needling of Razumikhin and mock-playful needling of Raskolnikov. The answer given "with surprising gravity" does not advocate the utilitarian view of crime, which Porfiry mockingly adopted the previous night to toy with Razumikhin and his friends. Rather, Porfiry is suggesting that crimes are shaped by what society values and what it denigrates. After making this assertion, Porfiry turns to Raskolnikov to say, "Apropos all these questions, crimes, the environment, and little girls, I am reminded of ... your little article 'On Crime.'"[32] By explicitly linking Raskolnikov's article with the topic of "crimes ... and little girls," Porfiry insinuates a parallel between patriarchal society's denigration of women with Raskolnikov's discussion of the relative value of different lives, and the "extraordinary men" who get to judge this value.

Two men recognize Raskolnikov's guilt early on in *Crime and Punishment* and actively plot to bring him to justice: Porfiry Petrovich and "the tradesman in the robe" who witnesses Raskolnikov's self-destructive outburst at the pawnbroker's apartment after the murder.[33] Both are suggestively feminized with the same terminology. The tradesman "strongly resembled a peasant woman from a distance [очень походившему издали на бабу]."[34] Porfiry is described by the adverb *"бабье"*, which Pevear and Volokhonsky render as "something womanish" and Slater as "something of a peasant woman."[35] In addition to its gendered significance, the word *"баба"* has age, marital status, and class connotations, with the term typically applying to married, lower class women.

---

[31] *PSS*, 6: 197.

[32] *PSS*, 6: 198.

[33] Porfiry and the tradesman share a number of characteristics and are never seen together, leading Valentina Vetlovskaia to suggest the tradesman in the robe may be Porfiry in costume. See Valentina Vetlovskaia, "Literary and Real-Life Prototypes of Dostoevsky's Heroes: The 'Tradesman in the Robe' in *Crime and Punishment*," in *The New Russian Dostoevsky: Readings for the 21st Century*. Edited by Carol Apollonio (Bloomington, IN: Slavica, 2010), 123–38.

[34] *PSS*, 6: 209.

[35] Fyodor Dostoevsky, *Crime and Punishment*. Translated by Richard Pevear and Larissa Volokhonsky (New York: Alfred A. Knopf, 1992), 250; Fyodor Dostoevsky, *Crime and Punishment*. Translated by Nicolas Pasternak Slater (Oxford: Oxford University Press, 2017), 221.

Thus, the adverb could be accurately rendered as "matronly," and Porfiry's figure as having "something matronly about it."[36] Porfiry even shakes his head in an effeminate way "with some kind of matronly gesture [с каким то бабьим жестом]."[37] It emerges, then, that in Raskolnikov's war against women, the resistance is feminized. Further, the specific terminology applied to Porfiry and the tradesman is also significant. As we will see in the next section, the most productive type of comedy in Dostoevsky is practiced by married, middle-aged women, or matrons.

In addition to sharing feminine features, Porfiry and the tradesman also share a fondness for theatrical gestures. The "tradesman in the robe" springs up as if from underground to accost Raskolnikov, like an incarnation of the Furies who hound the matricide in Aeschylus' *Oresteia*. He also collaborates with Porfiry to set the stage for what they hope to be Raskolnikov's confession, when the tradesman hides behind a partition in Porfiry's office to startle Raskolnikov into the truth. While Porfiry is relying on the dramatic surprise to finish the job, he also works to unsettle Raskolnikov with his laughter. As he paints the picture of the killer's eventual confession, "'No, I see that you don't believe me, you still think that I am making innocent little jokes,'—Porfiry carried on, while growing more and more jolly, incessantly giggling with pleasure and starting to circle the room again."[38] Meanwhile, joking is the farthest thing from Raskolnikov's mind in that moment, as he is actually imagining strangling his tormentor. But Porfiry continues, "well, you are, of course, right; God saw fit to shape my figure in such a way that it arouses nothing but comic thoughts in others [у меня и фигура уж так самим богом устроена, что только комические мысли в других возбуждает]," and curiously labels himself with the theatrical term "buffoon [буффон]," an actor typecast into exclusively comic roles.[39] Hilariously, the thoughts Porfiry's matronly figure inspires in Raskolnikov are, of course, not comic, but homicidal, as Porfiry knows full well that Raskolnikov cannot stand being laughed at. Just as he is about to break down, Raskolnikov is rescued by a deus ex machina in the shape of a sectarian house painter. But Mikolka's false confession to the murder fails to convince Porfiry, whose visible displeasure at this turn of events even causes him to briefly break character.

[36] *PSS*, 6: 192.
[37] *PSS*, 6: 194.
[38] *PSS*, 6: 262.
[39] *PSS*, 6: 262–3.

What is it about Porfiry that helps him to see through Raskolnikov so clearly? Why does he remain convinced of Raskolnikov's guilt on the basis of flimsy circumstantial evidence? It is a matter of perspective; the same perspective that gives him insight in the conversation about "crimes ... and little girls" with Razumikhin. In addition to playfully taking on alternative viewpoints, Razumikhin reports that Porfiry is very fond of playing elaborate practical jokes on his friends. The year before, he convinced all his friends that he was going off to join a monastery and managed to keep up the ruse for two months. His next joke was a fake wedding. "He even had a new outfit made," reports Razumikhin. "We all started to congratulate him. But there was neither a bride nor anything else—it was all a mirage!"[40] Porfiry retorts that, in fact, it was the new outfit that prompted the performance, rather than the other way around, with his comic improvisation drawing inspiration from the costume change. When we combine Porfiry's feminized description and gestures, his subversive playfulness and elusiveness, with the fact that his practical jokes center on his personal life or lack thereof, we can see that the reader is being invited to play detective about the police inspector via the lexicon of nineteenth-century queer spotting. Further, in the Russian context, Porfiry's yellowish skin, and rounded, ambiguously gendered figure may also imply membership in the Skoptsy or Castrate sect, whose rejection of procreative sex was seen as a serious threat to patriarchal norms and therefore the tsar's rule.[41] David Halperin writes that "Queer is by definition *whatever* is at odds with the normal, the legitimate, the dominant."[42] Porfiry's interest in criminal psychology may have prepared him to take note of Raskolnikov's guilty behavior, but it was his liminal perspective that saw through Raskolnikov's philosophizing in "On Crime" to patriarchal society's violence against those it marginalizes.

The Unruly Women of Uncle's Dreams

Dostoevsky's preoccupation with "crimes, the environment, and little girls" is matched only by its complement—his persistent indictment of predatory paternal figures. In that sense, Dostoevsky's "daddy issues" are much more radical and

---

[40] *PSS*, 6: 198.
[41] For more on the Castrates, see Laura Engelstein, *Castration and the Heavenly Kingdom: A Russian Folktale* (Ithaca: Cornell University Press, 2003).
[42] David Halperin, *Saint Foucault: Towards a Gay Hagiography* (Oxford: Oxford University Press, 1997), 62. Quoted in Connor Doak, "Myshkin's Queer Failure," 4 n. 9.

wide-ranging than Freud intimated in his preface to *The Brothers Karamazov*.[43] Dostoevsky's indictment is already on display in his first published work. In *Poor Folk* (1846), an old lecher visits Varenka and says that he would like to offer her his "fatherly affection."[44] Disturbingly, his wording replicates Devushkin's and thus insinuates that Devushkin's motives are likewise not as "fatherly" as he would like to claim. *Poor Folk*'s insipient critique is writ large in *Notes from the Dead House* (1860–2), which chronicles Dostoevsky's experience in a Siberian prison camp. Karla Oeler notes the way the semi-autobiographical text exposes Russia's patriarchal institutions and society via its radical critique of the "traditional" family and religion:

> One kind of 'monstrous fact' that takes Gorianchikov by surprise, leading him repeatedly to record such 'facts' in his notes, concerns the violent power relations underlying the cultural structures—family and religion—traditionally seen as curbing violence by transmitting ethics. In particular, the memoir reveals how the ideal of the 'good father' masks the violence of Russia's patriarchal society and the moral bankruptcy of its institutions.[45]

The interpolated narrative of "Akulka's Husband" is illustrative in this regard, since Akulka is mercilessly beaten by her parents in the name of their version of morality before she is handed over to be abused and ultimately murdered by her husband. Oeler's analysis of the text concludes that "When 'father' refers to sadists, murderers, and a class of oppressors … the basic structure by which an ethical tradition is presumably handed down is destroyed."[46] The question becomes how to counteract this deadening oppression. Dostoevsky's answer in *Notes from the Dead House* emerges in the joyous scenes of the convicts' comic theater. The comic interludes feature classic carnivalesque reversals: the adulterous wife hiding lovers in low places, the sneaky servant laughing at his master. The convicts and even the guards all come together during the performance, while the topsy-turvy world conjured by their plays brings the *Dead House*, ever so briefly, to life.

---

[43] See Sigmund Freud, "Dostoevsky and Parricide," *The International Journal of Psychoanalysis*, vol. 26 (1945): 1–8. Originally published in German in 1928.

[44] Dostoevsky, *Poor Folk*, PSS, 1: 72.

[45] Karla Oeler, "The Dead Wives in the *Dead House*: Narrative Inconsistency and Genre Confusion in Dostoevskii's Autobiographical Prison Novel," *Slavic Review*, vol. 61, no. 3 (Autumn 2002): 523.

[46] Ibid., 528.

After his ordeal in the prison camp, Dostoevsky immediately turned to theatrical comedy, suggesting that the genre was integral to processing his experience. He wrote *The Village of Stepanchikovo and Its Inhabitants* and "Uncle's Dream" in 1858 and published both in 1859, a year before *Notes from the Dead House*. *The Village of Stepanchikovo* rewrites Molière's *Tartuffe* in the figure of the petty tyrant Foma Opiskin. "Uncle's Dream" is equally inflected with comic theater. A novella with a vaudeville plot, feuilleton-style narration, and a dash of Gogol's special provincial sauce, "Uncle's Dream" revisits Dostoevsky's love of vaudeville theater that dates back to the 1830s and 40s.[47] The garrulous narrator of "Uncle's Dream" relates that he has taken up a "worthy and tempting subject" in the figure of Marya Aleksandrovna Moskaleva. "My novella," he explains, "contains the whole and remarkable story of the elevation, fame and the triumphant fall of Marya Aleksandrovna and her entire household in Mordasov."[48]

Marya Aleksandrovna is a shameless and ingenious comic heroine who terrorizes her henpecked husband and hilariously outwits would-be representatives of patriarchal authority. It helps that in Mordasov the patriarchy is literally falling apart, decomposing in front of us in the figure of the senile prince K, who is variously described as "half-dead and counterfeit," a "corpse on springs," and a mummy in a youth's costume.[49] "Prince K. was not as old as all that, and yet, in looking at him you would inadvertently be overcome with the thought that he will fall apart that very minute: this is how decayed or, to put it better, worn out he was."[50] Recalling Edgar Allen Poe's "The Man That Was Used Up" (1839), prince K. is made up of prosthetics that comprise nearly his entirety: a glass eye, fake hair, glued-on sideburns and goatee, extensive make-up, a corset, a wooden leg, and fake teeth. But whereas Poe's "The Man That Was Used Up" utilizes prostheses to fabricate a model of stereotypical masculinity, Dostoevsky's prince K. embodies its dissolution. "People were saying that he spent more than half a day on his toilette, and it seemed that he was composed

---

[47] "Uncle's Dream" twice references the vaudeville "Husband away, wife to Tver'" ("Муж в дверь, а жена в Тверь"), which premiered in 1845 and saw publication in *Repertuar i Panteon* in the same year. The plot centers on the jealousy of an older husband (played by the inimitable Pyotr Karatygin in 1845) toward his younger wife. For references to the vaudeville, see *PSS*, 2: 318–19 and 376.

[48] Fyodor Dostoevsky, "Uncle's Dream," *PSS*, 2: 299. While the heroine's name is Mar'ia (Марья), I use Marya for ease of reading and to distinguish from Maria (Мария).

[49] *PSS*, 2: 301 and 310.

[50] *PSS*, 2: 300.

entirely from bits and pieces. Nobody knew when and where he managed to fall apart so much."[51]

The satire is hardly subtle, as prince K.'s physical decay parallels both his disjointed babbling and his degraded morality. In a particularly jarring scene, the elderly prince shows an ardent interest in a young girl's dance performance:

- ... Well, and that girl that was dan-cing, she is also ... formed ...
- You mean Sonechka? But she is still a child, prince! She is only fourteen!
- Well, yes ... but, you know, she is so dexterous, and she also has ... such forms ... forming. So lo-ve-ly! And that other one who was dan-cing with her is also ... forming ...[52]

Prince K.'s senile pedophilia is not an obstacle for Marya Aleksandrovna, however, as she plots to marry him to her beautiful daughter Zina. Her goals are quite unoriginal, of course, but her complete lack of shame and the creativity with which she pursues these ends both impress. The narrator ironically compares the provincial mother to Napoleon preparing for battle. "Having scanned the field of battle, she noticed with pleasure that the lecherous old man was practically smacking his lips when he looked at Zina, and her parental heart fluttered with joy."[53] In devising her plan, Marya Aleksandrovna looks forward to seeing Zina become a wealthy widow in a few years' time and uses all her considerable verbal virtuosity to convince her daughter that she would be doing the prince a favor by taking care of him in his old age.

Obviously, Marya Aleksandrovna is hardly a candidate for mother of the year. She is also a schemer, a gossip, and a sharp-tongued social climber in the vein of Becky Sharpe from *Vanity Fair* (1848). Like Becky Sharpe, however, her verve and creativity inspire respect. Even her daughter says, "I also find, mommy dearest, that you have too much poetic inspiration. You are a woman-poet in the full sense of the term; that is what everyone calls you here. You always have projects. Their impossibility and absurdity do not stop you."[54] But Marya Aleksandrovna also employs her "poetic inspiration" for mundane projects, including miraculously maintaining an impressive household in Mordasov without a corresponding income stream. Her husband lost his position in the provincial bureaucracy due

---

[51] *PSS*, 2: 300.
[52] *PSS*, 2: 342.
[53] *PSS*, 2: 341.
[54] *PSS*, 2: 321.

to incompetence and their fortunes depend entirely on her ingenuity. She exiled her husband Afanasy Matveevich to her small country estate, which is also their only modest source of income. But the strain of managing the family's shaky fortunes pours out onto Afanasy Matveevich's thick head as unbridled fury on the rare occasions that the spouses see each other.[55]

Norms dictate that, despite his uselessness, Zina's father would need to give his blessing for a potential marriage. Thus, Marya Aleksandrovna is forced to collect him to briefly reinstall him as a figurehead at the family table. When she arrives at the country house, Marya Aleksandrovna can't help but lash out at her husband for his blissful ignorance of her struggles:

> As she was entering the room, Marya Aleksandrovna planned to greet Afanasy Matveevich much more benevolently, but seeing that he is fresh from the bathhouse and contentedly drinking tea, she could not restrain herself from the bitterest of outrage. Indeed, while she has so many worries and tasks, her good for nothing ne'er-do-well gets such blissful quietism. This contrast wounded her right in the heart. Meanwhile the blockhead, or, to put it a bit more delicately, the one who was called a blockhead, sat by the samovar in a senseless fright, his mouth hanging open and his eyes bulging, and stared at his wife, who had nearly turned him to stone with her arrival.[56]

Most of the comedy in "Uncle's Dream" takes place at the expense of its male characters, thanks to their nearly unbelievable combinations of incompetence and dimwittedness. This scene with Afanasy Matveevich exhibits this pattern well, as his wife tries to whip him into presentable shape for his brief reinstatement:

> – You've sucked out all my juices, you slob!—said Marya Aleksandrovna.— Bend down more, bend down!
> – With what, my dear, did I suck out your juices?—sputtered her husband, bending his head down as low as he could.
> – Blockhead! You don't understand allegory![57]

---

[55] My co-editor, Lynn Patyk, pointed out that this dynamic of a furious woman married to an ineffectual, and even parasitic man recurs throughout Dostoevsky's texts, for example in the Marmeladov and Epanchin marriages in *Crime and Punishment* and *The Idiot* respectively, and Varvara Stavrogina and Stepan Verkhovensky's relations in *Demons*. To be sure, their interactions are exaggerated and patently hilarious in "Uncle's Dream," but the comic strains remain in the later works. For example, the scene of the drunk Marmeladov being pulled around by his hair (which the narrator is sure to tell us is already much too thin) is quite funny on its own, albeit the physical comedy becomes jarring in the context of the spouses' tragic ends.

[56] *PSS*, 2: 358.

[57] *PSS*, 2: 359–60.

Marya Aleksandrovna's fury at her husband is, as ever, excessive for the situation and quite vividly expressed. In combination with his literal response, it creates a scene of undeniable hilarity, while also highlighting her central comic trait. Marya Aleksandrovna is excessive in more than just her hatred for her "blockhead" husband, but also in her fanciful plans, her effusive language, her sharp barbs directed at "enemy" provincial ladies.

The fact that Marya Aleksandrovna's very appearance "nearly turned him to stone" alludes to the myth of the Medusa. While on the one hand the mythological reference serves a similar purpose to Marya Aleksandrovna's comparison with Napoleon—that of comic effect through incongruity—on the other hand, a female figure whose glance petrifies men (turning them into objects in, one might say, a role reversal) is a rather apt reference point for a text that is as theatrical and woman-dominated as "Uncle's Dream."[58] As Kathleen Rowe explains, "Medusa, like Bakhtin's grinning pregnant hags, contains some of the earliest outlines of the unruly woman, an ambivalent figure of female outrageousness and transgression with roots in the narrative forms of comedy and the social practices of carnival."[59] While "the closeness between laughter and anger produces deep constraints on how women may express or participate in both," the unruly woman is both funny and furious, representing "a special kind of excess differing from that of the femme fatale … or the madonna."[60] This type will also evolve further in Dostoevsky's later works, culminating with *The Idiot*'s explosive and endearing Madame Epanchina, whose henpecked husband "respected and sometimes feared her so much that he even loved her [*до того уважал и до того иногда боялся ее, что даже любил*]."[61]

While Marya Aleksandrovna reserves one kind of intemperance for interactions with her overawed husband, a different verbal extravagance emerges in conversations that require persuasion rather than terrorization. When Mozgliakov, the (also not-too-bright and ironically named) young man who has been courting Zina, eavesdrops on their conversation and discovers

---

[58] For a suggestive examination of Medusa's threat to the patriarchy, see Hélène Cixous, "The Laugh of the Medusa," in *New French Feminisms*. Edited by Elaine Marks and Isabelle de Courtivron (Brighton: Harvester, 1980), 245–64.

[59] Kathleen Rowe, "The Unruly Woman: Gender and the Genres of Laugher," in *Understanding Inequality: The Intersection of Race/Ethnicity, Class, and Gender*. Edited by Barbara A. Arrighi (Lanham: Rowman & Littlefield Publishers, Inc., 2001), 263.

[60] Ibid., 271 and 263.

[61] Dostoevsky, *The Idiot*, PSS, 8: 15.

that Marya Aleksandrovna plans to marry Zina to his uncle, she has to use all of her creative powers to persuade him of the marriage's benefit to all, including even himself, if he gives Zina up for the time being. "Imagine that you come to her," Marya Aleksandrovna suggests,

> and you say: 'Zinaida! I love you more than my own life, but familial reasons are parting us. I understand these reasons. They are for your own happiness, and I dare not oppose them any longer, Zinaida! I forgive you. Be happy if you can!' And here you would gaze at her—with the gaze of a sacrificial lamb, if one can put it like that,—imagine all this and think what kind of an effect these words would have on her heart![62]

Beginning to be carried away by the vision of romantic sacrifice, Mozgliakov is still confused as to how it could possibly benefit him, so Marya Aleksandrovna continues her poetic outpouring, borrowed though it might be from Pushkin's *Eugene Onegin*:

> No, no, no, my friend! Do not interrupt me! I want to paint the entire picture for you without fail with all its consequences in order to virtuously astound you. Imagine, then, that you meet her again, after some time has passed, in high society; you meet somewhere at a ball, with splendid lighting, with intoxicating music, amongst magnificent women and amidst this whole celebration, you stand alone, sad, thoughtful, pale, leaning against a column somewhere (but so that you would be noticeable), and watch her amidst the whirlwind of the ball.[63]

She manages to persuade Mozgliakov in that moment that he would have a better chance of success with Zina via a noble sacrifice and a magnificent reunion once she is a wealthy widow. But Mozgliakov eventually realizes that he is not exactly in a position to give Zina up, since she has already flatly rejected him. He seizes on the opportunity to spoil the marriage plans by convincing his uncle that the brief courtship Marya Aleksandrovna stage-managed had been a dream. The curtain closes on the scandalous non-event, but it would seem that the narrator was not entirely truthful in his oxymoronic promise that his story ends with the "triumphant fall" of Marya Aleksandrovna's house.

During a trip several years later, Mozgliakov finds himself at an opulent ball given by the region's recently appointed governor. To his shock, he recognizes Zina in the governor's proud, beautiful wife. Without realizing it, Mozgliakov is

---

[62] Dostoevsky, "Uncle's Dream," *PSS*, 2: 353.
[63] *PSS*, 2: 352.

to such an extent still under the influence of her mother's poetic vision that he attempts to enact the scene painted for him years before:

> A gloomily distracted look and caustic Mephistophelean smile did not leave his face for the entire evening. He picturesquely leaned against a column (the hall, as luck would have it, contained columns) and for the duration of the whole ball, for several hours straight, he stood in the same place, following Zina with his eyes. But alas! All of his tricks, all of his incredible poses, disillusioned expression, etc., etc.—all of it was for nothing. Zina did not notice him at all. Finally, furious, with aching feet from standing for so long, hungry—since he obviously could not stay for dinner in his capacity as a suffering lover—he returned to his apartment completely worn out and feeling as if someone had beaten him.[64]

Mozgliakov's performance is for naught, while the wound to his ego feels like a beating, echoing Mikhailovsky's sympathetic response to the torments of Dostoevsky's insecure men. Mozgliakov never manages to speak to Zina, but he does exchange a few words with her mother, who has already built a reputation in her new town as an exceedingly clever woman. Like her predecessor Becky Sharpe, it seems that Marya Aleksandrovna has also managed to resurrect herself for a second act.

Conclusion

Just as *Crime and Punishment* is not a "superman" manual, Marya Aleksandrovna is not being held up as a model of morality, despite her success within the story's comic paradigm. As Davis explains, "The point about such portraits is that they are funny and amoral: the women are full of life and energy, and they win much of the time."[65] In "Husband Under the Bed" and "Uncle's Dream," the comic types of the cuckold and henpecked husband underscore patriarchal anxieties, while a refreshingly obnoxious woman runs the show. Having tracked this comic paradigm in these vaudeville-inspired texts, we can also notice its elements at work in even Dostoevsky's most disturbing novels. While space does not allow me to give it the detailed treatment here that it deserves, I want to briefly turn

---

[64] *PSS*, 2: 398.
[65] Davis, "Women on Top," 134–5.

to *The Idiot*, by way of an illustration of both the perseverance and continued importance of the "unruly woman" to this late novel.

In her discussion of "The Unruly Woman," Kathleen Rowe argues that, while women's anger and laughter are both socially pathologized and suppressed, "those structures for expressing women's anger do exist—in the genres of laughter, and, at least in rudimentary form, in the structure of narrative itself."[66] *The Idiot*—long singled out for its impossible structure and held up as perhaps the most hopelessly dark of Dostoevsky's novels, despite being continuously punctuated by laugher—presents a fascinating case study for Rowe's suggestion.[67] Indeed, Nastasya Filippovna seems to back Rowe's claim, when she tells her old abuser that she wants nothing so much as "to laugh at you to my heart's content, because now I too finally want to laugh."[68] I invite us to take her at her word and to think seriously about *The Idiot* as a novel about women's rage and its expression through laughter.

While the main character of the Prince makes a 180-degree turn through the novel's evolving drafts (indeed, he is initially conceived as a rapist!), references to rape and women who fight back against their abusers dominate the draft's first pages and remain driving forces of the plot, emphasizing the extent to which *The Idiot* concentrates on issues of gender. Barbara Heldt deems *The Idiot* to be Dostoevsky's "most thorough consideration of women's status," wherein "'Female' submissiveness is allotted to Prince Myshkin, while the two women protagonists dominate every situation of the plot."[69] More recently, Connor Doak's insightful article argues that Dostoevsky's "queer" Myshkin "destabilized the masculinity norms of the Russia of his time," making way for "openings that reveal the absurdity of the gender system and the possibility of a different, more equitable and just society."[70]

As Doak notes, it is not simply Myshkin's passivity, but also the assertiveness of *The Idiot's* female characters that destabilizes gender norms (and the novel's

---

[66] Rowe, "The Unruly Woman: Gender and the Genres of Laugher," 261.

[67] In regard to the novel's structure and its implications, Nina Pelikan Straus notes that "the novel remains particularly interesting in terms of the woman question because it displays in its own narrative structure a confusion about one part's relation to another, about orders and hierarchies, and about subordinations and dominations that have gendered connotations." See *Dostoevsky and the Woman Question Rereadings at the End of a Century* (New York: St. Martin's Press, 1994), 63.

[68] Dostoevsky, *The Idiot*, PSS, 8: 37.

[69] Barbara Heldt, *Terrible Perfection: Women in Russian Literature* (Bloomington: Indiana University Press, 1987), 35.

[70] Doak, "Myshkin's Queer Failure," 4 and 6.

narrative structure, as their imperatives drive the plot). Nastasya Filippovna refuses to be a meek and silent victim, and instead chooses her own fate, self-destructive though it may be. Heldt argues that her case demonstrates that "Dostoevsky's conservatism does not allow an abused woman the right to remain angry and alive."[71] Rather, it is Nastasya Filippovna's radicalism that refuses to compromise with the world that has been thoroughly defiled for her.[72] Her provocative performances fit within a paradigm Judith Wilt dubs "maiden comedy": "She expresses rather than represses; she piles no sandbags on the dikes of the collapsing world; she exposes and deflates, in fundamental comic style, finding no role *in* the world which fundamentally satisfies her."[73] But, in Wilt's description, as well as in Dostoevsky's depiction, her time is short, as she is destined to succumb to either love or early death. If Cupid's arrow fells her, then the maiden comic may well join the ranks of the matriarchs, who practice within a competing comic paradigm. For Wilt, "matriarchal comedy" is conciliatory rather than radical, championing fertility and community.[74] Both modes feature in *The Idiot* as divergent, but potentially complementary responses to their degraded world.

In *The Idiot*, Nastasya Filippovna's angry comedy and Elizaveta Prokofievna's comic anger alternate between rejection and the possibility of reconciliation, but both share the author's disgust with society's hypocrisy and the abuse it enables. Elizaveta Prokofievna Epanchina is pragmatic (a trait she shares with Marya Aleksandrovna of "Uncle's Dream" and Dostoevsky's other unruly matrons), but she is no less furious for being so. Usually referred to via her husband's military title, she is associated with explosive imagery and can be seen "exploding like a bomb [*разрывалась как бомба*]" when she confronts the group of self-declared radicals who take advantage of Prince Myshkin.[75] Elizaveta Prokofievna commands every scene she takes part in, whether by the force of her comic explosions at her hapless husband and the other incompetent men around her, or the physical comedy of her gestural excess. The narrator reveals that long ago

---

[71] Heldt, *Terrible Perfection*, 35–6.
[72] For a fascinating discussion of Nastasya Filippovna's feminist provocation, see Lynn Ellen Patyk, Chapter 3: "'That a Girl!' Dostoevsky's Feminist Provocation in *The Idiot*," in *Dostoevsky's Provocateurs* (Evanston: Northwestern University Press, 2023), 65–92.
[73] Judith Wilt, "The Laughter of Maidens, the Cackle of Matriarchs: Notes on the Collision between Comedy and Feminism," in *Gender and Literary Voice*. Edited by Janet Todd (New York: Holmes & Meier, 1980), 180–1.
[74] Ibid, 176.
[75] *PSS*, 8: 273.

she "had the weakness to believe that her gaze was incredibly striking [*у неё была слабость поверить, что взгляд ее необыкновенно эффектен*]," and she is still all too fond of glaring, wide-eyed like a would-be Medusa.[76] As we can see, Elizaveta Prokofievna is not immune to being the subject of laughter. Sharing that trait with the unruly mother of "Uncle's Dream," she is more comically productive than Nastasya Filippovna, who is never the subject of laughter herself. A much better mother than Marya Aleksandrovna, Madame Epanchina is similarly successful at navigating society and hilariously unrestrained in her attacks on her cowed husband, whom she nonetheless calls her tyrant. But more importantly, she is fiercely loving and empathetic to the point of eccentricity. For example, at one point she is so worried about Myshkin's illness that her concern turns to anger when she realizes he is not as ill as she feared. The impish Kolya intentionally neglects to tell her that Myshkin is better prior to their meeting, "slily anticipating Madame Epanchina's future comic anger [*комический гнев*], when she would ... inevitably get angry having found her good friend the Prince in good health."[77] But her comic anger is always quick to turn to empathy and compassionate action, as when, for example, her fury at Ippolit's behavior suddenly turns to tears of compassion and a plan to help when she realizes the extent of his illness. Her empathy aligns Madame Epanchina with Myshkin, and she herself recognizes that the two share this characteristic, hilariously taking the comparison to an absurd level to assert, "I consider your character absolutely identical to mine and I am very glad; we are like two drops of water. Except you are a man and I am a woman, and I have never been to Switzerland; that is the extent of our difference."[78]

A powerful mother figure is conceived early in *The Idiot*'s first draft. The third sentence of the novel's plan reads: "The principal force is in the Mother—a noble character worthy of respect, but eccentric. [*Главный форс у Матери—особа достойная уважения и благородная, но взбалмошная*]."[79] This force is realized in Madame Epanchina, "the novel's most endearing comic figure .... [N]o matter how many times she loses her temper, she is quick to acknowledge her faults and quirks and to restore peace. Most importantly, she has the last word

[76] *PSS*, 8: 44.
[77] *PSS*, 8: 201.
[78] *PSS*, 8: 65.
[79] *PSS*, 9: 140.

in the novel, thus affirming its hidden comic vision."[80] In his thought-provoking analysis of *The Idiot*'s latent comedic potentiality, John Givens points out that "As one of the novel's outsized comic characters, Mme Epanchina fittingly brings the novel to a close with a confirmation of the common sense that reasserts itself at the end of comedies and an implied affirmation of Russia itself."[81] Like Nastasya's pragmatic take-down of Raskolnikov's "thinking" in *Crime and Punishment*, Elizaveta Prokofievna's closing words admonish the youth to forget about their Westernized illusions and return home to mother Russia. Madame Epanchina's conclusion highlights the importance of the matrilineal strand in Dostoevsky's comedy, which opens up pathways for salvation and reconciliation in even his darkest works by setting laughter's bombs to explode.

Bibliography

Andrew, Joe. "The Seduction of the Daughter: Sexuality in the Early Dostoevskii and the Case of *Poor Folk*," in *Narrative, Space and Gender in Russian Fiction: 1846–1903*. Edited by Joe Andrew, 23–42. Amsterdam: Rodopi, 2007.

Andrew, Joe. *Women in Russian Literature: 1780–1863*. London: Macmillan, 1988.

Apollonio, Carol. *Dostoevsky's Secrets: Reading against the Grain*. Evanston: Northwestern University Press, 2009.

Ashimbaeva, Natalia. "Comedy between the Poles of Humour and Tragedy, Beauty and Ugliness: Prince Myshkin as a Comic Character," in *Reflective Laughter: Aspects of Humour in Russian Culture*. Edited by Lesley Milne, 49–56. London: Anthem Press, 2004.

Bakhtin, Mikhail. *Problems of Dostoevsky's Poetics*. Edited and Translated by Caryl Emerson. Minneapolis: The University of Minnesota Press, 1984.

Baym, Nina. "The Madwoman and Her Languages, or Why I Don't Do Feminist Literary Theory," *Tulsa Studies in Women's Literature*, vol. 3, no. ½ (Spring–Autumn, 1984): 45–59.

Briggs, Katherine. *How Dostoevsky Portrays Women in His Texts: A Feminist Analysis*. Lewiston: The Edward Millen Press, 2009.

Busch, Robert. *Humor in the Major Novels of F. M. Dostoevsky*. Columbus: Slavica Publishers, 1987.

Christa, Boris. "Raskolnikov's Wardrobe: Dostoevsky's Use of Vestimentary Markers for Literary Communication in Crime and Punishment," 14–20. In Dostoevsky on the

---

[80] John Givens, "A Narrow Escape Into Faith? Dostoevsky's *Idiot* and the Christology of Comedy," *The Russian Review*, vol. 70 (January 2011): 101.

[81] Ibid., 116–17.

Threshold of Other Worlds: Essays in Honor of Malcolm V. Jones. Edited by Sarah Young and Lesley Milne. Ilkeston: Bramcote Press, 2006.

Cixous, Hélène. "The Laugh of the Medusa," translated by Keith Cohen and Paula Cohen, *Signs*, vol. 1, no. 4 (Summer 1976): 875–93.

Davis, Natalie Zemon. "Women on Top," in *Society and Culture in Early Modern France: Eight Essays*, 124–51. Stanford: Stanford University Press, 1975.

Doak, Connor. "Masculine Degeneration in Dostoevsky's *Demons*," in *Writers and the Fin de Siècle: The Twilight of Russian Realism*. Edited by Katherine Bowers and Ani Kokobobo, 107–25. Cambridge: Cambridge University Press, 2015.

Doak, Connor. "Myshkin's Queer Failure: (Mis)Reading Masculinity in Dostoevskii's *The Idiot*," *Slavic and East European Journal*, vol. 63, no. 1 (2019): 1–27.

Dostoevsky, Fyodor. *Crime and Punishment*. Translated by Nicolas Pasternak Slater. Introduction by Sarah J. Young. Oxford: Oxford University Press, 2017.

Dostoevsky, Fyodor. *Crime and Punishment*. Translated by Richard Pevear and Larissa Volokhonsky. Introduction by W. J. Leatherbarrow. New York: Alfred A. Knopf, 1992.

Dostoevsky, Fyodor. *Polnoe sobranie sochinenii v tridtsati tomakh*. Leningrad: Nauka, 1972–1990.

Engel, Barbara. "The 'Woman Question,' Women's Work, Women's Options," in *Dostoevsky in Context*. Edited by Deborah Martinsen and Olga Maiorova, 58–65. Cambridge: Cambridge University Press, 2015.

Engelstein, Laura. Castration and the Heavenly Kingdom: A Russian Folktale. Ithaca: Cornell University Press, 2003.

Erman, Irina. "'Husband under the Bed': Specular Enclosures, Cuckoldry, and Logorrhea in Dostoevsky's Early Works," *The Russian Review*, vol. 76, no. 2 (April 2017): 311–30.

Finney, Gail (ed.) *Look Who's Laughing: Gender and Comedy*. Langhorne: Gordon and Breach, 1994.

Fusso, Susanne. *Discovering Sexuality in Dostoevsky*. Evanston: Northwestern University Press, 2006.

Fusso, Susanne. "Husbands and Lovers: Vaudeville Conventions in 'Another Man's Wife,' 'The Jealous Husband,' and *The Eternal Husband*," in *Before They Were Titans: Essays in the Early Works of Dostoevsky and Tolstoy*. Edited by Elizabeth Cheresh Allen, 61–91. Brighton: Academic Studies Press, 2015.

Gillooly, Eileen. *Smile of Discontent: Humor, Gender, and Nineteenth-Century British Fiction*. Chicago: University of Chicago Press, 1999.

Gindele, Karen. "When Women Laugh Wildly and (Gentle)Men Roar: Victorian Embodiments of Laughter," in *Look Who's Laughing: Gender and Comedy*. Edited by Gail Finney, 139–60. Langhorne: Gordon and Breach, 1994.

Givens, John. "A Narrow Escape into Faith? Dostoevsky's *Idiot* and the Christology of Comedy," *The Russian Review*, vol. 70 (January 2011): 95–117.

Gozenpud, Abram. *Dostoevskii i muzykal'no-teatral'noe iskusstvo*. Leningrad: Sovetskii Kompozitor, 1981.

Grenier, Svetlana. *Representing the Marginal Woman in Nineteenth-Century Russian Literature: Personalism, Feminism, and Polyphony*. Westport: Greenwood Press, 2001.

Heldt, Barbara. *Terrible Perfection: Women in Russian Literature*. Bloomington: Indiana University Press, 1992.

Hengren, Shannon (ed.). *Performing Gender and Comedy: Theories, Texts, and Contexts*. Amsterdam: Gordon and Breach, 1998.

Hingley, Ronald. *Undiscovered Dostoyevsky*. London: Hamish Hamilton, 1962.

Hoisington, Sona Stephan (ed.). *A Plot of Her Own: The Female Protagonist in Russian Literature*. Evanston: Northwestern University Press, 1995.

Ivanits, Linda. *Dostoevsky and the Russian People*. Cambridge: Cambridge University Press, 2008.

Knapp, Liza. "Dostoevsky and the Novel of Adultery: *The Adolescent*," *Dostoevsky Studies*, New Series, vol. XVII (2013): 37–71.

Knapp, Liza. "Mothers and Sons in *The Brothers Karamazov*: Our Ladies of Skotoprigonevsk," in *A New Word on the Brothers Karamazov*. Edited by Robert Louis Jackson, 31–52. Evanston: Northwestern University Press, 2004.

Knapp, Liza. "Myshkin through a Murky Glass, Guessingly," in *Dostoevsky's the Idiot: A Critical Companion*. Edited by Liza Knapp, 191–215. Evanston, IL: Northwestern University Press, 1998.

Kreienbrock, Jörg. *Malicious Objects, Anger Management and the Question of Modern Literature*. New York: Fordham University Press, 2013.

Krieger, Murray. "Dostoevsky's *Idiot*: The Curse of Saintliness," in *Dostoevsky: A Collection of Critical Essays*. Edited by René Wellek, 39–52. Englewood Cliffs: Prentice-Hall, 1986.

Lapshin, I. I. "Komichekoe v proizvedeniiakh Dostoevkogo," in *O Dostoevskom: Sbornik Statei*. Edited by A. L. Bem, 101–20. Paris: Amga Editions, 1986.

Leatherbarrow, William J. *A Devil's Vaudeville: The Demonic in Dostoevsky's Major Fiction*. Evanston, IL: Northwestern University Press, 2005.

Lesage, Julia. "Women's Rage," in *Marxism and the Interpretation of Culture*. Edited by Carol Nelson and Lawrence Grossberg, 419–28. Chicago: University of Illinois Press, 1988.

Levinton, G. A. "Dostoevskii i 'nizkie' zhanry fol'klora," *Literaturnoe Obozrenie* (1992, special issue on "Erotika v russkoi literature: Ot Barkova do nashikh dnei"): 46–53.

Marullo, Thomas Gaiton. *Heroine Abuse: Dostoevsky's "Netochka Nezvanova" and the Poetics of Codependency*. Ithaca: Cornell University Press, 2015.

Marx, Nick and Matt Sienkiewicz (eds.). *The Comedy Studies Reader*. Austin: University of Texas Press, 2018.

Matich, Olga. "Dostoevsky's Troubled Temporalities: New Approaches to *The Idiot*," *Slavic and East European Journal*, vol. 60, no. 3 (2016): 422–46.

Matich, Olga. "*The Idiot*: A Feminist Reading," in *Dostoevski and the Human Condition after a Century*. Edited by Alexej Ugrinsky, Frank S. Lambasa, and Valija K. Ozulis, 53–60. New York: Greenwood, 1986.

Merrill, Lisa. "Feminist Humor: Rebellious and Self-Affirming," in *Last Laughs: Perspectives on Women and Comedy*. Edited by Regina Barreca, 271–80. New York: Gordon and Breach, 1988.

Milne, Lesley (ed.). *Reflective Laughter: Aspects of Humour in Russian Culture*. London: Anthem Press, 2004.

Mochulsky, Konstantin. *Dostoevsky: His Life and Work*. Princeton: Princeton University Press, 1967.

Murav, Harriet. "Reading Woman in Dostoevsky," in *A Plot of Her Own: The Female Protagonist in Russian Literature*. Edited by Sona Stephan Hoisington, 44–57. Evanston: Northwestern University Press, 1995.

Overton, Bill. *The Novel of Female Adultery: Love and Gender in Continental European Fiction, 1830–1900*. New York: St. Martin's Press, 1996.

Patyk, Lynn Ellen. "'That a Girl!' Dostoevsky's Feminist Provocation in *The Idiot*," in *Dostoevsky's Provocateurs*, 65–92. Evanston: Northwestern University Press, 2023.

Rowe, Kathleen. *The Unruly Woman: Gender and the Genres of Laugher*. Austin: The University of Texas Press, 1995.

Rowe, Kathleen. "The Unruly Woman: Gender and the Genres of Laugher," in *Understanding Inequality: The Intersection of Race/Ethnicity, Class, and Gender*. Edited by Barbara A. Arrighi, 261–76. Lanham: Rowman & Littlefield Publishers, Inc., 2001.

Rozenblium, L. M. "Iumor Dostoevskogo," *Voprosy literatury*, vol. 1 (1999): 141–89.

Russo, Mary. "Female Grotesques," in *Feminist Studies/Critical Studies*. Edited by Teresa de Laurentis, 213–29. Bloomington: Indiana University Press, 1986.

Shneider, Vadim. "The Greasy-Haired Pawnbroker and the Capitalist *Raskrasavitsa*: Dostoevsky's Businesswomen," in *Dostoevsky at 200: The Novel in Modernity*. Edited by Katherine Bowers and Kate Holland, 61–80. Toronto: Toronto University Press, 2021.

Spiegel, John. *Dimensions of Laughter in Crime and Punishment*. Selingsgrove: Susquehanna University Press, 2000.

Straus, Nina Pelikan. *Dostoevsky and the Woman Question: Rereadings at the End of a Century*. New York: St. Martin's Press, 1994.

Straus, Nina Pelikan. "'Why Did I Say Women?' Raskolnikov Reimagined," *Diacritics*, vol. 23 no. 1 (Spring 1993): 53–65.

Terras, Victor. *The Young Dostoevsky (1846–1849): A Critical Study*. Paris: Mouton, 1969.

Vetlovskaia, Valentina. "Literary and Real-Life Prototypes of Dostoevsky's Heroes: The 'Tradesman in the Robe' in *Crime and Punishment*," in *The New Russian*

Dostoevsky: Readings for the 21st Century. Edited by Carol Apollonio, 123–38. Bloomington, IN: Slavica, 2010.

Weber, Samuel. *The Legend of Freud*. Minneapolis: The University of Minnesota Press, 1982.

Wilt, Judith. "The Laughter of Maidens, the Cackle of Matriarchs: Notes on the Collision between Comedy and Feminism," in *Gender and Literary Voice*. Edited by Janet Todd, 173–96. New York: Holmes & Meier, 1980.

Notes on Contributors

Fiona Bell is a Ph.D. Candidate in the Department of Slavic Languages and Literatures at Yale University. Her dissertation traces how the Russian peasant woman became a sex symbol—and a privileged symbol of white femininity—in the nineteenth century, both in Russia and in the European and US imaginaries. Her research interests include performance studies and histories of race and racialization in the Russian Empire.

Caryl Emerson is A. Watson Armour III University Professor Emeritus of Slavic Languages and Literatures at Princeton University. Her work has focused on the Russian classics (Pushkin, Tolstoy, Dostoevsky), Mikhail Bakhtin, and Russian music and opera. Recent projects include the modernist Sigizmund Krzhizhanovsky (1887–1950), the allegorical-historical novelist Vladimir Sharov (1952–2018), and the co-editing, with George Pattison and Randall A. Poole, of *The Oxford Handbook of Russian Religious Thought*.

Irina Erman is Associate Professor of Russian Studies at the College of Charleston. She has published articles on Dostoevsky, nineteenth- and twentieth-century Russian literature and contemporary literature in *The Russian Review*, *The Journal of Popular Culture*, the *Russian Literature* journal. Her article on A. K. Tolstoy won the inaugural Levin Article Prize for best article published in *The Russian Review* in 2020.

Melissa Frazier is Professor of Russian Language and Russian and Comparative Literature at Sarah Lawrence College. Her current book project, *Signs of the Material World*, sets Dostoevsky and the nineteenth-century novel in the context of a contemporary science of mind and body.

Susanne Fusso is Marcus L. Taft Professor of Modern Languages and Professor of Russian, East European, and Eurasian Studies at Wesleyan University. Her most recent book is *Editing Turgenev, Dostoevsky, and Tolstoy: Mikhail Katkov and the Great Russian Novel* (2017). She has translated the novels of Sergey Gandlevsky and the prose of Nikolai Gogol, Fyodor Sologub, and Vladimir Trubetskoi. She is now working on a new translation of Dostoevsky's novel *The Adolescent*.

Tatyana Kovalevskaya is Chair of the European Languages Department at the Linguistics Institute of the Russian State University for the Humanities. Her research interests focus on Dostoevsky, cultural studies, and comparative literature. She has published extensively on Dostoevsky, authoring over 100 articles. Her most recent book is a bilingual volume entitled *Fyodor Dostoevsky on the Dignity of the Human Person* (2020).

Chloe Papadopoulos is Assistant Professor (LTA) in the Department of Russian Studies at Dalhousie University. Her current research focuses on Russian reform-era historical fiction, drama, and the plastic arts, and their contemporary reception in newspapers and the periodical press. Her article "Speaking Silently and Overnarrating in Fyodor Dostoevsky's 'Krotkaia'" appeared in *Dostoevsky Studies* in 2021.

Lynn Ellen Patyk is Associate Professor of Russian at Dartmouth College and works at the intersection of culture, media studies, and political communication/performance. Her first book, *Written in Blood: Revolutionary Terrorism and Russian Literary Culture, 1861–1881* (a Choice Outstanding Title for 2018), traced Russian literary culture's contribution to the emergence of revolutionary terrorism. Her second book, *Dostoevsky's Provocateurs*, argues that provocation is Dostoevsky's creative and communicative macrostrategy. She currently serves as associate editor of *The Russian Review* and has published articles and reviews on Dostoevsky, revolutionary terrorism, provocation, and more in *The Russian Review*, *Slavic Review*, *Slavonic and East European Review*, *The American Historical Review*, and the *L.A. Review of Books*.

Alina Wyman is Professor of Russian Language and Literature at the New College of Florida. Her research interests focus on nineteenth-century Russian literature, Russian and German philosophy and literary theory and the work of Mikhail Bakhtin and Max Scheler. She has published *The Gift of Active Empathy: Scheler, Bakhtin, and Dostoevsky* (2016) as well as articles on Bakhtin, Scheler, Gogol, Dostoevsky, Tolstoy, and on medieval Slavic literature.

Index

Aleksandrinskii Theater 74
Allen, Woody 4, 4 n.8
Andrin, Muriel 75
Aquinas, Thomas 13, 16
Aristotle, *Nicomachean Ethics* 157
Averintsev, Sergei 45–7, 46 n.56

Bakhtin, Mikhail 3, 10, 25 n.2, 29 n.14, 142 n.63
   carnival 4, 8–9, 11, 14, 14 n.34, 19, 27, 34–42, 46–7, 166
   carnivalesque 36, 77, 206
   chronotope 25, 35, 42, 45
   dialogue 37–8
   Discourse and the Novel 11
   double-voiced word 180, 185–6
   genre memory 27, 34
   heteroglossia 11
   laughing genres 19, 26, 28, 29 n.14, 30, 34, 47
   metaphysics of laughter 19, 26, 28–30, 33, 44
   negation 30–1
   polyphony 12, 27, 52, 60
   Problems of Dostoevsky's Poetics 4, 202
   Rabelais and His World 26, 33, 36
   "seriousification" 3, 3 n.4, 36, 38, 40, 42
   utopia of laughter 36
balagan puppet theater 74, 92
bathos 77
Beer, Gillian 106, 110–12
   Darwin's Plots 106
Berger, Peter 10 n.27, 14, 16–17, 18 n.49
Bergson, Henri 5, 7, 29, 31–3, 47, 94, 165
   Le Rire (Laughter: An Essay on the Meaning of the Comic) 7, 31, 31 n.20, 113–14
Berlant, Lauren 8, 13
Bernard, Claude, *Introduction to the Study of Experimental Medicine* 103, 105–6

Bethea, David 153
Bird, Robert 26, 31, 46–7
Blanchot, Maurice 155
Blank, Ksana 30, 30 n.16
Boebert, Lauren 186
Bowser, Eileen 75
Boyd, Brian 10, 10 n.25
Brooks, Peter, *The Melodramatic Imagination* 72, 73, 75
Busch, R. L., *Humor in the Major Novels of Dostoevsky* 4

capitalism 20, 72, 76, 80, 82, 86, 95
Chakhachiro, Raymond 54
Chaplin, Charlie 75, 76, 81, 85
   Modern Times 81, 89
   Tramp 76, 81, 85–6, 89, 95
Chernow, Ron 183
Chernyshevsky, N. G. 20, 99–101, 104–5, 107–9, 113, 154, 193
   New People 104
   What Is To Be Done? 99–100, 104–5, 193
Christianity 6, 13, 17
Clayton, Alex 75
clown 12, 43–5, 73–4, 76, 78, 81–3, 85–8, 92–5
Colescott, Robert 180
Collins, Wilkie
   The Moonstone 110
   The Woman in White 108
Combs, Sean 183
comedy 3–6, 8, 15, 17–21, 40–1, 62
   coefficient 20, 121, 135, 135 n.41
   gender and 19, 21–2, 167, 192–3, 196–8, 202–3, 213–14
   maiden 214
   matriarchal 214
   slapstick 20, 71–2, 75, 78, 86, 88–9, 95
   stand-up 51, 121
   commedia dell'arte 32, 40, 74–5, 80–1

Corrigan, Yuri 176
Coulson, Jesse 66
Critchley, Simon 13 n.32, 17, 99, 114
cuckold play 73, 92
Cynic Peregrinus 141, 143

Daly, Nicholas 108
Darwin, Charles 101, 103, 106, 107 n.29, 110, 112
Davies, Christie 14 n.34
Davis, Natalie Zemon 201, 212
devil 16–17, 17 n.43, 18, 59, 101–4, 114–16
Diggs, Daveed 186–7
Doak, Connor 202 n.29, 213
Dobroliubov, Nikolai 152
Dostoevskaia, Anna (nee Snitkina) 1, 9, 195
Dostoevskaia, Liubov' Fyodorovna 194
Dostoevsky, Aleksandr Andreevich 194
Dostoevsky, Fyodor 1–4, 18–22, 51, 194–5
   Adolescent 133
   The Brothers Karamazov 11, 20, 37, 41–2, 55, 101–3, 177, 206
   Crime and Punishment 13, 15, 18, 21, 55–6, 71–2, 74, 80, 82, 84, 86, 95, 107, 107 n.32, 115, 152, 167, 192, 195, 197, 202–3, 212
   Demons 21, 58, 74, 99, 109, 114, 149–58, 162
   The Devils 21, 42, 58, 60, 62, 171–3, 175–7, 179, 181, 183, 187
   The Double 71, 77, 84, 199
   genre trouble in 72–7
   "The Husband under the Bed" 21, 200–1, 212
   The Idiot 20–1, 111, 121–3, 134–46, 193, 195, 199, 210, 213–16
   Notes from the House of the Dead 74, 89, 196, 206–7
   Notes from Underground 4, 60, 66, 107, 122, 125, 125 n.11, 127–30, 134, 138
   "One of the Modern Falsehoods" 150, 159 n.47
   ontological mockery in 122–7, 134, 145
   play in 9–13
   Poor Folk 195–6, 206
   "Uncle's Dream" 193, 195, 199, 205–12, 209 n.55, 210, 212, 214–15
   The Village of Stepanchikovo 72, 74, 199, 207
dual-aspect monism 101–2, 107, 110, 113, 117
Duck Soup (film) 79
Dyson, Michael Eric 182

Emerson, Caryl 95, 166
Erman, Irina 73, 92

Fantina, Richard 108
Feuerbach, Ludwig 100
Fisher, Philip 156, 168
fool 14, 19, 41–5, 102, 200
"Founding Fathers" 21, 173, 177–80
Frede, Victoria 100
Freud, Sigmund 7, 199, 206
Froula, Christine 202
Fusso, Susanne 73, 201

gags 71, 75–6, 79–80, 83, 87–8, 92
Garnett, Constance 56–9, 61, 65–6, 68
Gates, Henry Louis Jr. 180
gender and comedy 19, 21–2, 167, 192–3, 196–8, 202–3, 213–14
genre
   laughing 19, 26, 28, 29 n.14, 30, 34, 47
   memory 10, 27, 34
   trouble 72–7
Gillota, David 14 n.34
global joke 123, 128–9, 132, 134 n.37, 136, 144–5
Gogol, Nikolai 3, 3 n.5, 131
   Petersburg Tales 80 n.30, 82
Goncharov, Ivan 152–3
   Oblomov 85 n.53, 152
Groskop, Viv, *The Anna Karenina Fix* 51
Gunning, Tom 76

Halperin, David 205
heroine abuse 196, 196 n.11
heuristic irony 19, 54
Hirschkop, Ken 25, 25 n.2, 28, 29 n.14
Hobbes, Thomas 13, 14 n.34
Hoffmann, E. T. A. 131
Huizinga, Johan, *Homo Ludens* 1, 9, 15–16

humor 10, 13–17, 14 n.34, 19, 53–4, 149–50
   cognitive theory of 6–10
   ethnic 14–15, 14 n.34
   incongruity theory of 7–8, 12–15, 21, 102, 136, 144, 150, 164–5, 167, 171, 178, 210
   physiological theory of 6–8
   relief theory of (aggression theory) 7–8, 14 n.34, 150, 166, 166 n.78
   scalar shifts 8
   spiritual potential 130–3
   superiority theory of 6, 8, 13–14, 14 n.34, 197
   theory of 5–8
Hutcheon, Linda 171–2

impatience 20–1, 149–52, 154–7, 159, 159 n.47, 160–3, 168
irony 11, 13, 54, 56, 69, 91, 143, 145
Ivanova, Maria 191–4
Ivanov, Viacheslav 3 n.6, 73 n.3

Jackson, Robert Louis 60, 66, 171
Jakim, Boris 66, 68
joke(s) 5
   April Fools 9
   ethnic 14 n.34
   global 123, 128–9, 132, 134 n.37, 144–5
   ontological 121–3, 128, 133–46
   practical 191–2, 205

Kajikawa, Loren 182–3
Kant, Immanuel 6–7, 21, 32, 164–5
Karepin, Aleksandr 193–5
Karepin, Pyotr 194–5, 195 n.9
Katz, Michael 57–8, 103, 126 n.16
Keaton, Buster 71, 77–8
Kentish, Jane 67–8
Khamitov, M. 142 n.63
Kitzinger, Chloë 105
Kliger, Ilya 27, 47, 152, 167
Kornblatt, Judith Deutsch 133–4 n.37
Kostalevsky, Marina 110 n.42

Lapshin, I. I. 135 n.39, 141–3, 143 n.69, 145
Latour, Bruno 101

laughter 5–6, 31–5, 133 n.37, 141 n.61, 166–7
   carnival 14, 14 n.34, 16, 37, 42
   holistic theory of 6–7
   and "living life" 113–17
   metaphysics of 19, 26, 28–30, 33, 44
   sensation 20, 101, 107–13
Leatherbarrow, W. J. 114 n.61
Lebedeva, O. B. 138 n.52, 141, 144
Levine, George, *Dying to Know* 106
Lewes, George Henry 101, 106–7, 107 n.32
   Problems of Life and Mind 107
Lipovetsky, Mark 45, 45 n.55
Lounsbery, Anne 85 n.53
Lucian of Samasota 141–4, 142 n.63
Ludovici, Anthony 5

Maguire, Robert 59, 61, 65
Mansel, Henry 108–9, 111
Martinsen, Deborah A. 74
Marx, Groucho 79
mask 14, 19, 38–45, 47, 206
material determinism 104–6, 108–9, 113
materialism 20, 102–7, 117
Maxwell, James Clerk 101, 106–7, 116
McDuff, David 56
McNeill, Daniel 39–40
melodrama 72, 73–7, 93
Menand, Louis 106–7
Mikhailovsky, N. K. 109–11, 199–201, 199 n.21, 212
   "A Cruel Talent" 109–10, 199
Miller, D. A. 108
Miranda, Lin-Manuel, *Hamilton* 21, 172–3, 176–87, 178 n.24
misogyny 21, 192–6, 202 n.29
Mochulsky, Konstantin 72
Monteiro, Lyra D. 180–1, 185–6
Morreall, John 9–10
Morson, Gary Saul 52, 173 n.3
Muecke, D. C. 54
Mulligan, Christina 186
Murav, Harriet 196
murder 11, 13, 15, 19, 57–8, 71–2, 84–6, 134 n.38
murder scene 71–2, 87–95

Ngai, Sianne 8, 13, 81–2, 155, 157, 168
Nietzsche, Friedrich 122, 124–5, 125 n.11, 144
  Beyond Good and Evil 124
  Toward a Genealogy of Morals 124
nihilists 20–1, 30, 101, 103–4, 109, 113, 115–17, 153, 160, 165, 167, 174–5, 177, 182, 187
novel of sensation 101, 108, 110
Nussbaum, Martha 79–80

Oliphant, Margaret 108–9
ontological jest 13, 20, 122, 122 n.3, 124, 134–6, 135 n.39
ontological joke 121–3, 128, 133–46

Pan'kov, Nikolai 46–7
parody 21, 84, 160, 163, 171–3, 172 n.1, 173 n.3, 175–80, 187
Patyk, Lynn Ellen 166, 209 n.55
Peregrinus 141–4
Pevear, Richard 56–7, 59, 61–2, 203
physical humor 12
Plato, *Theaetetus* 18 n.49
play 9–13
  defined 9
Podosokorsky, N. 142 n.63
Ponkratova, E. 51
Pumpiansky, Lev 20, 130–2, 134 n.38, 141 n.61
pun 55–6, 128, 133, 138, 140
puppet 73–4, 78, 90–1
Pushkin, Alexander, *Eugene Onegin* 183, 211

Rabelais, François 25–6, 34
  culture of laughter 35
radicalism 149–50, 214
rap 179–85, 181 n.35
Ready, Oliver 57
ressentiment 20, 122–5, 125 n.11, 127, 129–30, 134, 134 n.38, 135 n.41, 144–5
restorative parody 21, 172–3, 175–7, 179–80, 187
revolutionary terrorism. *See* terrorism
ridicule 8, 14, 19, 30–1, 121, 123, 129, 132, 140, 197
Ronen, Omry 181

Rowe, Kathleen 210, 213
Rozanov, Vasily 177
Rozenblium, Liia (L. M.) 53
Rylance, Rick 106

Saltykov-Shchedrin, Mikhail 68 n.49
satire 19, 25–6, 29–30, 33–4, 37, 53, 141, 144, 208
scandal 25, 27, 37, 109, 141, 150, 211
Scheler, Max 124–5, 127, 130, 134, 145
sensation 20, 101, 107–13
Shestov, Lev 126, 126 n.14
Shklovsky, Viktor 31
Shneyder, Vadim 82, 86, 111
silent film comedy 75
Sistine Madonna 21, 173, 173 n.4, 175–9
slapstick
  comedy 20, 71–2, 76, 78, 86, 89, 95
  detouring 76, 87
  gags 71, 75–6, 81, 83, 87–8
  humor 173–4
  and labor 80–7
  violence 78
Soloviev, Vladimir 130, 131 n.29, 132–3
  La Sophia 130–1
Spencer, Herbert 7, 32
Spiegel, John, *Dimensions of Laughter in Crime and Punishment* 141 n.61
Straus, Nina Pelikan 202, 213 n.67
Suls, Jerry M. 165–6

Tapley, Robin 15
Taranovsky, Kiril 181
Terras, Victor 196 n.12
terrorism 150–4, 151 n.7
Thorstensson, Victoria 153
Tihanov, Galin 28, 33
Tikhomirov, Boris 122, 122 n.3, 135
Tkachev, P. I. 109–11
Tolson, Franita 186
Tolstoy, Lev 163
Tynianov, Yuri 171–2, 185

vaudeville 74–5, 77, 192, 200–1, 207, 212
verbal humor 12, 174
Verhoeven, Claudia 151–2
Vinogradov, V. V. 78, 79 n.30, 83
Vinokur, Val 152–3
violence 75, 77–8, 82, 93, 196–7, 200–2

Vogüé, Eugène-Melchior de, *Le Roman Russe* 4
Volokhonsky, Larissa 56–7, 59, 61–2, 203
vulgar materialists 20, 100–1, 104, 117

Weiner, Adam 16 n.43
Wilks, Ronald 68
Wilt, Judith 214
"The Woman Question" 193–4, 196, 213 n.67
wordplay 55, 140

youth 149–50, 157–60

zanni 80–1, 85, 95
zany/zaniness 81–3, 85–7, 89–91, 95
Zhernokleyev, Denis 30–1, 31 n.18
Zhukovsky, V. A. 176–7
Zupančič, Alenka 20, 102, 113–14, 114 n.57, 117
  The Odd One In: On Comedy 99–100, 113

www.ingramcontent.com/pod-product-compliance
Lightning Source LLC
Chambersburg PA
CBHW052037300426
44117CB00012B/1854